SHAKESPEARE, SEX, AND LOVE

SHAKESPEARE,

Sex, & Love

STANLEY WELLS

OXFORD

UNIVERSITY PRESS

OXFORD

UNIVERSITY PRESS

Great Clarendon Street, Oxford OX2 6DP

Oxford University Press is a department of the University of Oxford.
It furthers the University's objective of excellence in research, scholarship,
and education by publishing worldwide in

Oxford   New York

Auckland   Cape Town   Dar es Salaam   Hong Kong   Karachi
Kuala Lumpur   Madrid   Melbourne   Mexico City   Nairobi
New Delhi   Shanghai   Taipei   Toronto

With offices in

Argentina   Austria   Brazil   Chile   Czech Republic   France   Greece
Guatemala   Hungary   Italy   Japan   Poland   Portugal   Singapore
South Korea   Switzerland   Thailand   Turkey   Ukraine   Vietnam

Oxford is a registered trade mark of Oxford University Press
in the UK and in certain other countries

Published in the United States
by Oxford University Press Inc., New York

British Library Cataloguing in Publication Data
Data available

Library of Congress Cataloging in Publication Data
Library of Congress Control Number: 2009941605

Typeset by SPI Publisher Services, Pondicherry, India
Printed in Great Britain
on acid-free paper by
Clays Ltd., St Ives Plc

ISBN 978–0–19–957859–7

1 3 5 7 9 10 8 6 4 2

PREFACE

All Shakespeare quotations are from *William Shakespeare: The Complete Works*, General Editors Stanley Wells and Gary Taylor (Oxford, 1986; 2nd edn, 2005). *King Lear* refers to the play printed as *The Tragedy of King Lear* in that edition unless otherwise stated.

I am grateful for encouragement from Andrew McNeillie and Jacqueline Baker, of Oxford University Press, and for specific points of information to Dr Jane Kingsley-Smith and Dr Duncan Salkeld. The staff of the library of the Shakespeare Birthplace Trust have been unfailingly helpful. Dr Paul Edmondson has as always been generous with perceptive, good-humoured and friendly comment and criticism at all stages of my work.

S. W.

CONTENTS

LIST OF ILLUSTRATIONS

Figures

Plates

INTRODUCTION

I n this book I aim to discuss aspects of Shakespeare's treatment of human sexuality in a wide range of his plays and poems, and to set it within its literary, social, and intellectual context. During the eighteenth and nineteenth centuries, especially, attempts were frequently made, both on the page and on the stage, to suppress or deny the sexuality in Shakespeare's language. Alexander Pope, in his edition of 1725, attributed some of the riskier passages to interpolations by 'the actors', signalling them with what he called his 'mark of reprobation'. Notoriously, Henrietta and Thomas Bowdler removed what they saw as indecency and obscenity (as well as profanity) in their frequently reprinted 'Family Shakespeare', published in part in 1807 then complete, in ten volumes, in 1820. Theatre texts too were cleaned up, so that for example the word 'whore' was removed from nineteenth-century acting texts of *Othello*.[1] It was often assumed that when Shakespeare used overtly sexual language he did so out of a desire to please the groundlings, patronizingly equated with spectators of low taste: early in the twentieth century the Poet Laureate Robert Bridges wrote that 'Shakespeare should not be put into the hands of the young without the warning that the foolish things in his plays were written to please the foolish, the filthy for the filthy, and the brutal for the brutal.'[2] Certainly Shakespeare wrote to entertain a broad spectrum of playgoers, but there is no reason to suppose that he did so with a sense of self-abasement or of condescension.

Well into the twentieth century school editions regularly expurgated their texts. Editors even of scholarly editions, some of them still current, evaded frankness in their glosses by using Latinisms such as 'pudendum'—which, heaven help us, means something of which one

1

should be ashamed—for the female sexual organs, and phrases such as 'with a bawdy quibble' or 'with an obscene pun' to avoid explaining a sexual quip.

On the other hand, during, especially, the later part of the twentieth century serious attempts have been made to dig beneath the surface meanings of what Shakespeare wrote in the effort to elucidate sexual significances that would have been apparent to his earlier readers and hearers but which have been submerged by the passage of time. Shakespeare sometimes unambiguously signals sexual wordplay. 'Out upon you, what a man are you!' says the Nurse in *Romeo and Juliet* after Mercutio has talked about the 'bawdy hand of the dial' being 'upon the prick of noon' (2.3.104–6). But certain words that have an innocent surface meaning may have carried sexual overtones to his earliest readers, and he may have wished his audiences to pick them up.

A well-known example is Hamlet's exhortation to Ophelia, 'get thee to a nunnery', followed by the question 'Why wouldst thou be a breeder of sinners?' (3.1.123–4). The editor of the play in the second Arden series, Harold Jenkins, wrote in his gloss '*Nunnery* was sometimes used sarcastically for a house of *unchaste* women, and awareness of this may add a bitter undercurrent as the dialogue proceeds; but to insist on it…at the expense of the literal meaning, itself so poignant in the context, is perverse.' And he devotes one of his 'Longer Notes' to an ample, somewhat vacillatory discussion of the topic, admitting with exemplary scholarly caution—if not with total lucidity—that 'additional evidence of the word's ironic usage has made me less persuaded than I once was…that we can altogether dismiss an inherent ambiguity'. His successors, the editors of the third Arden edition, are more summary: 'It has been suggested that *nunnery* is used here in a slang sense meaning "brothel", though it does not seem very relevant, given that Hamlet is trying to deter Ophelia from "breeding".' (Not that brothels are designed as breeding-grounds.) The evidence supplied by these editors and by Gordon Williams in his scholarly and sensible *Glossary of Shakespeare's Sexual Language* (1997) seems to me to be enough to suggest that whatever Shakespeare's no-longer-discernible intentions may have been, it would have been impossible for the 'slang sense' of the words—roughly equivalent to 'Fuck off!'—not to flicker across the minds of at least some members of his audiences.

More disputable is the gloss in the RSC edition, of 2008, to Boyet's statement in *Love's Labour's Lost* that since Armado was in Rome 'he wore none but a dishclout' of Jaquenetta's, and that he wears it next his heart 'for a favour' (their 5.2.710). Here, 'dishclout' is explained as 'dish-cloth, with play on menstrual rag'. No evidence is given for the subsidiary sense, nor is any provided by the *Oxford English Dictionary*, nor is it suggested even by Frankie Rubinstein in her over-the-top *Dictionary of Shakespeare's Sexual Puns and their Significance* (1984). Shakespeare uses the word once elsewhere, when the Nurse in *Romeo and Juliet* says that 'Romeo's a dishclout to him' (i.e. compared to Paris; 3.5.219). 'When is a dishcloth not a dishcloth?' I should require evidence that the word was used in the proposed subsidiary sense in Shakespeare's time to be persuaded of this interpretation of its meaning in *Love's Labour's Lost*.

There are also somewhat complex instances of words which may have had a sexual meaning to Shakespeare's contemporaries, which, however, Shakespeare uses without apparently wishing to draw on this significance, but where modern audiences may be conscious of it. In *A Midsummer Night's Dream* Titania says to Bottom, 'I have a venturous fairy that shall seek | The squirrel's hoard, and fetch thee off new nuts' (4.1.34–5). 'Nuts' could mean 'testicles'—'balls' in the vernacular—to Shakespeare's audience as to ours, but he does nothing to signal a pun here, nor is the subsidiary sense particularly relevant to the dramatic situation. In Michael Boyd's Stratford production of 1999 Titania clearly intended the sexual sense, and Bottom was pleased and amused by it, even though there was nothing to indicate that he was in need of rejuvenation in that area. This could be regarded as a gratuitous imposition upon the text; on the other hand, it might also be argued that, especially at school matinees, some members of the audience might have sniggered at the implied sense, and that it was wiser to acknowledge that possibility by playing up to it rather than denying it.

It is also possible for words to acquire a special sense in a particular performance. Dr Caius in *The Merry Wives of Windsor* frequently uses 'by Gar' as a substitute for 'By God'. When Greg Hicks played the role at Stratford in 2002 he gave it a pronunciation which inescapably resembled 'bugger', and caused much amusement by doing so. Thus a euphuism for a profanity ingeniously became a foreigner's mispronunciation of an obscenity. And there are straightforward mistakes. Judi Dench tells how, in the casket scene of *The Merchant of Venice*, 'Michael Williams was standing in the centre of the stage as Bassanio, about to make his choice. There was a wind band at the back of the stage, Peter Geddes as Gobbo, Polly James waiting to sing "Tell me where is fancy bred", and my brother Jeff and Bernard Lloyd as monks. I was supposed to say

> I speak too long, 'tis but to peize the time,
> To eke it, and to draw it out in length,
> To stay you from election.

But I said "erection." The band just put down their instruments and walked off' unable to control their laughter, 'as did the monks, leaving Polly James to sing on her own.'[3]

Moreover, words that have acquired a sexual meaning since Shakespeare's time may convey that meaning to a modern audience: Richard II's declaration that he will give his '*gay* apparel for an almsman's gown' (3.3.148) is an example, especially since it is not uncommon for actors to portray the King as homosexual.[4]

*

Whenever Shakespeare uses the word 'sex', some seventeen times throughout his writings, he always does so in the sense simply of gender, as when Benedick describes himself as 'a professed tyrant to their sex' (*Much Ado About Nothing*, 1.1.160–1). And according to the supplement to the *Oxford English Dictionary*, it was not until 1929, in a work by D. H. Lawrence, that 'sex' came to be used in the sense of sexual intercourse.

But one of the greatest of love poets, Shakespeare's contemporary John Donne (see Plate 2), comes at least close to this sense in his poem 'The Ecstasy', where, envisaging a pair of lovers lying enraptured together all day long 'like sepulchral statues', hand in hand in wordless spiritual communion, he writes that this 'ecstasy'—the abstracted state of being in which they find themselves—helps them to understand 'what we love':

> We see by this it was not sex;
>> We see we saw not what did move;
> But as all several [distinct] souls contain
>> Mixture of things, they know not what,
> Love these mixed souls doth mix again,
>> And makes both one, each this and that.

The poet goes on to ask why for so long they 'forbear' the use of their bodies in a sexual communion which would complement their spiritual oneness. There is something of a 'descent' in the movement from a spiritual to a physical ecstasy, but it is a liberating resolution, one that reveals 'Love's mysteries':

> So must pure lovers' souls descend
> To' affections, and to faculties
> Which sense may reach and apprehend;
> Else a great Prince in prison lies.
> To'our bodies turn we then, that so
> Weak men on love revealed may look.

I quote this poem because it helps us to understand Shakespeare's vocabulary of love. Both writers, seeking to express their sense of what love means, speak of it in metaphysical, religious terms of 'soul' and

'spirit', as a transcendental state of being which reaches earthly frui-
tion in sexual union; the richest kind of human communion which,
though it may seem like a 'descent' to earthliness from spirituality, yet
is the nearest that 'weak man' can attain to the communion of the gods.
So for example Biron in *Love's Labour's Lost* says that 'when love speaks,
the voice of all the gods | Make heaven drowsy with the harmony'
(4.3.320–1), the poet in Sonnet 151, which is one of Shakespeare's most
explicitly sexual poems, remarks that 'My soul doth tell my body that
he may | Triumph in love', and when Othello arrives in Cyprus he
greets his new wife Desdemona as 'my soul's joy' and decrees that

> My soul hath her content so absolute
> That not another comfort like to this
> Succeeds in unknown fate.   (2.1.192–4)

In passages such as these the words 'soul' and 'spirit' are virtually inter-
changeable, if difficult to define, referring to the concept of a spiritual
as opposed to the bodily part of man, the quintessence of something.

The slipperiness of the language, however, is demonstrated by the
fact that both words could also be used in the sense of 'semen'; Gordon
Williams writes that 'Exchange of souls'—such as Donne writes
about—'confuses with physiological ideas on the mingling of
seed…indeed *soul* like **spirit**, sometimes clearly carries a semen-
sense'.[5] This gives a sexual undertone to Faustus's reaction to Helen of
Troy in Marlowe's play: 'Her lips suck forth my soul: see where it flies.'[6]
The idea that the parting of the soul from the body is akin to the emission of semen relates also to the ubiquitous notion that orgasm was a
species of little death—*la petite mort*—illustrated by Fletcher's 'many a
handsome wench that loves the sport well | Gives up her soul so in her
lover's bosom' (*The Mad Lover*, 2.1.15–16). And the sexual sense of 'spirit'
is clearly present in Shakespeare's Sonnet 129, 'Th'expense of spirit in
a waste of shame | Is lust in action', with its puns on 'spirit' (semen)
and 'waste' ('waist' as well as 'waste land').

Shakespeare's writings are full of a sense of the tension between the spiritual and the earthly, and awareness of the difficulty of understanding when and how the sexual faculty, which may be terribly abused in the search for sensual gratification and the wielding of power over other individuals, may nevertheless become the key that, in Donne's terms, releases 'a great Prince' from prison. When, Shakespeare often seems to be asking, does desire stop being lustful and start being love? What is the relationship between lust and love? He explores the theme repeatedly in both plays and poems, and it will recur in later pages of this book. (It is akin to the question of where, in the visual arts, artistic portrayal of nakedness or of sexual behaviour shades into pornography.)

There are important studies of Shakespeare's sexual language, mostly reference works, ranging from Eric Partridge's pioneering *Shakespeare's Bawdy* (1947), through Hilda Hulme's chapter on 'The Less Decent Language of the Time' in her *Explorations in Shakespeare's Language* (1962), and two studies mentioned above, Frankie Rubinstein's over-heated book and Gordon Williams's invaluable *Glossary*. A more critical study is E. A. M. Colman's *The Dramatic Use of Bawdy in Shakespeare* (1974). There are also studies of specialized aspects of sexuality in Shakespeare's time and in his works, some of them heavily theorized, and not all of them focusing principally upon Shakespeare. I refer to some of these when relevant, and list them in my Further Reading section (pp. 265–6). My own *Looking for Sex in Shakespeare* (Cambridge University Press, 2004) is a short series of three chapters, originally given as lectures, which confines itself to a critique of over-sexualized interpretations of *A Midsummer Night's Dream*, an essay on the originality of the sonnets, and a study of gay interpretations on page and stage.

Despite a growth in tolerance and understanding over the past half-century, the word 'sex' is still liable to provoke sniggers. The use of 'bawdy' in two of the titles that I have cited suggests concentration on the lubricious use of the language of sex rather than an attempt to discuss the subject in all its fullness. It is still too common to imply that sex is something to be ashamed of, that sexual language is a matter for titters and for semi-concealment, that explication of a sexual subtext will titillate rather than illuminate. Jonathan Bate promoted the Royal Shakespeare Company edition (2008) as the 'filthiest' edition of Shakespeare ever to be published, as if its main appeal would be to readers looking to its notes for sexual thrills; and 2006 saw the publication of *Filthy Shakespeare: Shakespeare's Most Outrageous Sexual Puns* by Pauline Kiernan, described as 'a brilliant giftbook' which 'contains 100 of Shakespeare's most shocking, tantalizingly-coded sexual subtexts, ranging from Wanking to Dildos', and in which 'Each filthy passage is "translated" into modern English and the hidden sexual meanings of the words explained in a glossary.' An example is her paraphrase of Coriolanus's 'Measureless liar…"Boy"! O slave' (5.6.104–5), which reads 'You buggered cock-less coward. You dare to call me "bum-boy"? O sodomite!' The paraphrase of 'liar' as 'bugger' is justified with a note 'Punning on the Italian *bugiare* meaning to lie', as if audiences or readers would automatically dig into their memories for translation of perfectly ordinary words in any language they happened to know in the effort to find a double meaning in them. In the same passage, 'Stain all your edges'—sides of your blades—'on me' (5.4.113) is glossed 'stain all your swords with my blood, smear all your cocks with my spunk' (pp. 209–10). Kiernan's book is a work of grotesque caricature, inventing rather than elucidating sexual meanings.[7] It is pornographic.

No one could deny that Shakespeare often uses sex as a subject for comedy, that some of his characters talk 'greasily', as one of them puts it (*Love's Labour's Lost*, 4.1.136), that (especially in his earlier years) he delighted in sexual wordplay and expected audiences to share his delight. I examine this aspect of his work particularly in Chapter 4, 'The Fun of Sex'. Despite this there is a degree of fastidiousness in

Shakespeare's use of the language of sex and of bodily functions. As Colman observes, his bawdy is often indirect, metaphorical, or allusive. Only at its least subtle does it use blunt, unequivocal terms of sexual description, the familiar four-letter words. Shakespeare invariably suppresses these in favour of euphemistic or pseudo-euphemistic substitutes: a man's *yard* (*penis*, as an English word, came later) will less often be joked about under its own name than under the thin disguise of *prick* or *pike* or *weapon*. *Cunt* and *fuck* do not reach print in Shakespeare's text at all, except through puns (*count, focative*). Again you find substituted words carrying the ideas—*case, foin*, and the like.

Similarly, as if from personal fastidiousness, Shakespeare never directly uses some of the more basic four-letter words, such as 'arse' (except in 'open-arse', see p. 157), 'fart', 'shit', or 'turd' (except as a pun, *Merry Wives of Windsor*, 3.3.225) for bodily functions or their effects— even 'piss' is rare. Nor does he refer to sodomites, or to passive partners in male/male sex as ingles, catamites, or pathics, as for instance Ben Jonson does. A consequence of this is that editors who insist on using these and related words in their glosses may be truer to the literal sense of the original than to the tone in which it is spoken. It is also worth remembering that Shakespeare's language is polyphonic; rather as, in listening to music played on a keyboard, our ears may pick out a note of a melody while subordinating its harmonies in our consciousness, so in a passage of Shakespearian verse, though we may subconsciously acknowledge the possibility of a sexual undertone, that sense forms only a small part of our apprehension of what is said. So, for example, in Romeo's last words, 'Thus with a kiss I die' (*Romeo and Juliet*, 5.3.120), though we may recognize in the conjunction of 'kiss' and 'die' the possibility of a reference to sexual orgasm, nevertheless this sense is likely to be relegated to the back of our minds in apprehension of the poignancy of what Romeo is saying.

Equation of sexuality with filth is demeaning and reductive. Shakespeare is profoundly and continuously interested in sex as a fundamental human instinct and activity, as a source not only of comedy but also of joy, of anguish, of disillusionment and of jealousy, of nausea as well as of ecstasy, as a site of moral and ethical debate, and, at its best, as a natural fulfilment of spiritual love. Moreover the attitudes that he expresses to it can be seen as changing and developing over the course of his career in ways that are interesting in themselves, and that could be plausibly related to his psychological development. My book aims to discuss sex as it matters in its poetic and dramatic context, seeing it as a major source of comedy, drama, debate, and passion in Shakespeare's works, not isolating it from their other concerns but considering it in relation to their overall patterns and effect. Perhaps most importantly, it seeks to illuminate Shakespeare's profound though often troubled reflections on the relationship between sex and love.

PART I

Life & Times

I
n the first part of this book I write about aspects of sexuality and love in Shakespeare's time. Chapter 1 offers a discussion of various aspects of sexual behaviour and attitudes towards it with special emphasis first on Stratford-upon-Avon—the community where he grew up—and then the worlds of the court and the theatre in London. Chapter 2 looks particularly at depictions of sexuality in the poetry of the period. In it I suggest that during the time at which Shakespeare was writing his narrative poems, and at least some of the Sonnets, a group of poets—Christopher Marlowe, Richard Barnfield, and Michael Drayton—catered especially for readers with homoerotic interests, and I consider how, if at all, Shakespeare fits into this milieu. Chapter 3 is concerned with Shakespeare's own sex life, and that of his immediate family.

1

Sexuality in Shakespeare's Time

T his and the following two chapters form a preliminary to a critical study of the way that Shakespeare portrays sexuality in his plays and poems. First, how much can we discover about the sexual behaviour of his fellow townsmen and women, and how did they think about sex? Were their behaviour and attitudes essentially different from those that prevail today? Were there discrepancies between precept and practice? In asking these questions we have to admit the likelihood that both behaviour and attitudes were as diverse then as they are now, but maybe we can hope at least to identify some norms and to think about interesting divagations from them. We shall want to look at how both secular and ecclesiastical authorities attempted to regulate sexual behaviour and to punish those who offended against their codes.

The Church took the lead: Elizabethans were well accustomed to being told how wicked they were. One of the homilies read in church when there was no sermon, the Homily against Whoredom and Uncleanness, begins

Though there want not (good Christian people) great swarms of vices worthy to be rebuked (unto such decay is true godliness and virtuous living now come), yet above other vices, the outrageous seas of adultery (or breaking of wedlock), whoredom, fornication and uncleanness have not only burst in, but also overflowed almost the whole world...so abundantly, that through the customable use thereof, this vice is grown into such an height, that in a manner among many, it is counted no sin at all, but rather a pastime, a dalliance, and but a touch of youth: not rebuked, but winked at: not punished, but laughed at.

And so on for paragraph after paragraph, culminating in the threat that 'whoremongers shall have their part with murderers, sorcerers, enchanters, liars, idolaters, and such other, in the lake which burneth with fire and brimstone, which is the second death'. They couldn't say they hadn't been warned.

The State too had its say, with a mass of legislation designed to buttress the Church's teachings and to punish offenders, often with a severity and brutality that seem shocking to civilized societies of today, but that can still be paralleled in some parts of the world.

From Stratford it will be appropriate to pass on to London, which appears to have been Shakespeare's other main place of residence and work, and which was certainly the centre of the theatre industry and indeed of the sex industry. Then as now, the theatrical profession was particularly associated in the public mind with sinful and aberrant sexuality. Many citizens regarded playhouses and those who worked in them, or even who simply attended them, as inherently wicked. Puritan opponents of the theatre, in particular, were liable to attack it as a stimulus to sexual vice. And indeed several prominent theatrical personnel, including Philip Henslowe, Edward Alleyn, and George Wilkins—who collaborated with Shakespeare—had interests in inns that doubled as brothels or in brothels themselves. Rumours about the morals of actors and their relationships with both boy players and women members of the audience circulated—one of the best known of these directly concerns Shakespeare (see p. 71). And, as we shall see, there were more than rumours of sexual immorality among players. A playgoer, Simon Forman, who left us the fullest surviving accounts of performances of plays by Shakespeare, is the author also of intimate diaries that afford unique insights into the sexual behaviour of a middle-class citizen of the period and of those whom he encountered.[1]

The theatre was associated with the court, and courtiers were notoriously promiscuous. Queen Elizabeth herself, the 'Virgin Queen', was regarded, officially at least, as a personification of chastity (though there was gossip about her, too), and endeavoured, not always successfully, to control the morals of her maids of honour; but standards were far more lax at the court of her successor, King James I. Some of his courtiers were the objects of notorious scandals, and the King himself gave rise to gossip, even scandal, because of his intimate relationships with handsome young men. Other prominent public figures were known, or are now known, to have participated in same-sex relationships. We know or can reasonably conjecture something of the sexual proclivities and outlooks of a number of the literary figures of Shakespeare's time, including John Donne, Ben Jonson, Christopher Marlowe, Richard Barnfield, and Michael Drayton, as well as Shakespeare himself, and we can observe literary transmutations of their sexual interests in their writings. Let's consider just a few manifestations of the relationship between the personal lives and the writings of some of these men. In traversing this topic we'll concentrate on aspects that seem most relevant to a study of its reflections and transmutations in the life and work of William Shakespeare.

*

It is in the nature of things that sexual behaviour that does not offend agreed norms makes no special stir. Even so it may be revealing. People masturbate, woo, marry, copulate, and give birth. Of these events the law requires only that marriages and, in Shakespeare's time, baptisms rather than births be recorded. Analysis of such records may in itself illuminate the sexual *mores* of the period and, indeed, of Shakespeare and his family. We know, for example, that between 1570 and 1630 the average age for first marriage among men in Stratford-upon-Avon, calculated on the basis of 106 known cases, was between twenty and thirty, though legally they could marry from the age of fourteen, with the 'greatest number of marriages (fifteen) taking place when the bridegroom was twenty-four'.[2] There was a practical reason for this: it would have given time for the men to have 'become settled in work at the expiry of their apprenticeship', which normally lasted for seven years. On the other hand, women by and large married younger: though the average age of brides at first marriage, based on sixty known cases, was also twenty-four, the favoured ages were 'either seventeen or twenty-one'. The youngest bride married at the age of only twelve—the earliest legal age for a woman, younger even than Shakespeare's thirteen-year-old Juliet—though she did not have a child until she was sixteen, which may (or may not) mean that the marriage was not initially consummated.[3] 'The men of Stratford', we learn, 'rarely looked farther afield than the outlying hamlets of the parish and, provided it was agreeable to the family, their choice usually seems to have been dictated by mutual attraction. Arranged marriages were only for the rich.'[4]

Marriage is not a prerequisite for births, and records of baptism sometimes reveal sexual irregularity, as in the entry in the Stratford register on 5 May 1592 of the birth of 'John, son of Katherine Getley, a bastard.' There is a slight Shakespeare connection, as the mother's father owned the cottage in Chapel Lane, close to Shakespeare's house New Place, and which Shakespeare bought in 1602.[5] In this case the simple entry in the parish register can be supplemented with legal evidence. Five months later Katherine and a man named William Sanford were called to court—but failed to appear—on a charge of fornication. After failing to turn up on a second occasion they were excommunicated. This information comes from the Act Books of the Ecclesiastical Court, popularly known as the 'Bawdy Court' because it dealt with sexual (as well as many other) offences. Only in 1964 did it become known that substantial records of this kind for Stratford survive, in, as it happens, the Kent Archives Office. They provide much information pertaining to sexual offences in Stratford. One of the most frequently named of them is 'incontinency', which seems to refer to either premarital or extramarital sex. In *As You Like It* Rosalind envisages the possibility that love at first sight will lead to incontinency: 'your brother and my sister no sooner met but they looked; no sooner looked but they loved; no sooner loved but they sighed; no sooner sighed but they asked one another the reason; no sooner knew the reason but they sought the remedy; and in these degrees have they made a pair of stairs to marriage, which they will climb incontinent, or else be incontinent before marriage' (5.2.31–8)—as of course Shakespeare, whose first child was born 6 months after his marriage, was.

Records of burials as well as births may inform us about sexual behaviour. The most conspicuous example of this in relation to the Shakespeare family is found not in Stratford records but in the parish registers of St Giles, Cripplegate, in London. Shakespeare had a brother named Edmund, sixteen years younger than himself. The registers tell us that a base-born—illegitimate—child named 'Edward, son of Edward Shakespeare, player' was buried on 12 August 1607. The names Edward and Edmund were often confused, and the child's father was probably the 'Edmund Shakespeare, a player' who was buried across the river at St Saviour's, Southwark—now Southwark Cathedral—on the last day of the same year 'with a forenoon knell of the Great Bell' costing a pound and paid for, presumably, by his prosperous brother. Nothing whatever is known of the child's mother, and indeed this is almost all we know of his father. It seems ironical that, not long before this, Shakespeare had given his name to the Bastard in *King Lear*.

Negative evidence, too, may be suggestive. Edmund was the youngest of Shakespeare's three brothers who survived infancy. He would have been only 27 when he died. The other two brothers lived longer: Gilbert, two years younger than William, is said to have become a haberdasher; his name occurs in legal records in Stratford and London and he died aged 45, four years before William. Nothing is known of the middle brother, Richard, except the dates of his baptism in 1574 and his burial in 1613 at the age of 38. Neither is known to have had any liaison, whether legal or not, or to have begotten offspring. Jeanne Jones, noting that 'The state of marriage was thought a desirable one, both for mutual comfort and support, and for raising children to carry on the family name', remarks that 'Bachelors aged more than thirty were rare; so much so that the compilers of the 1595 list of maltsters felt it necessary to explain than John Page "a smith by trade" was "a man never married".'[6] At the time that Richard and Gilbert died William's son Hamnet was also dead, so they would have known that there was no male heir to carry on the Shakespeare name. Whether the fact that William married when he was only eighteen whereas two of his brothers appear to have been confirmed bachelors tells us anything about their relationships with their mother is a matter for psychoanalysts after the fact rather than for literary historians.

The Stratford records give many instances of prosecutions for fornication, 'incontinence', and straightforward adultery. Some of these cases had resulted in pregnancy. Sex before marriage was an offence for which the culprits could be required to do public penance in church even after they were married. So for example a Stratford shoemaker, John Davis, was reported to the ecclesiastical court on 7 January 1625 on suspicion of 'incontinence' with Elizabeth Wheeler. He soon applied for a marriage licence, but was accused again of incontinence two weeks later. Probably the couple were living together. They married on 31 January, but less than five weeks later Davis appeared in court on the charge of 'begetting his wife with child before marriage'. No doubt either her pregnancy had become very visible or the child was already born. Both of them had to acknowledge their sin in church. They were spared the most ignominious form of penance, imposed on for example Isabella Hall for begetting a bastard in the same year. She was required

> to stand upon a mat or seat in the middle aisle of the church during all the time of Morning Prayer and Sermon in white sheets hanging down from her shoulders to her feet and holding a white rod in her hand and at the end of the sermon to confess according to the schedule

—that is, to spill all the beans—and to bring a document certifying that she had done all this to the court the next day. Davis and his wife were not required to provide this amount of entertainment for the congregation. They simply had to acknowledge their sin in church, though not during service time, before the Bailiff, an Alderman, and the curate.[7]

In *Measure for Measure* Shakespeare portrays the punishment of a man, Claudio, for getting a woman to whom he is engaged pregnant before marriage. Shakespeare is at pains to make clear that Claudio's offence only just comes within the compass of the law:

> Upon a true contract
> I got possession of Julietta's bed.
> You know the lady: she is fast my wife,
> Save that we do the denunciation [public announcement] lack
> Of outward order.   (1.2.133–7)

Claudio's words 'a true contract' imply that the lovers had entered into a formal agreement to marry, which might be accomplished by so simple a ceremony as an unwitnessed 'handfasting', to be followed by a religious rite.[8] In Shakespeare's England it was not uncommon for contracted couples to 'risk each other's chastity in anticipation of matrimony'.[9] And there was a specific, though perhaps not wholly admirable, financial reason for delaying the formalities of this marriage:

> This we came not to
> Only for propagation of a dower
> Remaining in the coffer of her friends,
> From whom we thought it meet to hide our love
> Till time had made them for us.   (1.2.137–41)

('Only for propagation of a dower | Remaining in the coffer of her friends' seems to mean 'only for want of the release of a dowry held in trust by her relatives.') But Juliet's pregnancy has become visible:

> …it chances
> The stealth of our most mutual entertainment
> With character too gross is writ on Juliet.   (1.2.141–3)

For all the extenuating circumstances, Claudio is sentenced to death. If this is anything to go by, Shakespeare was lucky to get away scot free—so far as we know.

Stratford was a hotbed of small-town gossip, and the records reveal many cases of slander involving accusations of adultery, cuckoldry, and whoredom. 'Whore', literally implying prostitution, was a common and much resented term of abuse. In 1622 one Thomas Faux called Alice Brunt a 'filthy whore and said he would prove her to be a whore', and two years later Richard Wheeler had to perform penance for having called the wife of Richard Brooks 'whore and sowlike whore, with divers other filthy speeches'.[10] There is evidence of the kind of sexually transmitted disease that would have been associated with whoredom in the casebooks of Shakespeare's son-in-law, Dr John Hall, who treated several cases of gonorrhoea or syphilis—the diseases were frequently confused. Masturbation, not being a criminal offence, is not mentioned in the records. Moralists wrote disapprovingly of it, but others more realistically saw it as a natural and healthy release of sexual tension, especially among the unmarried.[11]

As for prostitution, there appear to be no surviving Stratford records of sex for sale, though this surely must have happened in the town's inns and taverns, and is probably subsumed in the allegations of incontinence and fornication. Germaine Greer suggests that 'more and more women fleeing disgrace in the church courts or actually driven out of town by the parish authorities for "unlawful pregnancy" were arriving in London every week to swell the ranks of prostitutes'.[12] Many of them gave birth to unwanted babies; it has been estimated that 'a thousand children were cast out each year, many at the doorsteps of city leaders'. We know of an unmarried mother who, when prosecuted at Bridewell, 'explained that she was advised to leave her new born [sic] "at some rich man's door and it will be better kept than thou canst keep it".'[13] And records survive of a young Stratford woman who actually did become a prostitute in London.

The records of Bridewell prison show that around 1594–5 Elizabeth Evans, daughter of a Stratford cutler named Robert who was executed for 'quoininge'—presumably coining, forging money—arrived in London where for some years she led a colourful life as a prostitute, adopting false names and moving frequently from one place of residence to another. In March 1598 one Mary Holmes declared on oath that she had 'sometimes served' Elizabeth (whom she referred to as Dudley), but 'perceiving that she was of ill report and an ill woman of her body did much repent her coming to her and that she stayeth not with her above a month but sought to get from so bad a service'. Mary spoke of Elizabeth's relations with two brothers, John and Henry Pears, 'who did often resort thereto and did call the said Elizabeth "cousin".' She had not seen any evil in Henry, but she had seen Elizabeth and John in bed together on two or three occasions. It looks as if Elizabeth was keener on John than he was on her, because Elizabeth 'would beg and entreat the said John Pears to come to bed to her and hath locked him into her chamber when he hath made show to be willing to run away'; John had made the servant 'help him off with his boots and stockings', presumably after changing his mind about the attractions of Elizabeth's bed. Maybe he needed help in removing his leg-wear because he was somewhat corpulent.

Another man, called Saunders, had also 'resort[ed]' to Elizabeth but Mary could not 'charge him nor any other to be caught with her' except John. Once, however, Henry 'did knock at the door when John Pears was in bed with' Elizabeth, so the maid 'did convey the said John Pears into another chamber and carried his clothes after him, he rising without his clothes'. I can only imagine that Elizabeth was trying to hide from Henry the fact that she had been in bed with John, and that she managed to delay Henry's entry into her room till she could compose herself. At about the same time, Shakespeare was portraying a somewhat similar incident with Falstaff hiding in a laundry basket (*The Merry Wives of Windsor*, 3.3). It's clear that Henry was resentful of John's relations with Elizabeth since he later asked the witness whether John 'had at any time lain with' Elizabeth, and on hearing that he had, exclaimed, 'O Lord, would she do so! I am sorry that ever I did speak for her.' Elizabeth had claimed to have 'three hundred pounds a year to live on', but Mary's wages went unpaid.

Not long afterwards, on 1 April, Elizabeth was in court; one of the witnesses was a woman named Joyce Cowden, who said that as a girl she went to school with Evans in Stratford-upon-Avon, and 'knew her father', but on that occasion Elizabeth was released without punishment on the intervention of Sir William Howard, brother of the Lord Admiral, patron of the Lord Admiral's Men, who may have been one of her clients.[14] She made a fulsome testament of repentance and 'purpose of amendment of my life'. Nevertheless, a couple of weeks later she was back in court because she had 'enticed a little child of the age of five years and would have begged with it and did strip it of the clothes that she had. The child was one Griffin Powell.' This time Elizabeth was detained and punished.

This case, at once farcical and poignant, is of interest not only for the light it throws on sexual behaviour, but also because it appears to be our only clear record of any formal education being available for girls in Stratford; it was probably only at the level of petty, or dame's, school, but Elizabeth was able to sign her name, whereas the maid testified with her mark only.

Events such as these may seem to cry out for dramatization, and in fact plays were based on similar real-life cases. A sensational later series of episodes formed the basis for a play with no Stratford links called *Keep the Widow Waking*, written by Thomas Dekker, John Webster, John Ford, and William Rowley. Though the play itself has not survived, we know of it and of the events upon which it was based from exceptionally vivid legal records of a court case of 1624. If we had only the play without the legal documents we should have been likely to assume that its events were fictional. As it is, we know that it portrayed truths stranger than many fictions. It combined two stories linked only, it would seem, by the fact that its two central characters were up for trial on the same day.

On 3 September 1624 Tobias Audley was prosecuted at the Old Bailey for felony, and Nathaniel Tindall for murder. The widow in the case was one Anne Elsdon, a sixty-two-year-old woman of means who had the misfortune to attract the attentions of Tobias Audley 'of Wood Street in your [the Queen's] City of London, a keeper of a tobacco shop and a most notorious lewd person and of no worth of [or?] credit.' He was about twenty-five years old. Audley paid court to the gullible widow, and on the evening of 21 July 1624 they met together in a private room in the Greyhound Tavern on Fleet Street with, among others, a prostitute, her madame, and two unscrupulous clergymen. Audley had promised substantial rewards to his cronies for helping him to win the widow and her wealth, by fair means or by foul. They plied her with drink, and she spent the next four days in a state of alcoholic stupor. A witness admitted 'with weeping tears' that Anne 'was very sick and senseless and yet the defendants did pour down such vials of hot waters [spirits] down her throat that she thought was able to kill a horse'. Audley made no attempt to conceal his mercenary motives, saying when one of the company expressed a fear that Anne would die, 'Let her be hanged, I'll have her goods and let them take her lands.' She was put through a marriage ceremony while too stupefied to know what was happening to her. A male witness, going, presumably ironically, to congratulate her, 'found her sitting in a chair, leaning her body all on one side, and drivelling'. 'Speaking somewhat loud unto her, and shaking her, and bidding God give her joy, she was unable to speak unto him again.' When Anne sobered up, her attempts to deny that she was married were met with insults. The prostitute suggested to Audley that he should 'make much of her, and so stop her exclamations', but he replied 'that he had as lief go to bed to an old sow.' She was soon dead drunk again.

Revelries continued at great expense, Audley looted his unwitting bride's house, and Anne was heard 'crying out…"I will [wish to] go home, I will go home"…making great moan that she was detained there against her will, diverse persons…telling her that she should not go'. After a few days, Audley, alarmed by the efforts of Anne's daughter and son-in-law to rescue her, abandoned her, and she lay 'in a manner speechless' for nine or ten days. Violence ensued, Audley was prosecuted and jailed on more than one charge, and the cases dragged on until well after Anne died, on 24 March 1626.

In the meantime both a play and a ballad which summarizes and advertises it, with the refrain 'keep the widow waking', had entertained fellow Londoners. The two-part ballad, in seventeen stanzas, ends:

> Thus sometimes that haps in an hour
> That comes not in seven year,
> Therefore let young men that are poor
> Come take example here,
> And you who fain would hear the full

> Discourse of this match-making,
> The play will teach you at the Bull
> To keep the widow waking.

Heartlessly, the ballad was sung repeatedly under Anne Elsdon's window.

At the time of the trial the play dramatizing the terrible happenings for which Audley and Tindall were prosecuted had already been acted on the stage of the Red Bull in Clerkenwell, which had a particular reputation as a playhouse that catered for the lower end of the market. The play entwined Anne Elsdon's story with that of the unhappy young Nathaniel Tindall's murder of his mother by stabbing her with a knife in the throat and the left breast, which provoked two ballads, one entitled 'The Penitent Son's Tears for his Murdered Mother', the other 'A Most Bloody Unnatural and Unmatchable Murder Committed in Whitechapel by Nathaniel Tindall upon his own Mother'. Tindall confessed to the crime, and was sentenced to be 'hanged near the house where he committed the murder'.[15]

The records of the Stratford Bawdy Court offer no instances of prosecutions for rape, homosexuality, or bestiality, which would have been 'referred to high judicial authority, for they were capital crimes, punishable by death'.

In all, 'forty cases of bestiality handled by the secular authorities' have been identified during the reigns of Elizabeth and James I, mostly with mares.[16] But 'It would seem…as if the awfulness of the penalty, and a desire not to notice that such outrages had been committed, had the effect of ensuring that there were very few prosecutions for them, and even a degree of tolerance.'[17] And there are horrifying records of such offences against children in the Bridewell records, including 'a girl aged 6, sodomized; another, 10, assaulted repeatedly by a man who brandished a knife and threatened "that if she either told or cried he would stick her"; a boy, 10, taken into a "blind alley" to be abused "by the way of buggery"; a child, 7, raped by her father both vaginally and anally and told that if she complained "he would stop her breath", or her mother's or that of a neighbor."[18]

In other respects too the scene becomes more colourful when we move to London. The professional life that Shakespeare entered was the source of much opposition from both Church and State, and strenuous, if often unavailing, efforts were made to regulate it. We should not believe everything that was said by Puritan opponents of theatre, who liked to give the impression that audiences were made up largely of thieves and whores. Some of the documents most frequently cited as evidence date from the early years of professional theatre and may be regarded almost as expressions of fear as to what might happen rather than as evidence of what did. Even two years before playgoing became established in London with the construction of The Theatre in 1576,[19] the strongly Protestant Geoffrey Fenton was complaining how often 'the majesty of God' was 'offended in those two or three hours'[20] that those plays endure, both by wicked words, and blasphemy, impudent gestures, doubtful slanders, unchaste songs, and also by corruption of the wills of the players and the assistants'.[21] Notoriously, one preacher blamed the plague on the players: 'the cause of plays is sin, if you look to it well; and the cause of sin are plays; therefore the cause of plagues are plays'.[22] That simple syllogism comes from a sermon by Thomas White preached in 1577, only one year after James Burbage built The Theatre.

Three years later Anthony Munday, a playwright who did not scruple to befoul his own nest, wrote of 'the chapel of Satan—I mean The Theatre' where visitors would find 'no want of young ruffians, nor lack of harlots utterly past all shame, who press to the forefront of the scaffolds to the end to show their impudency [demonstrate their shamelessness] and to be as an object to all men's eyes'. And the tub-thumping Puritan Philip Stubbes wrote in 1583 that 'these goodly pageants being done, every mate sorts to his mate, everyone brings another homeward of their way very friendly, and in their secret conclaves covertly they play the sodomites or worse'.[23] (Sodomy could refer to any kind of sexual transgression.)

Attacks like these may represent an extreme point of view, but it is undeniable that theatre was reasonably associated in many people's minds with sexual licence. On the one hand, some actors seem to have been highly respectable citizens. Shakespeare's close and long-time colleagues John Heminges and Henry Condell became churchwardens and so far as we know led blameless lives. But the prohibition of playing within the City of London meant that playhouses were located outside the City bounds, especially in Southwark, south of the Thames, which for centuries had been the main location of the stews, or brothels. Some theatre owners and practitioners, most conspicuously Philip Henslowe and his son-in-law, the great actor Edward Alleyn, also owned inns which doubled as brothels, and made a lot of money out of them. The Swiss physician Thomas Platter, who toured England in 1599, wrote that 'although close watch is kept on them, great swarms' of prostitutes 'haunt the town in the taverns and playhouses'.[24]

Theatre is a sexy business. The relationship between actors and audiences, then as now, was sexually charged. Just as in our own time actors are the frequent object of gossip, scandal, and desire, so in Shakespeare's time there is ample evidence that playgoers looked on them with admiration for more than their acting skills. To give only one example, in Thomas Middleton's comedy *A Mad World My Masters* a Courtesan is so taken with an actor playing a Prologue in a play that she exclaims:

> O' my troth, an I were not married, I could find in my heart to fall in love with that player now, and send for him to a supper. I know some i'th'town that have done as much, and there took such a good conceit of their parts into th' two-penny room, that the actors have been found i'th'morning in a less compass than their stage [that is, in bed], though 'twere ne'er so full of gentlemen.[25]

(The 'two-penny room' appears to have been a private room in the theatre used for entertaining.)

In the Cambridge University play *The Second Part of The Return from Parnassus*, written anonymously around the turn of the century, the admiration of young women is counted among the rewards of the profession: the actor Will Kemp, speaking to students who have ambitions to go on the stage, says 'There's not a country wench that can dance Sellenger's Round [probably a euphuism for 'engage in sexual activity'] but can talk of Dick Burbage and Will Kemp.'[26] And a ballad on the burning of the Globe playhouse scurrilously advises the actors to save the money they would otherwise have spent on whores to buy tiles in place of thatch for the new theatre.[27]

These are light-hearted enough examples, but we know also of more serious cases of sexual licence among players, and specifically on the part of an actor who was at one time a member of Shakespeare's company. Christopher Beeston, born about 1580, seems to have begun his career during the 1590s as a boy player with the Lord Chamberlain's Men, and was to have a long and influential career as a theatre manager until he died in 1638. He married in September 1602, and only a few weeks later a woman who had been imprisoned in Bridewell for 'having a child in whoredom' accused him of raping her. Beeston, she said, boasting of having 'lain with a hundred wenches in my time', had 'committed with her the abominable sin of adultery in most filthy and brutish manner in one Winter's house in an alley without Bishopsgate on Midsummer Eve last'. Beeston denied the charges but he 'and others his confederate players did very unreverently demean themselves to certain governors and much abused the place'. The charges appear to have been dropped.[28] As the scholar who discovered the case points out, it resonates interestingly with Shakespeare's *Measure for Measure*, which takes place partly in a prison:

> The case provides a striking context for *Measure for Measure*, performed in December 1604, in which Angelo threatens Isabella with rape,

Lucio vehemently demeans himself to the Duke, and Barnardine refuses to leave his cell. *Measure for Measure* seems to have enabled the company (now the King's men) to acknowledge the controversy and parody the Bridewell court at the same time, resolving the risks of legal procedure into an uneasy fiction. Shakespeare used a variety of literary sources to compose that play, but it is hard to imagine that he did not have in mind Beeston's experience too.[29]

We come even closer to Shakespeare if we think about his fellow playwright George Wilkins, who wrote a play, *The Miseries of Enforced Marriage*, for Shakespeare's company in or around 1607, and with whom Shakespeare, it is now generally agreed, collaborated on the composition of *Pericles*. As we shall see, this is the play of Shakespeare's which offers the most sordid portrayal of life in a brothel.

Wilkins, who led a complex and largely disreputable life, was often in trouble with the law, was more than once prosecuted for violence against women, and kept an inn, which clearly doubled as a brothel, in an area of London notorious for prostitution.[30] The darkest side of such establishments is graphically portrayed by Thomas Nashe in his pamphlet *Christ's Tears over Jerusalem*, published in 1593. In order to evade the law, he writes, prostitutes in London brothels seek out 'back doors to come in and out by undiscovered. Sliding windows also, and trap-boards in floors, to hide whores behind and under, with false counterfeit panes in walls, to be opened and shut like a wicket.' They allow a gentleman in '*sans* fee' and give him 'free privilege thenceforward in their nunnery, to procure them frequentance'. (The use of 'nunnery' here for a brothel resonates interestingly with Hamlet's consigning of Ophelia to a 'nunnery.' See p. 204 below.) Anyone can 'set up a shop of incontinency' on the strength of 'but one letter of an honest name'. 'In such a place dwells a wise woman that tells fortunes, and she under that shadow hath her house never empty of forlorn unfortunate dames married to old husbands.' (This seems to imply a brothel with male prostitutes catering for women clients.)

Figure 1. This composite portrayal of the multiple goings-on in a sixteenth-century bath-house and brothel was engraved by the German artist Virgil Solis (1514–62).

In another corner inhabiteth a physician and a conjuror who hath corners and spare chambers to hide carrion in, and can conjure up an unphysical [diseased] drab at all times. In a third place is there a gross-pencilled painter who works all in oil-colours, and under cover of drawing of pictures draws more to his shady pavilion than depart thence pure vestals.

Nashe seems ahead of his time in advocating 'public stews'—licensed brothels—rather than letting rogues 'keep private stews as they do'. The proprietors of such establishments know about

positions and instructions…to make their whores a hundred times more whorish and treacherous than their own wicked affects, resigned to the devil's disposing, can make them. Waters and receipts have they to enable a man to the act after he is spent, dormative potions to procure deadly sleep, that when the hackney he hath paid for lies by him, he may have no power to deal with her, but she may steal from him whiles he is in his deep *memento* [*memento mori*, i.e. sleep] and make her gain of three or four other.[31]

This is Nashe in sermonizing mode; later we shall find him writing more tolerantly of a visit to a brothel.

Elizabethan London was a close-knit society in which one name frequently links easily with another. Wilkins was a witness in the lawsuit brought by Stephen Bellot against his father-in-law, Christopher Mountjoy, in which Shakespeare gave evidence; and Mountjoy's wife Marie had been a client of the Simon Forman whose notebooks, as I have mentioned, throw floods of light on sexual behaviour at the time. Forman frequently records his sexual adventures, employing the code word 'halek' to mean fuck—so for example, apparently writing up notes in the form of a chronicle, he records that in May 1593 'I made my gown with velvet fur. The 11th of June I did halek Alice Blague, and the 15th of July. The 13th of August I redeemed my ring that was in pawn. The 8th day of October I went first a-wooing to Mrs. Lodcaster. The 29th of November, Thursday at 3 p.m. Avis Allen'—a cheese-monger's

Batfauch del.   Godfrey Sc.

D.ᴿ SIMON FORMAN,

ASTROLOGER.

Engraved from the Original Drawing

in the Collection of the Right Honᵇˡᵉ

LORD MOUNTSTUART.

Publish'd July 1.ˢᵗ 1776 by F. Blyth N.º 87. Cornhill.

Figure 2. This eighteenth-century engraving is presumably based on the portrait of himself that Simon Forman had painted around the time of his marriage, in 1599.

wife—'and I first osculavimus [kissed]. She rose and came to me; et halek Avis Allen prius [first] the 15th December, Saturday p.m. at 5.'[32] He needed precise records of the timing of his exploits in order to work out the astrological chances of further encounters, and perhaps because such records 'might come in handy for denying paternity'.[33]

Forman's notebooks also include information about Emilia Lanier, who was identified by A. L. Rowse with the so-called 'dark lady' of Shakespeare's[34] Sonnets, an identification which, while I regard it as highly dubious, has nevertheless been more recently at least provisionally endorsed by Michael Wood and René Weis.[35] Emilia seems not to have been exactly a prostitute—courtesan might be a more appropriate term. She underwent a religious conversion in later life, wrote a remarkable volume of sacred verse, *Salve Deus Rex Judaeorum* (1611), and later started a school. Nevertheless at the time she visited Forman she was the mistress of the elderly patron of Shakespeare's company, Lord Hunsdon, by whom she had a son. He kept her 'in great pride' though apparently with some concealment since when she became pregnant 'she was for colour [for the sake of appearances] married to a minstrel'—the musician Alfonso Lanier.

There was no shortage of sexual irregularity at the courts of either Elizabeth or James, though it was less blatant under the vigilant eye of the Virgin Queen. Let's look at a few examples which impinge more or less directly on Shakespeare. So far we have been concerned mainly with heterosexual activity. Historians of sexuality often tell us that homosexuality regarded as a psychological phenomenon did not exist until the later part of the nineteenth century, when indeed the word first came into being. But same-sex sexual activity certainly occurred in Shakespeare's time even if it is regarded as the expression of a taste rather than of an involuntary sexual identity. One writer even suggested that parental love might result in sexual transgression: 'what may be said of those that are so hellishly enamoured with their children as to commit incest or buggery with them?'[36] Though male sodomy was a capital crime, the punishment was rarely enforced. Bruce Smith notes that 'During the forty-five years of Elizabeth's reign and the twenty-three years of James I's reign only six men are recorded as having been indicted for sodomy in the Home County assizes,' all involving under-age victims, and there was only one conviction, in 1569, when a man was hanged for committing sodomy with a five-year-old boy. Moreover in general 'the conviction rate for sodomy is significantly lower than the rate for other categories of crime' with indictments for bestiality between 1553 and 1602 outnumbering indictments for sodomy six to one.[37] Smith sums up by saying that 'By and large, what the legal discourse addresses is the narrow case of forcible rape of an underaged boy by an adult male.'[38]

Male-to-male sexual relationships were common, even though later ages have often tried to submerge the fact. And there is good reason to believe that they were not regarded as subversive unless they involved rape of a child. Frank acknowledgement that one male can give pleasure to another male by sexual contact is not uncommon in societies where post-Freudian guilt feelings do not prevail. Alan Sinfield remarks, 'in early-modern England same-gender relations *were not terribly important*. In *As You Like It* and *Twelfth Night*, homoeroticism is part of the fun of the wooing...but it wouldn't be fun if such scenarios were freighted with the anxieties that people experience today.'[39] That is a generalization; certainly some moralists inveighed vehemently against same-gender sex, at least between adults and boys, but this very fact shows awareness of the possibilities of temptation: as Sinfield also writes, 'Moralists who complained about theatre and sexual licence took it for granted that boys are sexually attractive.'[40]

It was not exceptional for persons of the same gender at all levels of society to share a bed; 'schools, colleges, and the inns of court were *households* in both the literal and the figurative senses of the word: young men studied together, played together, ate together, and, like everybody else in the sixteenth century, slept together two to a bed'.[41] Shakespeare has a number of references to the practice with no necessary imputation of sexual contact. In *Henry V* Lord Scrope of Masham is spoken of as the King's 'bedfellow' (2.2.8); in *As You Like It* Celia says to Rosalind 'We still have slept together' (1.3.72); and the most explicitly homoerotic passage in the whole of Shakespeare is that in which Iago claims that the sleeping Cassio sought to make love to him as if he were Desdemona (see p. 177 below).

Sleeping together does not necessarily imply sexual contact; on the other hand a number of contemporary warnings about correct behaviour in these circumstances demonstrates awareness that suspicion and temptation might arise. A conduct book advises, 'If you are forced by unavoidable necessity to share a bed with another person of the same sex on a journey, it is not proper to lie so near him that you disturb or even touch him; and it is still less decent to put your legs between those of the other.'[42]

One modern scholar has uncovered fascinating evidence, centring on plays performed by the Whitefriars company of boy actors in the early seventeenth century, of the existence of what she calls 'a self-aware homoerotic community in early modern London'. 'Boy actors', she writes, 'appear to have been seen as a group with whom it was possible to become sexually intimate (and I would stress that women as well as men viewed them in this fashion).'[43] She shows too that the plays they acted in were exceptionally full of puns with homoerotic overtones. I shall suggest that before this, during the 1590s, too, a group of poets rather than dramatists may similarly have been consciously catering for a homoerotic public.

One reader who may have belonged to this group is the only person to whom Shakespeare personally dedicated any of his writings, Henry Wriothesley, 3rd Earl of Southampton, who has often been thought to figure in the supposed back story of Shakespeare's Sonnets. (See Plate 1) In 1598 he secretly married Elizabeth Vernon, to the Queen's great displeasure, and had a daughter by her in 1600. In the meantime, however, he was the subject of gossip reporting that while on military service in Ireland with the Earl of Essex, he had what was regarded as an unseemly relationship with one Captain Piers Edmunds. The writer of a letter says that Edmonds 'ate and drank at his table, and lay in his tent, the Earl of Southampton gave him a horse, which Edmunds refused a hundred marks for him [i.e. it was very valuable]. The Earl Southampton would clip and hug him in his arms and play wantonly with him.' A. L. Rowse, in his biography of Southampton, comments, 'Evidently there were compensations for service in the bogs.'[44]

This may be no more than malicious rumour-mongering, but homosexual behaviour and indeed crime among courtiers is well authenticated, notably in the case of the Earl of Oxford, who had theatrical interests—he kept a company of players and according to Francis Meres, in his *Palladis Tamia, or Wit's Treasury*, of 1598, which is a mine of information and opinion about the literary scene of his day, wrote comedies, none of which survive; he is often touted as a candidate for the authorship of Shakespeare's plays. While on an extended visit to Italy in 1575–6 Oxford consorted with both a well-known courtesan, Virginia Padoana, and a sixteen-year-old choirboy, Orazio Cogno, who entered Oxford's service and lived with him in London for close on a year as a page boy. A few years later two of Oxford's fellow noblemen, Henry Howard and Charles Arundel, accused him to the Privy Council of frequent pederasty, including having sodomized Orazio. They 'offered testimony from nearly a dozen victims, near-victims, and non-victim witnesses'. Orazio 'complained how horribly my lord had abused him, and yet would not give him anything'. (It sounds as if he might have been happier about what happened if he had been paid.) Arundel reported that Oxford's cook 'weeping to my Lord Harry and myself at Hampton Court confessed how my lord had almost spoiled him, and yet he durst not open his grief'; he could prove him a buggerer of a boy that is his cook, as well by that I have been an eye-witness of as also by his confession to[o] often to myself and to others that would not lie. It is most true that I have seen this boy many a time in his chamber two hours close locked together with him, ... and finding it so, I have gone to the back door to satisfy myself; at the which the boy has come out all in a sweat, and I have gone and found the beast [presumably Oxford] in the same plight.

It was even reported that Oxford committed, and boasted of, bestiality: 'he would often tell my lord Harry, myself, and Southwell that he had abused a mare; and that the Englishmen were dolts and idiots, for there was better sport in *passa pecora*, which they knew not, than in all their occupying.' (Passa pecora, writes Oxford's biographer, was 'an unorthodox [sexual] position, recorded by Aretino and translatable as the "grazing sheep"'; it appears to refer to oral sex.[45] And 'occupy' is said by the prostitute Doll Tearsheet in 2 *Henry IV* to have been 'an excellent good word before it was ill sorted' (2.4.144, quarto only).

That was during the reign of Queen Elizabeth. Her successor, James I, who married and had three children, was the source of continual gossip about his relationships with young men, gossip which he fostered both by overtly sexual behaviour in public and by semi-public statements such as his touchingly vulnerable words to the Privy Council in 1617:

I, James, am neither a god nor an angel, but a man like any other. Therefore I act like a man and confess to loving those dear to me more than other men. You may be sure that I love the Earl of Buckingham more than anyone else, and more than you who are here assembled. I wish to speak in my own behalf and not to have it thought to be a defect, for Jesus Christ did the same, and therefore I cannot be blamed. Christ had John, and I have George.

And in a private letter to Buckingham written during his last illness, in 1624, the King wrote

And yet I cannot content myself without sending you this billet, praying God that I may have a joyful and comfortable meeting with you, and that we may make at this Christenmass a new marriage, ever to be kept hereafter; for God so love me, as I desire only to live in this world for your sake, and that I had rather live banished in any part of the earth with you, than live a sorrowful widow-life without you. And so God bless you, my sweet child and wife, and grant that ye may ever be a comfort to your dear dad and husband.[46]

Whatever the difference in the way that men were accustomed to address each other between the seventeenth century and now, that surely leaves no room for doubt that the men had a sexual relationship, and that it was infused with deep affection, at least on the part of the King.

It is interesting that the King attempts to justify himself to the Privy Council by an appeal to Jesus' relationship with the beloved disciple John. Thomas Kyd had alluded to the supposedly sexual nature of that relationship in his famous letter of self-defence of 1593, a quarter of a century earlier. Accusing Marlowe of atheism, Kyd wrote in language that shies away from explicitness that Marlowe 'would report St John to be our saviour Christ's Alexis'—the man desired by Corydon in Virgil's second Eclogue—and, still not quite coming out with what he means, 'that is, that Christ did love him with an extraordinary love'.[47] The informer Thomas Baines similarly reported Marlowe as having said that 'St John the Evangelist was bedfellow to Christ and leaned always in his bosom [and] that he used him as the sinners of Sodoma.'[48] There is a difference in tone between Kyd's and the King's invoking of Christ. For Kyd, the very thought that Jesus and John might have been physical lovers is blasphemy, evidence of abhorrent atheism on Marlowe's part. In effect, if Marlowe had justified his atheism by speaking as Kyd and Baines said he had, Marlowe himself was adopting what we would now call a homophobic attitude: he was implying that homosexual behaviour was incompatible with holiness, with Christ's presumed divinity. James, on the other hand, was justifying his homosexual behaviour as no 'defect' on the grounds that no less a figure than the son of God had also taken a male lover. Moreover he speaks passionately, as he does in his letters to his three principal, consecutive lovers, of love as well as of desire. This is not a casual cruiser, but a man desperately trying to claim his right to love. If he had been entirely fair he would have mentioned that Jesus, unlike King James, was not married.

Clearly the Earl of Oxford, copulating with his pageboy as well as his wife, was what we would now term bisexual. So, if in a somewhat different fashion, was the King. Other men of the period were narrower in their tastes. Francis Bacon, who was frequently suspected of sodomy, especially with young Welshmen, entered into a marriage of convenience at the age of 45, when he took a 14-year-old bride from whom he became estranged in his later years; she appears to have been unfaithful. He died childless. The diarist Simonds D'Ewes wrote that even after his downfall he would not 'relinquish the practice of his most horrible and secret sin of sodomy, keeping still one Godrick a very effeminate faced youth to be his catamite'. As a result

> men began to discourse of that his unnatural crime which he had practised many years; deserting the bed of his lady, which he accounted as the Italians and Turks do, a poor and mean pleasure in respect of the other; and it was thought by some that he should have been tried at the bar of justice for it, and have satisfied the law most severe against that horrible villainy with the price of his blood.[49]

In France in 1586 Bacon's brother Anthony, who never married, was charged with sodomizing a pageboy, who said at the trial that 'there was nothing wrong in the practice of sodomy'; Bacon was lucky not to be burned alive. In a letter to a physician written when he was nearly 40 years old Anthony claimed that he had 'never been troubled with any kind of *leues veneria* [presumably a venereal disease] nor committed any act to occasion it, for the which modesty I have by some physicians been rather censured than commended, noting my *abundantia semenis* [abundance of semen].'[50]

The Roaring Girle.

OR

Moll Cut-Purse.

As it hath lately beene Acted on the Fortune-stage by
the Prince his Players.

Written by *T. Middleton* and *T. Dekkar.*

My cafe is alter'd, I muft worke for my liuing.

Printed at *London* for *Thomas Archer*, and are to be fold at his
fhop in Popes head-pallace, neere the Royall
Exchange. 1611.

Figure 3. The title page of *The Roaring Girl* shows Moll Frith with phallic
sword and pipe and in masculine guise, depicted as appearing on the stage
of the Fortune playhouse.

In a theatre where all female roles were played by males, cross-dressing was a matter of course, though it formed one of the moralists' objections to the drama, not least because it transgressed biblical injunctions. Little evidence appears to have survived about lesbianism in England during the period,[51] though there is a remarkable poem by John Donne, 'Sappho to Philaenis', which imagines same-sex desire between women:

> My two lips, eyes, thighs, differ from thy two,
>   But so as mine from one another do,
> And, oh, no more: the likeness being such,
>   Why should they not alike in all parts touch?
> Hand to strange hand, lip to lip none denies;
>   Why should they breast to breast, or thighs to thighs?[52]

There are also numerous records of women who dressed and behaved as men; one of them, Moll Frith, is portrayed as the central character of Thomas Middleton's play *The Roaring Girl*. In a court case of 1612 she declared that when clothed as a man at the Fortune playhouse she had 'told the company there present that she thought many of them were of opinion that she was a man, but if any of them would come to her lodging they should find that she is a woman'.[53] Though she did not take part in a play there, she 'played upon her lute and sang a song'. She was required to do public penance for this and other offences, appearing at Paul's Cross dressed in a white robe, having first fortified herself by drinking three quarts of sack.[54]

Shakespeare reflects the variety of sexual behaviour that he could have observed, heard about, and indeed experienced, in most of his writings. He clearly thought deeply about it in the context of the personal relationships that form the basis of his plays and that are mirrored in his poems. This is discussed mainly in Part II, but in the following chapter we shall concentrate on Shakespeare's poetry and that of some of his early contemporaries.

2

Sex and Poetry in Shakespeare's Time

We have focused so far mainly on historical and biographical matters. Now let's turn to art, and look at sexuality in the lives and work of some of Shakespeare's fellow poets. Drama will be touched on only lightly here, if only because in plays the writers are too easily confused with their characters.

The kind of crude sexuality exemplified in real life in the prostitution and promiscuity of some of the activities dealt with by the Bawdy Courts, and by the activities of brothel keepers such as George Wilkins and womanizers such as Christopher Beeston, finds a parallel in a mass of bawdy literature, ballads, pamphlets, and other writings, some of them distinctly sub-literary. There is, however, an interesting example in the work of one of the most original and eccentric writers of the period, Thomas Nashe, who is now believed to have collaborated with Shakespeare on *Henry VI, Part One*.[1]

Nashe was a poet, playwright, and pamphleteer who wrote and published many highly serious works along with others of a lighter nature, most famously his novel *The Unfortunate Traveller*, of 1594, which is not short on bawdy. It is written mostly in prose but includes a few lyrics, appropriately since the central character, Jack Wilton, is servant to the poet Henry Howard, Earl of Surrey, who introduced blank verse to English and wrote sonnets influenced by Petrarch. One of Nashe's poems, a sonnet addressed to a chaste woman, is nevertheless far from Petrarchan in its erotic fantasy:

> If I must die, O let me choose my death:
> Suck out my soul with kisses, cruel maid;
> In thy breasts' crystal balls embalm my breath,
> Dole it all out in sighs when I am laid.
> Thy lips on mine like cupping-glasses clasp;
> Let our tongues meet and strive as they would sting;
> Crush out my wind with one straight-girting grasp;
> Stabs on my heart keep time whilst thou dost sing;
> Thy eyes like searing irons burn out mine;
> In thy fair tresses stifle me outright;
> Like Circes change me to a loathsome swine,
> So I may live forever in thy sight.
> Into heaven's joys none can profoundly see
> Except that first they meditate on thee.

Nashe's comment on the poet's source of inspiration is interesting in its suggestion that he is writing more to show off his wit than to express his feelings: 'I persuade myself he was more in love with his own curious-forming fancy than her face; and truth it is, many become passionate lovers only to win praise to their wits.'[2]

Erotic to the point of pornography is Nashe's poem written some time before 1597, *A Choice of Valentines*, otherwise known as *Nashe's Dildo*—the 'choice' of the title lies between a real penis and an artificial one—which in its own time circulated only furtively, in manuscript.[3] It was printed privately in 1899, and then again, in a curiously shame-faced manner, in subscribers' copies only of R. B. McKerrow's great early-twentieth-century edition of Nashe's writings. Three manu-scripts survive, one of them abbreviated and written partly in cipher, as if in shame at its content, and one apparently dating from the late seventeenth century in a collection whose owner preferred to remain

anonymous when allowing McKerrow to use it. The editor wrote
'There can, I fear, be little doubt that this poem is the work of Nashe.'[4]
Nevertheless he manfully edited it with meticulous collation of the
variant texts, though it has still not been presented with the full
commentary that it deserves.

Nashe dedicates the poem 'To the Right Honourable the Lord S.'
(conjecturally identified with Ferdinando, Lord Stanley, a patron of
poetry and drama who died in 1594, and less frequently with the Earl
of Southampton), whom he calls the 'sweet flower of matchless poetry,
| And fairest bud the red rose ever bare.' (If Stanley is the dedicatee,
'red rose' would refer to his Lancastrian ancestry.) Describing the
poem in his dedication as a 'wanton elegy'—'elegy' links it with the
classical, especially the Ovidian tradition—Nashe asks not to be
accused of 'loose unchastity | For painting forth the things that hidden
are, | Since all men act what I in speech declare, | Only inducèd by
variety.' In other words, he's only saying what everyone knows to be
true, however they may pretend to deplore it.

It would be interesting to know in what circles this poem
circulated—the dedication suggests an aristocratic readership. The
inns of court are likely enough. The poem is like much of the literature
of this period in its indebtedness to writings of previous ages, in this
case particularly to Ovid, so it cannot be regarded as documentary
evidence about what really happened. Indeed Nashe claims that 'of love's
pleasures none did ever write | That hath succeeded [followed after] in
these latter times', which I take to be an excuse for his heavy dependence
on Ovid, whom he names in the poem's apologetic closing lines:

> Yet Ovid's wanton Muse did not offend.
> He is the fountain whence my streams do flow.
> Forgive me if I speak as I was taught.

But his poem certainly evinces a taste for bawdy descriptions of both
heterosexual and autoerotic activity which cannot be unrelated to the

contemporary scene. It recounts a visit to a brothel by a young man who loses his erection at the crucial point. After a lengthy description of sexual foreplay, the young man finds his

> limbs unwieldy for the fight,
> That spend their strength in thought of her delight.
> 'What shall I do to show myself a man?
> It will not be for aught that beauty can.
> I kiss, I clap, I feel, I view at will,
> Yet dead he lies not thinking good or ill.'
> 'Unhappy me', quoth she, 'and will't not stand?
> Come, let me rub and chafe it with my hand.
> Perhaps the silly worm is laboured sore
> And wearièd that it can do no more.'

Eventually she succeeds, and Nashe describes their coupling with uninhibited and detailed gusto. The woman yearns to prolong the ecstasy, but eventually 'the well' of the young man's 'instrument of lust' is dry. Still unsatisfied, she resorts to her 'little dildo', which 'bendeth not, nor foldeth any deal, | But stands as stiff as he were made of steel, | And plays at peacock⁵ 'twixt my legs right blithe, | And doth my tickling 'suage with many a sigh.' She speaks a paean to the instrument which 'gives young girls their gamesome sustenance' and describes it as 'a youth almost two handfuls high, | Straight, round and plump, yet having but one eye.' It may be 'attired in white velvet or in silk | And nourished with hot water or with milk, | Armed otherwhile in thick congealèd glass, | When he more glib to Hell below would pass. | Upon a chariot of five wheels [the woman's fingers?] he rides, | The which an arm-strong driver steadfast guides.'

And there is much more in the same vein. (Calling the vagina 'Hell' here recalls Shakespeare's Sonnet 144: 'I guess one angel in another's hell.')

By contrast with Nashe's explicitness, much writing about relationships between men and women in this period treats love in an idealized manner, often portraying women as unattainable objects of desire in a stylized, Petrarchan fashion. This is true of almost all Elizabethan love-sonnet collections, which avoid explicit suggestion of physicality in the relationship between lover and beloved. Shakespeare is one of only two exceptions—the other is Richard Barnfield, who is also uniquely like Shakespeare in having written sonnets addressed to a man. Shakespeare's so-called 'dark lady' sonnets include poems which treat sexuality—specifically heterosexuality—with an explicitness unparalleled in any other sonnet collection, and perhaps in any other serious verse, of the period. The most conspicuous example is Sonnet 151 with its vivid account of a male erection that in this case is wholly successful:

> My soul doth tell my body that he may
> Triumph in love; flesh stays no farther reason,
> But rising at thy name doth point out thee
> As his triumphant prize. Proud of this pride,
> He is contented thy poor drudge to be,
> To stand in thy affairs, fall by thy side.
>   No want of conscience hold it that I call
>   Her 'love' for whose dear love I rise and fall.

It is impossible to overemphasize how dramatically this poem breaks away from and challenges the sonnet conventions of the period. 'Conscience' in l. 13 may allude to the erect penis; Williams cites Florio, *'with a ready conscience, with a stiffe standing pricke'* adding, 'There may also be a pun on **con**- science = cunt knowledge.'[6] And in the 'I' of the couplet the poet identifies himself precisely with his rising and falling penis. He shows a brave, slightly playful yet at the same time harshly honest attempt to face up to the interdependence of his 'nobler part' and his 'gross body', to the fact that the spirituality of his love is indivisible from physiological reality. And the sonnets in which Shakespeare puns most insistently on the multiple meanings of the word 'will', especially Numbers 135 and 136, are little less frank, and even more

Figure 4. 'flesh stays no farther reason, / But rising at thy name doth point out thee / As his triumphant prize' (Sonnet 151). This wood engraving by Simon Brett (b. 1943) matches Shakespeare's poem in its explicitness. The lovers look apart from each other as if in shame, linked only by a cord around their necks apparently attached to lockets bearing portraits of two men, and by the woman's hand on Shakespeare's penis.

intellectually complex, in their multilayered exploration of sexuality.
Here is Number 135:

> Whoever hath her wish, thou hast thy Will,
> And Will to boot, and Will in overplus.
> More than enough am I that vex thee still,
> To thy sweet will making addition thus.
> Wilt thou, whose will is large and spacious,
> Not once vouchsafe to hide my will in thine?
> Shall will in others seem right gracious,
> And in my will no fair acceptance shine?
> The sea, all water, yet receives rain still,
> And in abundance addeth to his store;
> So thou, being rich in Will, add to thy Will
> One will of mine to make thy large Will more.
>   Let no unkind no fair beseechers kill;
>   Think all but one, and me in that one Will.

'Will' occurs thirteen times. When the sonnet was first printed, in the
1609 collection, attention to the word's potential ambiguities was
drawn by its being both capitalized and italicized. In editing it I
removed the italicization but preserved all the capitals of the original,
not out of slavish deference but because it seemed to me that these
were the uses of the word in which the personal name predominated.
But so many senses of 'will' are pertinent throughout the poem that it
is often difficult to say which is uppermost, or even whether particular
ones are present at any given point. And they may present themselves
to the reader even if they did not to the poet.

In the opening lines the name seems dominant—'Will' the poet is
subjugated to the woman's 'will' in the primary sense of 'sexual desire'.
The idea that she has 'will' in overplus may, in view of the following
line—'More than enough am I that vex thee still'—act simply as an
apology for continuing to trouble her, but could also imply that she is
oversexed, and must surely suggest too that this is the name of the
poet's friend with whom the woman is having an affair, as well as of

the poet. To my mind the fact that Shakespeare's name was 'Will' increases the likelihood that the poem has a real-life addressee. In lines 5–8 the senses successively of 'penis' and 'vagina' dominate, then in the poem's last six lines multiple meanings proliferate—'So thou, being rich in Will'—that is, in sexuality, and in the organs of the lovers named 'Will', 'add to thy Will | One will of mine to make thy large Will more'—that is, if she agrees to his demands she will increase her sexual appetite (and, however improbably, 'enlarge her vagina' by enclosing his penis in it along with all the others).

The most idealized of Shakespeare's Sonnets fall among those either clearly addressed to a male or nonspecific in their addressee. His explicitly sexual sonnets, all concerned with heterosexual love, suggest severe psychological tension in a man who must acknowledge his heterosexuality but who finds something distasteful about it, at least in its current manifestation. It is not unreasonable to be reminded of Angelo in *Measure for Measure*—'What's this? What's this? Is this her fault or mine? | The tempter or the tempted, who sins most?', etc. (2.2.168–92), and of King Lear in his anguished diatribes against female sexuality:

> Down from the waist
> They're centaurs, though women all above.
> But to the girdle do the gods inherit;
> Beneath is all the fiend's... (4.5.121–4)

Other writers of the period were able to write explicitly about sex in a more accepting, even transcendental manner. We know far more about John Donne's real-life personal relationships than we do about Shake-speare's, and we are able to see how he mutates them into totally serious poetry of a transcendental frankness that may even owe something to Shakespeare. There is no pussyfooting Petrarchism in poems such as 'The Sun Rising', or 'The Flea', or 'The Ecstasy' (see p. 5), with its passionate acknowledgement of the interdependence of spiritual and physical love. As Shakespeare's soul tells his body that it may 'triumph in love', so Donne's soul acknowledges that 'the body' is love's 'book'.

On the evidence of both his life and his writings, no one could doubt Donne's heterosexuality. His 'attitude to male homosexuality seems to have been conventionally negative'.[7] Even so, he draws on sexual, including homosexual, imagery in the daring Holy Sonnet in which he asks God to help him to 'rise and stand', expresses the wish to 'admit' God, wishes to be 'loved' by God, and climactically invites God to rape him:

> Batter my heart, three-personed God; for you
> As yet but knock, breathe, shine, and seek to mend;
> That I may rise and stand, o'erthrow me, and bend
> Your force to break, blow, burn, and make me new.
> I, like an usurped town to'another due,
> Labour to' admit you; but O, to no end.
> Reason, your viceroy in me, me should defend,
> But is captived, and proves weak or untrue,
> Yet dearly I love you, and would be lovèd fain,
> But am betrothed unto your enemy.
> Divorce me, untie, or break that knot again,
> Take me to you, imprison me, for I,
>   Except you enthral me, never shall be free,
>   Nor ever chaste, except you ravish me.

The life stories and writings of other poets leave more room for ambivalence, or even for certainty in the other direction. Marlowe is the most conspicuous example, in especially the depictions of homoerotic behaviour in his poem *Hero and Leander* and his plays *Dido, Queen of Carthage* and *Edward II*. And he had his followers. I mentioned (p. 35) that Mary Bly, on the evidence of a group of plays written for a particular company towards the end of the first decade of the seventeenth century, posits the existence of what she calls 'a self-aware homoerotic community in early modern London'. Similarly, I suggest, it is reasonable to maintain that a number of writers in the early years of the last decade of the sixteenth century, and especially around 1593 to 1596—the period when Shakespeare is likely to have been writing most of his sonnets—were aware of a body of readers specially attracted by homoerotic literature, and that they attempted to satisfy these readers' tastes.

As usual, chronology is a problem. We cannot be sure in what order Marlowe wrote the three works of his that I have mentioned. But *Edward II*, which of all Elizabethan plays is the one most clearly concerned with homoerotic behaviour, and which has become iconic in the gay canon (See Plate 3), was printed in 1594, the year after he died, and one line from it appears almost verbatim in one of Barnfield's longer poems, 'The Tears of an Affectionate Shepherd Sick for Love; or the Complaint of Daphnis for the Love of Ganymede', also published in 1594, which similarly is the most clearly homoerotic of Elizabethan verse collections. In *Edward II*, Gaveston says:

> Sometime a lovely boy in Dian's shape,
> With hair that gilds the water as it glides,
> Crownets of pearl about his naked arms,
> And in his sportful hands an olive tree
> To hide those parts that men delight to see,
> Shall bathe him in the spring.

Barnfield writes:

> I would put amber bracelets on thy wrists,
> *Crownets of pearl about thy naked arms.*

Either Barnfield remembered this from seeing the play acted or he was among the playbook's first purchasers—waiting at the stationer's door on the day of publication, perhaps. His poem is sensuously erotic in a manner that far exceeds any of the sonnet sequences addressed to women. Barnfield's Daphnis addresses his Ganymede in lines wide open to homoerotic interpretation:

> O would to God, so I could have my fee,
> My lips were honey, and thy mouth a bee.

> Then shouldst thou suck my sweet and my fair flower
> That now is ripe and full of honey berries;
> Then would I lead thee to my pleasant bower
> Filled full of grapes, of mulberries and cherries;
>   Then shouldst thou be my wasp or else my bee,
>   I would thy hive, and thou my honey be.[8]

It sounds like Titania attempting to seduce Bottom, in *A Midsummer Night's Dream*; she instructs her fairies 'feed him with apricots and dewberries, | With purple grapes, green figs, and mulberries; | The honey bags steal from the humble-bees, | And for night tapers crop their waxen thighs' (3.1.158–61).[9]

In his next book, *Cynthia, with Certain Sonnets on the Legend of Cassandra* (1595), Barnfield includes a sequence of sonnets also concerned with Ganymede which are explicitly and unashamedly homoerotic, full of physical desire:

> Sometimes I wish that I his pillow were,
>   So might I steal a kiss, and yet not seen.
>   So might I gaze upon his sleeping eyne,
> Although I did it with a panting fear.
> But when I well consider how vain my wish is,
>   'Ah, foolish bees', think I, 'that do not suck
>   His lips for honey, but poor flowers do pluck
> Which have no sweet in them, when his sole kisses
> Are able to revive a dying soul.
>   Kiss him, but sting him not, for if you do
>   His angry voice your flying will pursue.
> But when they hear his tongue, what can control
>   Their back return? For then they plain may see
>   How honeycombs from his lips dropping be.[10]

The poet's love, we learn, is unrequited; when he declares it, his friend assumes that he loves a woman:

> … what is she … whom thou dost love?

To which the poet, taking up a covered mirror, responds:

> 'Look in this glass', quoth I, 'there shalt thou see
> The perfect form of my felicity.'
> When, thinking that it would strange magic prove,
> He opened it, and taking off the cover
> He straight perceived himself to be my lover.[11]

Along with Shakespeare, Barnfield is one of the only two English poets who wrote love sonnets addressed to a man, though Barnfield did so under cover of mythological figures, and Shakespeare's are addressed to one or more anonymous persons. As well as quoting from Marlowe, Barnfield mentions Shakespeare by name, explicitly referring to *Venus* and *Lucrece* in his poem 'A Remembrance of Some English Poets', published in 1598.

Barnfield may well have known Shakespeare personally, and was influenced in his poetry by *Venus and Adonis*. The tone of the two poets' poems is very different, but Paul Hammond has convincingly demonstrated that Shakespeare engaged with poems by Barnfield in his Sonnets.[12] Barnfield's risky verse may have been responsible for his being regarded as the black sheep of his family; it was discovered in 1991 that he was disinherited in favour of his younger brother.[13]

Marlowe's interest in the relationship between Edward II and Gaveston is echoed in the work of another poet who wrote uncensoriously and indeed repeatedly about the love between the two men. This is Shakespeare's fellow Warwickshireman Michael Drayton, who spent much time close to Stratford, at the home of friends in Clifford Chambers, and who was treated for a tertian fever by Shakespeare's son-in-law, John Hall, who prescribed an emetic mixed with syrup of violets which 'wrought very well both upwards and downwards'. Drayton was a prolific, even garrulous poet who wrote much about ostensibly heterosexual love, including the sonnet sequence known as *Idea*, which includes the touching and well-known lines beginning

'Since there's no help, come let us kiss and part.' This sequence, which first appeared in 1594, underwent a long process of revision between then and 1619.

Drayton was involved in a curious lawsuit in 1627 when, in his 64th year, he was accused of 'suspicion of incontinency' with a married woman, Mary Peters. According to a keeper of a London lodging house, a maidservant had seen Mary Peters raise her skirts

> unto her navel before Mr Michael Drayton and that she clapped her hand on her privy part and said it was a sound [healthy] and a good one, and that the said Mr Drayton did then also lay his hand upon it and stroke[d] it and said that it was a good one.

Mrs Peters denied the accusation, launched a counter-suit, and called Drayton as a witness. He said he had seen nothing of the kind, and bawdily joked, when asked about his finances, that he was 'worth only 20 nobles, debts paid' but 'was worth at least 200 nobles in good parts.'[14] The author of the *Oxford Dictionary of National Biography* article on Drayton, Anne Lake Prescott, comments that 'Commending a woman's private parts, if only as a courtesy, would be out of character for Drayton', who in the anonymous play *The Return from Parnassus* (1605) is said to have lacked 'one true note of a Poet of our times, and that is this, he cannot swagger it well in a tavern nor domineer in a hothouse [brothel]'. Is that a snide hint that he prefers men to women? The object of his devotion, his 'Idea', is nominally Anne Goodere, daughter of Sir Henry, in whose house the young poet served as a page. He sustained his friendship with her till he died. There is no record of his having married.

The romantic explanation for this is that he was passionately but hopelessly in love with the lady both before and after her marriage, and for the rest of his life. A more realistic theory is that his love was a Petrarchan conceit, even a codified way of avoiding the admission of same-sex desire. Lest it be thought that this idea merely reflects modern preoccupations with homoeroticism it is worth mentioning that over one hundred years ago an American scholar wrote

> That Drayton addressed Anne Goodere in the strain of a lover is not a tenable theory. He is one of a large group of poets that indulged in a conventional literary expression. *Idea* may not be as shadowy as the nominal idol of some other sonneteers; but Drayton's pen has addressed her only in terms of the gallantry of the age, the homage of a friend.[15]

(Admittedly this may equally reflect early-nineteenth-century American preoccupations with homoeroticism.)

And more recently Anne Prescott remarks that 'the luxurious sympathy with which he could describe male beauty and imagine (if not explicitly approve) homoerotic desire could indicate that, except as a writer, he found heterosexual passion uninteresting.'[16]

Drayton, like Marlowe and, so far as we know, Barnfield, never married. He had good friendships, one of which is touchingly recalled in his autobiographical poem 'To my most dearly-loved friend Henry Reynolds Esquire; of Poets and Poesy'. This begins:

> My dearly lovèd friend, how oft have we
> In winter evenings—meaning to be free—
> To some well-chosen place used to retire,
> And there, with moderate meat, and wine, and fire,
> Have passed the hours contentedly with chat,
> Now talked of this, and then discoursed of that,
> Spoke our own verses 'twixt ourselves, if not
> Other men's lines which we by chance had got,
> Or some stage pieces famous long before
> Of which your happy memory had store.

And he goes on in his garrulous way to sketch the development of his taste in classical, English, and Scottish poetry, mentioning many famous and once-famous names along the way, and including a tribute to Shakespeare who had

> As smooth a comic vein,
> Fitting the sock,[17] and in thy natural brain
> As strong conception and as clear a rage
> As anyone that trafficked with the stage.

This seems innocent enough, but it has been claimed that 'Private reading together...signified intimate male friendship. The nexus of friendship and reading is a space of male, homoerotic intimacy.'[18]

Drayton's most overtly homoerotic writing comes in his long poem *Piers Gaveston Earl of Cornwall: His life, death, and fortune*, first published in 1593, which he tinkered with obsessively: it found a welcome readership, appearing in four later revisions, in 1595, 1596, 1605, and 1619. Drayton found the story interesting enough to take it up in two other works, *Mortemeriados* (1596) and *England's Heroical Epistles* (1597). The first poem portrays Gaveston as Ganymede to Edward's Jove, and relates how 'Frolic as May, a lusty life we led.' Drayton as well as Marlowe exercised a direct influence on Barnfield. Drayton writes that Gaveston's breast was the King's 'pillow where he laid his head, | Mine eyes his book, my bosom was his bed.' And in Barnfield's *The Affectionate Shepherd*, published in the same year as *Piers Gaveston*, Daphnis addresses Ganymede with

> And every morn by dawning of the day
>   When Phoebus riseth with a blushing face
> Silvanus' chapel clerks shall chant a lay,
>   And play thee hunt's up in thy resting place.
> My cot thy chamber, **my bosom thy bed,**
> Shall be appointed for thy sleepy head.[19]

Is this perhaps echoed in the phrase 'most most loving breast' in Shakespeare's Sonnet 110, which may or may not be addressed to a male?

Drayton's mode of writing is not laconic; the lines in which Gaveston describes his seduction of the King are too long to quote in full, but they include

My breast his pillow where he laid his head,
Mine eyes his book, my bosom was his bed.

.   .   .   .   .

His love-sick lips at every kissing qualm
  Cling to my lips to cure their grief with balm.

Like as the wanton ivy with his twine
Whenas the oak his rootless body warms,
The straightest saplings strictly doth combine,
Clipping the woods with his lascivious arms,
  Such our embraces when our sport begins,
  Lapped in our arms like Leda's lovely twins.

After this it is not easy to take seriously the moralistic criticism of the
King and his lover's behaviour implied in the lines

Some slanderous tongues in spiteful manner said
  That here I lived in filthy sodomy,
And that I was King Edward's Ganymede
  And to this sin he was enticed by me.

Of course he did, and of course he was!

Marlowe, Barnfield, and Drayton, then, form a group of poets with
linked interests in homoerotic subject matter for poetry, and there are
clear signs of direct influence and aesthetic fellowship among them. It
seems likely that they would have had especial appeal for a common
readership, perhaps the young gentlemen of the Inns of Court.[20] And
one of these writers also links directly with the theatre company
which catered for similarly specialized tastes: Drayton was a joint
lessee of the Whitefriars playhouse, and Mary Bly believes that he
worked on the script of one of the plays written for it, *The Turk*.[21]

*

How, if at all, does Shakespeare fit into this community? He is explicitly mentioned by both Drayton and Barnfield, and it is inconceivable
that he was not personally acquainted with his fellow playwright at the
Rose, Christopher Marlowe. Much of his non-dramatic poetry is

written around 1593–5, the time when the vogue for homoerotic verse seems to be at its height. On the other hand none of Shakespeare's verse is homoerotic in the manner of Marlowe, Barnfield, and Drayton. His two narrative poems, *Venus and Adonis* and *The Rape of Lucrece*, appeared respectively in 1593 and 1594, at the height of the vogue. Both are dedicated by the author to the Earl of Southampton, the second in exceptional terms that imply close intimacy: 'The love I dedicate to your lordship is without end…What I have done is yours; what I have to do is yours, being part in all I have, devoted yours.' And both poems were very popular, the former especially, being reprinted in at least ten editions before Shakespeare died, with another six by 1636, making it the most frequently reprinted of all his works during and shortly after his lifetime. Various tributes to the poems' contemporary success survive. Meres gives *Venus* (based on an episode from Ovid's *Metamorphoses*) as his example of how 'the sweet witty soul of Ovid lives in mellifluous and honey-tongued Shakespeare, witness his *Venus and Adonis*'.[22]

This poem appears to have been especially popular with young readers—'the younger sort takes much delight in' it, wrote Gabriel Harvey, and a character in the *Parnassus* plays, written for performance by members of St John's College, Cambridge, early in the seventeenth century, declares 'I'll worship sweet Master Shakespeare, and to honour him will lay his *Venus and Adonis* under my pillow.' It was associated in some minds with Marlowe's *Hero and Leander*, which clearly exercised homoerotic appeal. In general Shakespeare's poem seems to have been regarded as a stimulus to masturbatory and heterosexual fantasy or to positive wooing and seduction. In the second of the *Parnassus* plays, written for performance by members of St John's College, Cambridge early in the seventeenth century, a foolish student, Gullio, boasts of how he woos his mistress in speeches larded with quotations from *Venus and Adonis* and *Romeo and Juliet*. And a husband in Middleton's *A Mad World My Masters* declares that he has 'conveyed away' from his wife 'all her wanton pamphlets, as *Hero and Leander*, *Venus and*

Adonis; O two luscious mary-bone pies for a young married wife.'[23]
(Marrow-bones were thought of as aphrodisiac.) Heterosexual readers
no doubt enjoyed passages such as Venus's erotic self description:

> I'll be a park, and thou shalt be my deer.
> Feed where thou wilt, on mountain or in dale;
>   Graze on my lips, and if those hills be dry,
>   Stray lower, where the pleasant fountains lie.   (ll. 231–4)

On the other hand the descriptions of Adonis's beauty may well have
had the same kind of homoerotic appeal as Marlowe's of Leander. The
goddess of love herself praises Adonis as

> Thrice fairer than myself...
> The fields' chief flower, sweet above compare,
>   Stain to all nymphs, more lovely than a man,
>   More white and red than doves or roses are.   (ll. 7–10)

Shakespeare's descriptions of the boy are more ironic and detached
than Marlowe's sensuous lingering over Leander's beauty. Adonis is
wooed by a goddess, not by the male god Neptune, as is the naked
Leander as he swims the Hellespont. But Adonis's beauty, along with
his total inability to respond to Venus's persistent and violent efforts to
seduce him, and the contrast between the youth's frigidity and his
horse's lustful pursuit of its mare, might well have found a sympa-
thizing echo in the breasts of male readers with no interest in women.
And it is well known that, centuries later, the young John Addington
Symonds (1840–93) indulged his homosexual fantasies by identifying
himself with Venus in her attempts at seduction of the beautiful youth.
'In some confused way', he wrote, 'I identified myself with Adonis; but
at the same time I yearned after him as an adorable object of passionate
love.' For Symonds, 'Venus' hot wooing taught me what it was to woo
with sexual ardour. I dreamed of falling back like her upon the grass,
and folding the quick-panting lad in my embrace.'[24]

Venus and Adonis ends with a plangent threnody for the death of the young Adonis, but is generally witty, even playful in tone. In its dedication Shakespeare promises the Earl 'to take advantage of all idle hours till I have honoured you with some graver labour'. This had its outcome in the following year in the publication of *The Rape of Lucrece*, which, as Gabriel Harvey wrote, was likely, along with *Hamlet*, 'to please the wiser sort' than those who delighted in the earlier poem. Indeed its tone is so predominantly serious that it has been described as 'perhaps the only joke-free zone in Shakespeare's works'.[25] The earlier part of the poem, leading up to the rape itself, is full of heteroerotic tension, culminating in the description of Tarquin's sexual arousal as he is about to commit the crime. A critic has remarked that 'The claustrophobic moment during which Tarquin looks at Lucrece and gains his necessary erection is one of the most erotic passages in all of Shakespeare. The extra syllables at the end of each line [of the second stanza quoted below] imitate Tarquin's gradually stiffening tumescence':[26]

> So o'er this sleeping soul doth Tarquin stay,
> His rage of lust by gazing qualified,
> Slaked not suppressed for standing by her side.
> > His eye which late this mutiny restrains
> > Unto a greater uproar tempts his veins,
>
> And they like straggling slaves for pillage fighting,
> Obdurate vassals fell exploits effecting,
> In bloody death and ravishment delighting,
> Nor children's tears nor mothers' groans respecting,
> Swell in their pride, the onset still expecting.
> > Anon his beating heart, alarum striking,
> > Gives the hot charge, and bids them do their liking.
>
> His drumming heart cheers up his burning eye,
> His eye commends the leading to his hand.
> His hand, as proud of such a dignity,
> Smoking with pride marched on to make his stand

On her bare breast, the heart of all her land,
  Whose ranks of blue veins as his hand did scale
  Left their round turrets destitute and pale.   (ll. 423–41)

This is straightforward (if elaborately rhetorical) eroticism which might offer stimulus to any kind of fantasy. It has nothing to link it specifically with the vogue for homoeroticism in verse.

Then there is the curious case of *The Passionate Pilgrim*. This collection of 20 short poems, mostly amorous, some mildly erotic, first appeared in 1599 (or possibly in late 1598), with a reprint in the same year. The first edition, published by William Jaggard, survives only in one incomplete copy, which implies popularity, with an ascription to Shakespeare, though several of the poems are definitely by other writers, including Barnfield, Marlowe, Sir Walter Ralegh, and Bartholomew Griffin (who died in 1602, and wrote a Petrarchan sonnet sequence, *Fidessa*.). It was reprinted again in 1612, with additional poems by Thomas Heywood, who protested, remarking that Shakespeare 'was much offended with Master Jaggard that, altogether unknown to him, presumed to make bold with his name'.[27] This is presumably intended to exonerate Shakespeare from accusations of having plagiarized Heywood; the ascription to Shakespeare was dropped in a substitute title page.

The title of the book, *The Passionate Pilgrim*, may be paraphrased as 'the suffering', or perhaps 'pleading' lover (a 'passion' could be any sort of emotional speech), in the sense that Romeo portrays himself as a pilgrim (the literal meaning of 'Romeo') seeking Juliet's hand. But the title is only vaguely relevant to the volume's contents. Jaggard—or maybe a compiler of a commonplace book which he acquired—appears to have thrown together a collection of loosely related poems in an apparently successful attempt to exploit Shakespeare's growing reputation. The poet's name had appeared for the first time on a title page of a play—*Richard II*—in 1598 (it is not on the title pages of the narrative poems, but comes at the end of their dedications). And in the same year Francis Meres, in *Palladis Tamia*, praised him as 'mellifluous and honey-tongued Shakespeare', referring to his 'sugared sonnets among his private friends'. This is ambiguous. It might mean either 'sonnets that circulated among his closest friends' or, intimating an even closer knowledge on Meres's part, 'addressed to his intimates'. Moreover it does not necessarily refer to the sonnets eventually published in 1609, though in fact Jaggard's volume opens with versions of two of those (Nos. 138 and 144, neither of them, especially the latter—'Two loves I have of comfort and despair'—among those that might most obviously be described as 'sugared'; in fact the phrase 'sugared sonnets' had already been used by Barnfield in Sonnet 10 of his *Greene's Funerals* of 1594; p. 73). These must have been acquired from a manuscript source, perhaps in the possession of one of those 'private friends', which could also have included some of the poems printed by Jaggard, whether or not written by Shakespeare. The next poem is an extract in sonnet form from *Love's Labour's Lost*, which was printed as Shakespeare's in 1598 (and possibly earlier in a lost edition). But it is followed by a sonnet of unknown authorship which very briefly summarizes the story of Venus and Adonis, followed by another genuine Shakespearian piece, also in sonnet form, and adapted from *Love's Labour's Lost*. Next comes another Venus and Adonis sonnet, which could be by Shakespeare but is now generally attributed to Bartholomew Griffin imitating Shakespeare. Both of the Venus poems have potentially homoerotic appeal, the first simply in its portrayal of a young man, 'lovely, fresh and green', who declines the advances of the goddess of love, the second more positively in its titillating description of how Adonis, overseen by an amorous Venus,

> ...comes and throws his mantle by,
> And stood stark naked on the brook's green brim.

He jumps into the stream to conceal his nakedness, provoking the goddess to exclaim 'O Jove...why was not I a flood?'—a conclusion that could have come from one of Marlowe's translations of Ovid ('Jove send me more such afternoons as this' is the last line of his translation of the fifth Elegy). A third Venus sonnet (which lacks its second line) also shows the young man shying away from heterosexuality:

> 'Once', quoth she, 'did I see a fair sweet youth
> Here in these brakes deep-wounded with a boar,
> Deep in the thigh, a spectacle of ruth.
> See in my thigh,' quoth she, 'here was the sore.'
>   She showèd hers; he saw more wounds than one,
>   And blushing fled, and left her all alone.'

This is a far cry from the pleasure that Nashe's young man, in *A Choice of Valentines*, takes in the sight of his wench's private parts:

> Smock, climb apace, that I may see my joys.
> O, Heaven and paradise are all but toys
> Comparèd with this sight I now behold,
> Which well might keep a man from being old.   (ll. 105–8)

A fourth Venus and Adonis poem (No. 11), also generally ascribed to Griffin, shows the goddess attempting in vain to seduce the 'youngling' by describing how Mars seduced her; Adonis, however, skips away, 'And would not take her meaning nor her pleasure'. The narrator wishes he had had the boy's opportunities.

These poems then, even if they are not by Shakespeare himself, show a willingness to attribute to him verses that have an element of homoerotic appeal.

And there are Shakespeare's Sonnets as published in 1609—over a decade after the short-lived English vogue for love sonnet sequences, which began with the posthumous publication of Sir Philip Sidney's *Astrophil and Stella* in 1591, had petered out. Though Shakespeare's sonnets include expressions of love for a man, none of them is explicitly homoerotic in the manner of Marlowe, Barnfield, and Drayton. Some are love poems clearly addressed to or about a young man, or 'boy', others clearly to a woman, but many others are unspecific about the gender of the loved one. Not as many of the sonnets are necessarily addressed to a male as has been generally assumed. When Paul Edmondson and I were writing a book on the Sonnets we came to believe that critical thought about the poems has been bedevilled by a number of misconceptions. The three principal ones are as follows: First, that the sonnets form a genuine, authorially determined sequence in the manner of Sir Philip Sidney, Samuel Daniel, or Michael Drayton. We believe Shakespeare's Sonnets to be a largely miscellaneous collection of poems which, although it may have been put into the order in which it is published by the author, are only loosely linked together. Second, we think it is wrong to suppose that all the sonnets up to Number 126 are necessarily addressed to a male. In fact we were able to identify only 20 sonnets 'which can confidently be said, on the evidence of forms of address and of masculine pronouns, to be addressed to or to concern a male' along with another 21 'which might imply a male addressee, either because of their context, or because of their subject matter, but which could imply either a male or a female, if read independently'.[28] If we allow for the diversity of possible addressees that I propose, we must admit that some of the poems in the first part of the sequence could even be love poems addressed to his wife.[29] Number 27 is an example:

> Weary with toil I haste me to my bed,
> The dear repose for limbs with travel tired;
> But then begins a journey in my head
> To work my mind when body's work's expired;
> For then my thoughts, from far where I abide,
> Intend a zealous pilgrimage to thee,
> And keep my drooping eyelids open wide,
> Looking on darkness which the blind do see:
> Save that my soul's imaginary sight
> Presents thy shadow to my sightless view,
> Which like a jewel hung in ghastly night

> Makes black night beauteous and her old face new.
> Lo, thus by day my limbs, by night my mind,
> For thee, and for myself, no quiet find.

Coming as it does in the order in which the poems were printed immediately after one that begins 'Lord of my love', this poem has naturally enough been supposed to be addressed to the poet's male friend. But if we ignore context, as perhaps we should, it could indeed be the lament of a travelling player who was missing the company of his wife.

Or consider Number 116, 'Let me not to the marriage of true minds admit impediment'. It is one of the most famous love poems in the language, one frequently read at heterosexual weddings; yet it is among the long group of poems generally supposed to be addressed to a man. Paul Edmondson and I print tables indicating the nature of the poems' addressees.[30] And among the later printed group of Sonnets, Number 145, with its puns on 'hate' and 'hate away', is now generally agreed to be a poem of Shakespeare's courtship, and probably thus the first surviving example of his writing.[31]

The third misconception about the sonnets is to believe unnecessarily that all of those with male addressees are addressed to one and the same person. This point of view is of greater biographical than critical interest.

The most idealized of Shakespeare's Sonnets fall among those that either are clearly addressed to a male or are nonspecific in their addressee. His explicitly sexual sonnets, all concerned with a woman, suggest severe psychological tension in a man who must acknowledge his heterosexuality but who finds something distasteful about it, at least in its current manifestation.

> My love is as a fever, longing still
> For that which longer nurseth the disease,
> Feeding on that which doth preserve the ill,
> Th'uncertain sickly appetite to please.
> My reason, the physician to my love,

Angry that his prescriptions are not kept,
Hath left me, and I desperate now approve
Desire is death, which physic did except.
Past cure I am, now reason is past care,
And frantic mad with evermore unrest.
My thoughts and my discourse as madmen's are,
At random from the truth vainly expressed;
    For I have sworn thee fair, and thought thee bright,
    Who art as black as hell, as dark as night.   (Sonnet 147)

Those of the poems that celebrate love between the poet (whether conceived of as simply a poetic persona or as Shakespeare himself) and a 'lovely boy' are not explicitly sexual in the manner of the frankest of the 'dark lady' sonnets. But it is undeniable that many of these poems would have had, and continue to have, a special appeal to homoerotic readers, and also that they have met with castigation from homophobic readers for this very reason, as the history of their reception over the centuries makes abundantly clear.[32] For this reason Henry Hallam—father of Tennyson's friend Arthur—wrote that he found it 'impossible not to wish that Shakespeare had never written them' (i.e. he wishes Shakespeare hadn't written them!), and Benjamin Jowett, the translator of Plato and master of Balliol College, Oxford, wrote that 'the love of the sonnets which [Tennyson] so strikingly expressed was a sort of sympathy with Hellenism [Greek love, i.e. homosexuality].'[33] On the other hand, the abundantly homosexual Oscar Wilde profoundly admired them, and some of them can be, and often have been, read sexually, as the work of critics such as Joseph Pequigney shows.[34] And a number of the Sonnets are deeply passionate if idealized love poems which one can easily imagine being addressed to a young man with whom the poet was having a physical relationship. Consider for example Number 108, and compare it with Number 147, which I have just quoted:

What's in the brain that ink may character
Which hath not figured to thee my true spirit?

What's new to speak, what now to register,
That may express my love or thy dear merit?
Nothing, sweet boy; but yet like prayers divine
I must each day say o'er the very same,
Counting no old thing old, thou mine, I thine,
Even as when first I hallowed thy fair name.
So that eternal love in love's fresh case
Weighs not the dust and injury of age,
Nor gives to necessary wrinkles place,
But makes antiquity for aye his page,
    Finding the first conceit of love there bred
    Where time and outward form would show it dead.

That poem, addressed to a 'sweet boy', gives an echo, as Viola says, to the very seat where love is throned. It expresses an intensity of love which goes beyond the light-hearted eroticism of Barnfield, or the indirect, somewhat voyeuristic pleasure in the portrayal of male-to-male love in Drayton, to a profound expression of a 'hallowed' love that, like John Donne's (p. 5), knows no limits.

So perhaps we can say that Shakespeare succeeds in writing verse which, like that of the contemporaries I have been discussing, can certainly appeal to a homoerotic readership but which transcends the boundaries of subdivisions of human experience to encapsulate the very essence of human love. As we might have expected of him.

3

Shakespeare and Sex

What do we know, or what may we legitimately infer, about Shakespeare's own knowledge and experience of sex? The closeness of family life in his boyhood, along with the normal experiences of puberty, including gossip and, probably, furtive fumblings at school and elsewhere, would no doubt have informed his early sexual knowledge. Some of the literature that he read at grammar school would have been at least mildly erotic, some of it homoerotic. It has been said, for instance, that his reading there

> would have encompassed erotic verse by poets like Horace and Virgil, who wooed both genders. To have mastered classical Latin was to have received a reasonably candid sexual education from poets who were unabashedly libertine and bisexual. It is a fact that an English schoolboy in Shakespeare's day would have learned far more about homosexuality from his classroom reading than a student in the age of Kinsey.[1]

Shakespeare seems to have proceeded with exceptional speed from theory to practice, at least in heterosexuality. Between 1570 and 1630 the average age for first marriage among men in Stratford, calculated on the basis of 106 known cases, was between twenty and thirty, with the 'greatest number of marriages (fifteen) taking place when the bridegroom was twenty-four' (see p. 16). In itself this may seem an arid statistic, but to anyone interested in Shakespeare it springs to dramatic life when we learn that he was one of only three men in the town over the sixty-year period to be recorded as having married before he was twenty years old, and the only one whose bride was pregnant at the time. So early a marriage must suggest that he was an early developer sexually, especially since he lived at a time when the onset of puberty is generally believed to have been later than it is now. It may also count as negative evidence in the much debated question of whether he was apprenticed to his father, or indeed to anyone else, as glover or butcher or whatever. Laws were and are often broken, but the fact remains that it was against the law for apprentices to be married. (Is it even thinkable that Shakespeare got Anne pregnant so that he had to marry and therefore could avoid being apprenticed?!)

The evidence I have given about prosecutions for prenuptial forni-cation shows that Shakespeare was lucky to escape punishment for getting Anne Hathaway pregnant before marriage. We can only conjecture whether there was any special reason for his good fortune, such as his father's prominent position in the town's hierarchy. Desire to minimize scandal may also help to explain why the marriage did not take place in Stratford itself—it is not recorded in the parish regis-ters, which are full for this period. Where exactly it did is a matter for conjecture; the neighbouring villages of Temple Grafton and Luddington are among those often suggested, but there is no hard evidence. The Shakespeares' first daughter, Susanna, was born on 26 May 1583, within six months of the marriage. ('Oh, fie, Miss Susanna', wrote Thomas de Quincey in the seventh (1842) edition of the *Encylo-paedia Britannica*, 'you came rather before you were wanted.'[2]) Twins, Hamnet and Judith, followed about 21 months later—they were baptized on 2 February 1585, a normal time span allowing for the fact that conception within the period of lactation is unusual. There were no more children.

This is sometimes taken to suggest that Shakespeare ceased to have sexual relations with his wife at an early stage in their marriage. But there is no real evidence for this. Rates of fertility varied. Though Shakespeare himself was one of seven children born to the same parents over a period of 22 years, his father's brother, Henry, had only two children, and William's elder daughter Susanna (Hall), who married at the age of 24, had just one daughter, born only nine months after she married. Susanna too may have been pregnant at the time she married; if not, it was a near thing. Her daughter, Elizabeth, though twice married, died childless. The birth of Shakespeare's twins could have caused damage to their mother's womb. Miscarriages occurred but were unlikely to be recorded. Primitive methods of birth control, including interrupted, anal, and intercrural—between the thighs, in front or behind, without penetration—intercourse, could be practised. According to Lawrence Stone in his classic work *The Family, Sex and Marriage in England 1500–1800*, 'lay commentators and writers of marriage manuals unanimously recommended very restricted sexual activity in marriage'. On the other hand the physician Thomas Cogan wrote in *The Haven of Health* (1594, etc.) that 'the commodities which come by moderate evacuation thereof [semen] are great. For it procureth appetite to meat and helpeth concoction; it maketh the body more light and nimble, it openeth the pores and conduits, and purgeth phlegm; it quickeneth the mind, stirreth up the wit, reneweth the senses, driveth away sadness, madness, melancholy, anger, fury.'[3] Anthony Bacon's physician would have agreed (see p. 39).

We can only conjecture how much attention people paid to these varying recommendations. Shakespeare must often have been absent from home in pursuit of his profession, and temptation must often have been put in his way. As we have seen, stories about assignations between actors and members of their audience were rife. The best known of all such stories concerns Shakespeare himself:

> Upon a time when Burbage played Richard the Third there was a citizen grew so far in liking with him, that before she went from the play she appointed him to come that night unto her by the name of Richard the Third. Shakespeare, overhearing their conclusion, went before, was entertained and at his game ere Burbage came. Then, message being brought that Richard the Third was at the door, Shakespeare caused return to be made that William the Conqueror was before Richard the Third.

That is an entry dated 13 March 1602 in the notebook kept by the lawyer John Manningham, of the Middle Temple, which also contains the first recorded performance of *Twelfth Night*, in the same year. His joke was repeated, in different form, in the eighteenth century, in *Thomas Wilkes's General View of the English Stage* (1759). Wilkes cannot have got it from Manningham, whose diary remained unpublished until the nineteenth century. But the existence of two different versions of the same anecdote does not prove that it was true, only that it was thought to be a good enough story to be worth repeating.

There are also hints that boy actors held attractions for men as well as women. For instance John Rainolds, in his *Th'Overthrow of Stage Plays* (1599), asks 'what sparkles of lust to that vice the putting of women's attire on men may kindle in unclean affections, as Nero showed in Sporus, Heliogabalus in himself; yea certain, who grew not to such excess of impudency [shamelessness], yet arguing the same in causing their boys to wear long hair like women.'[4] Undeniably the appearance of men, especially of the aristocracy, in relation to clothes as well as to length of hair resembled that of women. The Earl of Southampton was proud of his long swathes of hair, which is conspicuous in a portrait painted around the time that Shakespeare dedicated poems to him. But it does not necessarily denote effeminacy. (See Plate 1)

Also relevant to the suggestion that Shakespeare had extramarital relationships is the legend that the poet and playwright William Davenant (1606–68), who was to adapt a number of Shakespeare's plays for the post-Restoration stage, was Shakespeare's illegitimate son. Mrs Jane (or Jennet) Davenant's husband was a wine-broker who, after working in London, moved to Oxford, which lies between Stratford and London, where he and his wife kept a large tavern, the Golden Cross, with twenty rooms in the centre of the city. The gossipy John Aubrey, who, though often demonstrably unreliable, was personally acquainted with two of William Davenant's brothers and his sister, and who had studied at Oxford, reported that Shakespeare 'was wont to go into Warwickshire once a year, and did commonly in his journey lie' at the Davenants' tavern. If so, this must have been as a guest of the family since taverns (unlike inns) were not lodging houses. Mrs Davenant 'was a very beautiful woman, and of a very good wit, and of conversation extremely agreeable'. William's brother Robert, a parson, had told Aubrey that Shakespeare 'had given him a hundred kisses' (presumably as a baby). There is a traditional belief, which Davenant's most scholarly biographer sees no cause to dismiss, that Shakespeare stood godfather to the boy William.[5] It may seem implausible that a married man should act as godfather to his bastard, though the relationship may have been unacknowledged. A possible objection is that though Shakespeare bequeathed a sum of money—'twenty shillings in gold'—to his acknowledged godson the seven-year-old William Walker, the ten-year-old Davenant is not named in his alleged godfather's will. But this might be explained if Davenant really was, as he liked to claim, Shakespeare's natural but unacknowledged son. Aubrey says that Davenant 'would sometimes, when he was pleasant [joking] after a glass of wine, say that it seemed to him that he writ with the very spirit that Shakespeare [did], and seemed contented enough to be thought his son'. (This might mean simply 'disciple', since for example Ben Jonson's followers were known as 'the sons of Ben'.) It is also of interest that Davenant is said to have owned the so-called Chandos portrait of Shakespeare, which has claims to have been painted during Shakespeare's lifetime.

In view of all this it is not surprising that Mrs Davenant has been identified with the so-called 'dark lady' of Shakespeare's Sonnets. Here again we have to face the problem of the degree, if any, to which these poems reflect actual incidents and participants in the poet's life. Was he promiscuous? Do they reflect a homoerotic disposition? In one of them, Number 31 (which is among those that may concern a male), the poet writes of 'the trophies of my lovers gone', which does not imply single-mindedness. But whereas the poems that may be addressed to a young man do not necessarily imply a sexual relationship, those relating to the woman unquestionably do, and some of them in distinctly unromantic terms. As Bruce Smith remarks, the Sonnets are exceptional in being 'focused on what love is like after sexual consummation, not before'.[6]

The implication of sexual laxity in Manningham's anecdote relates to a theory, propounded with particular force by two women biographers, Katherine Duncan-Jones and Germaine Greer, that a venereal disease, such as syphilis, may have been a direct or contributory cause of Shakespeare's death. Images of venereal disease appear especially in relation to Falstaff in a relatively light-hearted manner in the tavern scenes of *Henry IV Parts One* and *Two* and, probably by coincidence, become more frequent and more graphic in plays written in the four or five years soon following the date of Manningham's diary entry (see Chapter 9 below). They are most common in *Measure for Measure, Troilus and Cressida, Pericles, King Lear*, and *Timon of Athens*. There are also possible allusions in the two last-printed sonnets, which include references to

> ....a seething bath which yet men prove
> Against strange maladies a sovereign cure.
> But at my mistress' eyes love's brand new fired,

> The boy [Cupid] for trial needs would touch my breast.
> I, sick withal, the help of bath desired,
> And thither hied, a sad distempered guest,
>> But found no cure; the bath for my help lies
>> Where Cupid got new fire: my mistress' eyes.

There are at least two strong arguments against supposing that the allusions in the plays along with the sonnets imply that the author himself suffered from the diseases he writes about. One is, quite simply, that writers do not need to have personal experience of their subject matter. Shakespeare does not need to have been a rapist to have written *The Rape of Lucrece*, or a murderer to have written *Macbeth*. As for the sonnets, the final two in particular are, of all the poems in the collection, the ones with the clearest literary sources. Both go back to a Greek epigram in which

> Love slept, having put his torch in the care of the nymphs; but the nymphs said to one another 'Why wait? Would that together with this we could quench the fire in the hearts of men'. But the torch set fire even to the water and with hot water thenceforth the Love-Nymphs fill the bath.

Shakespeare's 'bath' is sometimes interpreted as a reference to the city of Bath, with its healing waters. It is true that hot mercury baths were used to treat syphilis, but 'editors who have imagined the poet setting off with his diseases to Bath to take the waters [ignore] the fact that sweating tubs must have been available in London'.[7] If any of the Sonnets are, as is often claimed, 'literary exercises', and therefore useless as biography, these highly derivative poems are they.

Nevertheless the theory that Shakespeare may have been venereally infected has been fuelled by accumulating evidence that in the composition of *Pericles* he collaborated, in one way or another, with George Wilkins, who besides writing plays kept at least one inn, on the notorious Turnbull (otherwise known as Turnmill) Street, which doubled as a brothel. Katherine Duncan-Jones assumes that Shakespeare was a client, writing that

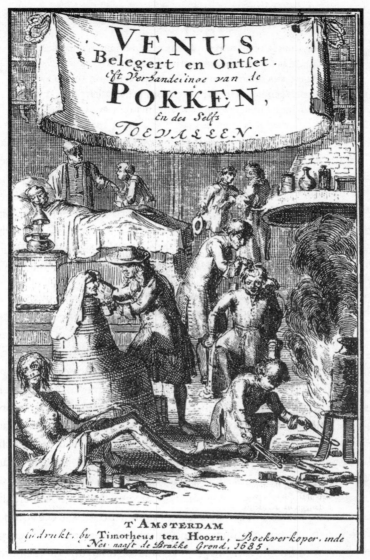

Figure 5. The title page of 'Venus besieged and liberated; or, an account of the pox and its ravages', 1685, by the Dutch physician Steven Blanckaert (1650–1702). The man in the bed salivates as a result of mercurial chemotherapy; the body of the man in a 'powd'ring tub of infamy' (*Henry V*, 2.1.73) is being exposed to mercury fumigation; beside him a patient is anointed with a preparation of mercury. In the foreground a woman in the late stages of syphilis displays her sores.

disturbing images of sweating tubs and venereal infection close both *Troilus and Cressida* and *Shakespeare's Sonnets*. Taken in conjunction with repeated gestures of retrospection and valediction in the late work, these images seem to me to support a supposition that Shakespeare's visits to Turnmill Street had left him with an unwanted legacy of infection, or at the very least, that he may have believed that they had done so. Again, it makes little difference whether, from about 1608, he was indeed venereally infected, or whether he merely thought he was.[8]

One might reasonably suppose that it would have made a lot of difference to him, and the alleged 'visits to Turnmill Street' are totally undocumented. And one might object on logical grounds that 'repeated gestures of retrospection and valediction' do not imply a diagnosis of any specific form of illness of either body or mind. So it seems to me that there is no reliable evidence whatever that Shakespeare suffered from a venereal infection.

Are there other ways in which the Sonnets may inform us about Shakespeare's personal sex life? The question of whether they are directly based on his own experience, or whether they are, as is often suggested, 'literary exercises', fictitious projections of imagined experiences, is hotly debated. It is a question to which there could, perhaps, be more than one answer: this to say, some of them could be more closely related than others to his personal life. I have emphasized what I believe to be the fallacy of reading the 154 poems as a unified collection, suggesting for instance that not all of the first 126 poems are necessarily addressed to a male, and that those so addressed are not necessarily all addressed to the same male. Similarly it is possible that some of the poems are more or less genuinely personal outpourings while others are more fictional imaginings. As a dramatist, Shakespeare spent most of his life imagining himself into the lives and minds of fictitious persons. The Sonnets might be as it were dramatic monologues with no basis in real life. Some of them could be straightforward exercises in lyric form.

If I must defend my personal belief, nevertheless, that some, indeed many of them, reflect circumstances of the author's own emotional and sexual life, it will be on several different grounds. One is that, while it is impossible to date the poems with any precision, there are good reasons for believing that many of them were written during the 1590s, when the love sonnet was a fashionable form, and that their late, and possibly unauthorized publication long after this fashion had died down suggests at least that they were not written as professional exercises, to make money and to enhance the poet's reputation, as the narrative poems clearly were.

Another, far more subjective reason is that to me the exploration of, especially, emotional situations of extreme anguish in some of the poems has the ring of authenticity. I should not be able to defend this position on purely intellectual grounds, since the man who could portray the emotional and sexual anguish of characters such as Troilus and Othello could have written no less convincingly of such passions in non-dramatic poems. But I could point to the fact that in the only poems in which the protagonist has a name, it is Shakespeare's own—Will. This distinguishes the collection from all others of the period, in which an addressee has a personal name, usually of a romantic cast such as Fidessa, Delia, or Stella.

Another reason for believing that some of the poems spring from personal experience is that they clearly hint at a love triangle between the poet, a male friend also named Will, and an unnamed woman who is sexually involved with both of them, in a manner that, seen as an attempt to relay to uninformed readers the sequence of events, is utterly incompetent, whereas viewed as a projection of events that the poet does not need or wish to spell out for readers, or indeed that he actively wishes to conceal from them, is more intelligible. This makes many of the poems rather like telephone conversations in which we are allowed to hear only one of the speakers, and it contributes greatly to their enigmatic quality. This differentiates them from anguished speeches in the plays, by characters such as Leontes and Posthumus, in that there the suffering is explained by its context.

It may also be worth noticing that of all the sonnet collections of the period, Shakespeare's is the most original, the one least clearly indebted to the continental tradition of Petrarchism. Indeed the poem with the closest links with this tradition parodies it: 'My mistress' eyes,' writes Shakespeare, 'are nothing like the sun.' And he declares that the reality of his love transcends convention.

So, if we think of these poems in autobiographical terms, what do they tell us? One, they show that he was indeed, and probably frequently, unfaithful to his wife. Furthermore we need to consider the triangular relationship involving friend and mistress adumbrated both in the poems printed earlier in the collection, up to Number 126, which include all those clearly addressed to a male, and in those printed later, from Number 127 onwards, which include the 'dark lady' sonnets.

It has been justly remarked that, uniquely among Elizabethan sonnet collections, 'for the first time in the entire history of the sonnet, the desired object [the writer assumes a single object] is flawed'.[9] Sonnet 35 alludes to an unnamed 'trespass', a 'sensual fault' which the poet forgives. Number 41 opens a mini-sequence with what starts as a mild enough admission that it is understandable that the friend's youth and beauty should cause a woman to woo him:

> And when a woman woos, what woman's son
> Will sourly leave her till he have prevailed?

But in the sestet the poet more bitterly expresses dismay that the woman with whom the friend is linked is the poet's own mistress:

> Ay me, but yet thou mightst my seat forbear,
> And chide thy beauty and thy straying youth

Who lead thee in their riot even there
Where thou art forced to break a two-fold troth:
  Hers, by thy beauty tempting her to thee,
  Thine, by thy beauty being false to me.

Then the next poem says that, though the poet dearly loved the woman, 'That she hath thee is of my wailing chief, | A loss in love that touches me more nearly.' Other poems, too, such as Sonnets 93, 95–6, and 120, show a troubled sense of a friend's transgressions.

The same theme emerges in the 'dark lady' poems. Sonnet 133 curses 'that heart that makes my heart to groan | For that deep wound it gives my friend and me.' Nothing is left. The woman has both betrayed the poet and enslaved his 'sweet'st friend', his 'next self', so that 'Of him, myself, and thee I am forsaken.' Sonnet 134 runs straight on to beg the 'covetous' woman to restore his 'kind' friend to him. But there is no hope: 'Him have I lost; thou hast both him and me; | He pays the whole, and yet am I not free.' Then, as we have seen (p. 48 above), in Sonnet 135 he puns tortuously and despairingly on the many possible senses of the word 'will' which include the name of both the poet and another man, desire, penis, and vagina. The following poem continues the word play, with seven uses of the word 'will', concluding categorically with 'my name is Will.'

I find it difficult not to read these poems as expressions of resentment at sexual infidelity on the part of both a male friend and a woman with whom he is linked. To me, the intensity of the poet's involvement with both one or more males and at least one woman suggests that he had both homosexual and extramarital heterosexual relationships. But there is everything to suggest that if he did so he was conscious of betraying ideals, of behaving out of unreasonable human frailty in ways that part of him deplored: his eyes 'know what beauty is, see where it lies, | Yet what the best is take the worst to be' (137); 'she that makes me sin | Awards me pain' (141); 'Love is my sin' and his mistress's lips 'have sealed false bonds of love as oft as mine, | Robbed others' beds' revenues of their rents' (142); 'Past cure I am, now reason is past care, | And frantic mad with evermore unrest' (147); 'In loving thee thou know'st I am forsworn…But why of two oaths' breach do I accuse thee | When I break twenty?' (152). He is, he acknowledges, the victim of lust which overwhelms reason:

> The'expense of spirit in a waste of shame
> Is lust in action; and till action, lust
> Is perjured, murd'rous, bloody, full of blame,
> Savage, extreme, rude, cruel, not to trust,
> Enjoyed no sooner but despisèd straight,
> Past reason hunted, and no sooner had
> Past reason hated as a swallowed bait
> On purpose laid to make the taker mad;
> Mad in pursuit and in possession so,
> Had, having, and in quest to have, extreme;
> A bliss in proof and proved, a very woe;
> Before, a joy proposed; behind, a dream.
>   All this the world well knows, yet none knows well
>   To shun the heaven that leads men to this hell.   (Sonnet 129)

This is a man with a conscience, betrayed by the turbulent sexuality that—if Shakespeare really is speaking of himself—led to his early marriage.

Shakespeare proclaims an ideal of marital constancy in the plangently lyrical if enigmatical poem beginning 'Let the bird of loudest lay', often known as 'The Phoenix and Turtle', published in 1601 without a title as one of the 'Poetical Essays' by various writers, including the playwrights Ben Jonson, George Chapman, and John Marston, in Robert Chester's *Love's Martyr; or Rosalind's Complaint*. The book is dedicated to Sir John Salusbury, and the poems appear to have irrecoverable allegorical significance. We do not know how Shakespeare came to be involved in the enterprise. Chester's long poem is described as 'allegorically showing the truth of love in the constant fate of the phoenix and turtle [dove]'. Clearly Shakespeare was writing to a prescribed theme, so his poem cannot be regarded as a totally personal utterance. Divided into three parts, it opens by summoning a convocation of benevolent birds, with a swan as priest, to celebrate the funeral rite of the phoenix and the turtle dove, who have 'fled | In a mutual flame from hence.' The birds then sing an anthem in which the lovers' deaths are seen as marking the end of all 'love and constancy'.

> So they loved as love in twain
> Had the essence but in one,
> Two distincts, division none.
> Number there in love was slain.

Their mutuality was such that 'Either was the other's mine.' Finally Love makes a threnos—funeral song—

> To the phoenix and the dove,
> Co-supremes and stars of love,
> As chorus to their tragic scene.

This part of the poem is set off by being composed in an incantatory style, each of its five stanzas having three rhyming lines, and the tone is one of grave simplicity. The pair died 'leaving no posterity', not because of 'their infirmity' but because of 'married chastity'. This last phrase in conjunction with absence of 'infirmity' appears to imply a deliberately sexless marriage, but is sometimes taken to signify one that was immaculate in its unity. In any case it sets forward an ideal that is antithetical to the poet's own situation as set forth in the Sonnets.

We have no documentary evidence deriving from legal sources of Shakespeare himself being involved, whether innocently or not, in sexual scandals. The same is true of his wife Anne. Domestically, the family stuck together. Shakespeare lived in several sets of lodgings in London, but there is nothing to show that he occupied them with anyone else. Or that he did not. There is no evidence of where the family lived in Stratford during the early years of marriage. It is usually assumed that they shared the family home with Shakespeare's parents, though Germaine Greer conjectures that they may have had a separate household before the purchase of the rather grand establishment, New Place, in 1597, fifteen years after they married.[10] If so, there is no trace of it in the records. From 1597 until they married, their daughters Judith and Susanna presumably lived in New Place with their mother, and with their father whenever he came back to Stratford.

The Sonnets appeared in print in 1609. The facts that they bear a dedication signed with the initials of the publisher, Thomas Thorpe, and that there is reason to believe that Shakespeare did not proofread the volume suggest that although the book was entered in the normal way in the Stationers' Register, on 20 May, the publication was unauthorized. Unlike the narrative poems, it seems to have been a publishing failure. The actor Edward Alleyn bought a copy in June, soon after it appeared.[11] But it did not go into a second edition, which suggests that, although the publisher seems to have regarded its appearance as something of a coup—'Shakespeare's Sonnets, never before imprinted', reads the title page—it flopped. Some scholars think that the book may have been suppressed, possibly on moral grounds, but this is mere conjecture. Others have supposed that, though Shakespeare may have wanted it to be published, he may have waited until after his mother died (she was buried on 9 September 1608) so as not to embarrass her. But his wife and daughters were still alive. Whether the publication of this apparent sequence of intimate revelations affected them, or the family's reputation, we simply do not know. Conceivably the revelation of marital infidelity through the publication of these poems affected his daughters' reputation: towards the end of his life both of them were involved in sexual scandals, though they appear to have been victims rather than offenders. Susanna was the subject of gossip which she was brave enough to challenge publicly. In July 1613 she sued one John Lane

SHAKE-SPEARES

SONNETS

Neuer before Imprinted.

AT LONDON
By *G. Eld* for *T. T.* and are
to be folde by *william Afpley.*
1609.

Figure 6. Title page of Shakespeare's Sonnets, 1609

for slander in the Consistory Court at Worcester on the grounds that he had reported that she 'had the running of the reins'—that is, a venereal infection—'and had been naught'—committed adultery—'with Ralph Smith', a Stratford hat maker. Her accuser, presumably unable to substantiate his charge, failed to turn up, and was excommunicated.[12] (This is the subject of Peter Whelan's 1998 play *The Herbal Bed*.) At the time of the accusation the Halls were living in New Place, no doubt with Anne and William, who by this time had virtually given up his literary career and was presumably spending more time at home.

In addition, scandal marred the marriage of Shakespeare's younger daughter, Judith, though it was not directly detrimental to her personal reputation. On 10 February 1616, at the age of 31, she married Thomas Quiney, a vintner and member of a prominent Stratford family. His father, Richard, was a neighbour of Shakespeare and wrote the only surviving letter addressed to him. Judith, like her mother and father before her, married in haste, failing to obtain the special licence required because it was Lent. As a result she and her husband were excommunicated. The reason for the haste must be related to the fact that the bridegroom had been carrying on an affair with another woman, Margaret Wheeler. On 15 March she and a child to whom she had given birth, presumably conceived by Quiney, were buried in Stratford. On 26 March, only six weeks after he married, he was brought to trial for incontinence with Margaret, and 'confessed that he had had carnal intercourse' with her. The vicar who had married him sentenced him to perform public penance 'clothed in a sheet (according to custom) for three Sundays' in Holy Trinity Church. In the event he was let down lightly; having offered five shillings to the poor of the town, he was required merely 'to acknowledge his fault in his own attire before the Minister of Bishopton [close to Stratford]...and to certify this at the next court.'[13]

Shortly before all this happened, probably in January, Shakespeare had drafted a will which shows great concern for family values. It apportions his money and property mainly between his two daughters, though also with bequests to other family members and to friends. His elder daughter, Susanna, and her husband, John Hall, are the main beneficiaries, as well as being appointed his executors. On 25 March, the day before Quiney appeared in court, Shakespeare made changes which suggest that in the light of what had happened, he was anxious to ring-fence Judith's interests. His bequests to her are substantial: £100 as a marriage portion and £50 more on condition that she surrender to Susanna her rights in a cottage on Chapel Lane, a silver-gilt bowl, and the interest on another £150 which would go to her or, if she had died, to her children three years after the date of the will; but she would receive this only as long as she was married, and her husband could claim it only if he settled lands of equal value on her. In the event, and despite its inauspicious start, her marriage was long-lasting and she had three children, all of whom died young. The eldest, baptized, like her sister's child, only nine months after she married, had the given name of Shakespeare, as if in tribute to his grandfather.

In writing of Shakespeare's sex life I have not attempted to draw evidence from his plays. It is clear from these that he had a deep understanding of sexual desire and of romantic love, of bodily rapture, and of sexual nausea; that he could imagine himself into the minds and imaginations of accepted and rejected lovers, that he had so vivid a sense of the torments inflicted by sexual jealousy that it would be easy, especially in the light of parallels with the Sonnets, to suspect more or less direct projections of his personal life in characters such as Othello and Leontes. I shall write of topics such as these in the ensuing chapters; but Shakespeare presents his dramas as fictions, and most of them derive partly from pre-existing literary and other sources. These are transformed by his imagination, which of course was fed by experience, but, as with the Sonnets, it is ultimately impossible to sift the imagined from the real.

PART II

Plays & Poems

I n the second part of this book I will complement my study of aspects of sexuality in Shakespeare's time by discussing the variety of ways in which he treats sexuality in his plays, and about the way in which he relates sexuality to love. First we will look at how he raises laughter out of the matter of sex, in both the language and the plotting of some of his comedies. After that we will consider his portrayal of sexual desire in relation to both lust and love. In one of his earlier plays, *The Two Gentlemen of Verona*, desire leads to attempted rape, and in another, *Titus Andronicus*, rape is accomplished. Sexual desire is central too to both *Measure for Measure* and *All's Well That Ends Well*; I shall suggest that the bed trick, by which a woman inveigles a man into having anonymous sex with her, represents a kind of rape of the man by the woman. Chapter 6, 'Sex and Love in *Romeo and Juliet*', is devoted to a single play because this is the one Shakespeare play in which he focuses most centrally on issues relating to sex, love, and the relation-ship between them. Chapter 7, 'Sexual Jealousy' examines the four plays—*Much Ado About Nothing*, *Othello*, *Troilus and Cressida*, and *The Winter's Tale*—in which jealousy figures most largely. There is a certain detachment in his portrayal of it in the first of these plays, followed by a far more intense and psychologically probing depiction of it in the others.

Chapter 8, 'Sex and Experience', endeavours to study Shakespeare's portrayals of, mainly, older lovers. As he—and the actors in his company—got older, he tended to portray more mature figures. *Hamlet* seems to me a watershed in his career—his longest, most technically ambitious, most stylistically varied, and above all most profoundly human play in which he reaches new levels of interiority. In it he juxtaposes love relationships between a young couple, Hamlet and Ophelia, and an older one, Gertrude and Claudius. We will consider the interactions between these strands of the play before going on to look at two later tragedies, *King Lear* and *Antony and Cleopatra*. Sex plays a relatively small, though still important part in the former; the latter, the counterpart in his later career to *Romeo and Juliet*, is his most ambitious examination of mature love and sexuality.

Chapter 9, 'Whores and Saints', is about his portrayals of the extremes of womanhood—the prostitutes in the *Henry IV* plays, *Timon of Athens*, and *Pericles*, and the virtuous maidens also in *Pericles* and in *The Winter's Tale* and *The Tempest*. A final chapter, 'Just Good Friends', considers Shakespeare's depiction of same-sex relationships that may be regarded as homoerotic.

4

The Fun of Sex

Like many of his contemporaries, Shakespeare derives much light-hearted comedy from the use of sexual wordplay, though it diminishes and darkens in his work with the passage of time. The comic effect of lewd puns results from the energy generated in the hearer's mind by the recognition that the innocent surface meaning of a word or phrase can be extended to encompass a sexual sense, which may or may not be signalled in the dialogue. Take the following passage from what is probably Shakespeare's earliest comedy, *The Two Gentlemen of Verona*. First Speed, referring to Proteus and Julia, says 'Why then, how stands the matter with them?' So far this may mean simply 'How are things going between them?' But then Lance introduces a comic dimension with 'Marry, thus, when it stands well with him it stands well with her.' An audience aware that 'stand' may mean 'have an erection' is invited to apply this meaning to the first use of the word and to admire Lance's ingenuity in so applying it. But Speed claims not to have seen that the word may have a double meaning.

What an ass art thou! I understand thee not.

The hearer is given a sense of superiority for having picked up the joke, and can identify with Lance's scorn of Speed as he responds with an additional pun, reinforced by stage business demanded by the dialogue, this time non-sexual:

> What a block art thou, that thou canst not! My staff understands me.
> SPEED   What thou sayst?
> LANCE   Ay, and what I do too. Look thee, I'll but lean, and my staff under-stands me.   (2.5.19–27)[1]

That this kind of word play is especially associated with Lance—whose name has clear phallic connotations—is recognized later in the play. After Speed asks him 'what news with your mastership?', a word defined some what stuffily by Schmidt in his *Shakespeare Lexicon* as 'a title of respect used by low people', Lance, pretending to understand 'mastership' as two separate words, makes the non-sexual pun 'With my master's ship? Why, it is at sea', provoking from Speed the response 'Well, your old vice still, mistake the word' (3.1.276–9).

Some sexual jests are so simple-minded that no pun is required to signal them. So when Lance, in the same play, says, 'This shoe with the hole in it is my mother' (2.3.17–18) the hearer needs little intelligence to understand why something with a hole in it may be identified with the female of the species. This is a kind of 'groan-joke'—so obvious that the hearer may even feel a kind of comic resentment at being expected to find it funny. Essentially it is the same sort of joke as at the end of *The Merchant of Venice* when Graziano says he will 'fear no other thing | So sore as keeping safe Nerissa's ring.' No pun is signalled here—unless by a knowing inflection of the actor's voice; it is left to the hearer, who has heard much of rings by this stage of the play, to make the connection between the wedding ring and the vagina. (That the pun has not always been obvious is shown by the fact that the lines were allowed to stand unaltered in the first version of Bowdler's edition.)

There are points in the plays at which the hearer is invited to admire both the author's and the characters' verbal ingenuity as each speaker picks up the opportunity offered by the other to take a potentially innocent word in a sexual sense. So, in Act 2, Scene 1 of *The Taming of the Shrew*, Petruccio sets things going by inviting Katherine to sit on his knee:

> PETRUCCIO
> ......Come, sit on me.

Katherine responds with an insult:

> Asses are made to bear, and so are you.

Petruccio turns it back on her by punning on 'bear' in the sense of 'bear a child':

> Women are made to bear, and so are you.

Katherine retaliates by calling him a 'jade', that is, a worn-out horse, with the implication that he is either too old or too feeble for her:

> No such jade as you, if me you mean.

Petruccio keeps the game going by suggesting that she is 'light', punning on the senses of 'light in weight' and 'morally suspect':

> Alas, good Kate, I will not burden thee,
> For knowing thee to be but young and light.

Katherine ingeniously picks on another sense of 'light', lighter in weight and therefore less in value, like a clipped coin:

> Too light for such a swain as you to catch,
> And yet as heavy as my weight should be.

Petruccio comes back at her with a pun on 'be/bee':

> Should be?—should buzz.

'Buzz' can mean 'rumour' or 'scandal', implying that he has heard rumours that Kate is 'light'. She responds with a mock-compliment, punning on 'ta'en' as 'understood' and 'captured':

> Well ta'en, and like a buzzard.

Remaining ornithological in his imagery, Petruccio calls her a turtle-dove—a gentle bird that would easily be seized by a bird of prey:

> O slow-winged turtle, shall a buzzard take thee?

Kate's reply 'Ay, for a turtle, as he takes a buzzard', is obscure, but provokes Petruccio's insult of calling her a wasp:

> Come, come, you wasp, i'faith you are too angry.

Katherine sustains the game with

> If I be waspish, best beware my sting.

To which Petruccio replies

> My remedy is then to pluck it out,

provoking Katherine's

> Ay, if the fool could find it where it lies.

There is still no overt sexuality, unless we are expected to hear this as a covert insult to Petruccio's manhood. But lewdness starts to rise to the surface as Petruccio responds provocatively with

> Who knows not where a wasp does wear his sting?
> In his tail.

'Tail' invites a jest on arse, or penis; Katherine attempts to correct him, incorrectly, with 'In his tongue', but in fact Petruccio is the better entomologist. He asks her 'Whose tongue?' 'Yours, if you talk of tales, and so farewell' says Katherine, to which Petruccio replies, in a tone of injured innocence, 'What, with my tongue in your tail? Nay, come again, | Good Kate, I am a gentleman.' The lewd image of a tongue (which could also evoke 'penis') in a tail ricochets back to the image of Katherine as a wasp, allowing us to admire the skill of the dramatist in creating the verbal circumstances which lead up to the climactic jest. It is a little like the passage in *The Comedy of Errors* in which Shakespeare, adopting the topos of the comic blazon or bodily geography—which he had already employed in *Venus and Adonis* (ll. 231–40)—has Dromio of Syracuse 'find out countries' in the kitchen maid Nell, culminating in the question 'Where stood Belgia, the Netherlands?', and Dromio's response 'O, sir, I did not look so low' (3.2.142–4). But whereas in *The Comedy of Errors* this bawdy is no more than part of a comic set piece, the one in *The Taming of the Shrew* serves a deeper dramatic function as a means of advancing the relationship between Petruccio and Katherine. Petruccio's initial introduction of bodily parts into the conversation surely constitutes a provocative invitation to sexual banter, and so could be understood as a courtship ploy. As the one speaker sparks off wit from the other, they grow in mutual understanding, in amused enjoyment of one another's company, and in acknowledgment of sexual attraction.

A slightly later development of what we may call a technique of accumulatively lewd wordplay comes in *Love's Labour's Lost* in one of the most sexually loaded passages in all of Shakespeare. It is sparked off by Costard's delivery to the Princess during a hunting expedition of a love letter which he mistakenly believes to have been written by Biron to Rosaline but is actually from Armado to Jaquenetta. Boyet, left alone by the Princess to sort it out, embarks on a game of teasing which starts with a hidden pun on 'suitor' and 'shooter' (4.1.107). I call this a hidden pun because, though there is nothing to signal it in the dialogue, an alert listener could recognize the word as its virtual homonym 'suitor' because of the preceding uncertainty about the recipient of a love letter—'From which lord to which lady?', asks the

Princess—and also 'shooter' meaning marksman. The objects of the hunt are deer, and the dialogue almost inevitably moves into a series of jokes on the topic of horns as the signs of a cuckold: 'My lady goes to kill horns, but if thou marry, | Hang me by the neck if horns that year miscarry.' Jokes about horns as the badge of a cuckold are ubiquitous in Elizabethan drama—Shakespeare deploys them most conspicuously in *The Merry Wives of Windsor* and *As You Like It*, and with deeper resonances in *Othello* and *The Winter's Tale*. The word could also convey the sense of 'penis'. Shakespeare's audiences would easily have picked up Boyet's remark as a comic insult meaning 'if cuckoldry is not a result' of the marriage; those with minds keenly attuned to the possibility of bawdy wordplay would also pick up the sense defined by the Arden editor, Henry Woudhuysen—whose notes are a model of frankness—as 'if penises don't get what they want'.

This raises the interesting question 'How dirty-minded do you have to be to understand the play?' The answer so far as the passage that follows is concerned is 'very dirty-minded indeed'. Maria says:

	You still wrangle with her, Boyet, and she strikes at the brow.
BOYET	But she herself is hit lower—have I hit her now?
ROSALINE	Shall I come upon thee with an old saying that was a man when King Pépin of France was a little boy, as touching the hit it?
BOYET	So I may answer thee with one as old that was a woman when Queen Guinevere of Britain was a little wench, as touching the hit it.
ROSALINE (*sings*)	Thou canst not hit it, hit it, hit it, Thou canst not hit it, my good man.
BOYET (*sings*)	An I cannot, cannot, cannot, An I cannot, another can. *Exit Rosaline*
COSTARD	By my troth, most pleasant! How both did fit it!
MARIA	A mark marvellous well shot, for they both did hit it.

BOYET   A mark—O mark but that mark! A mark, says my lady.

           Let the mark have a prick in't to mete at, if it may be.

MARIA   Wide o' the bow hand—i'faith, your hand is out.

COSTARD   Indeed, a must shoot nearer, or he'll ne'er hit the clout.

BOYET   An if my hand be out, then belike your hand is in.

COSTARD   Then will she get the upshot by cleaving the pin.

MARIA   Come, come, you talk greasily, your lips grow foul.

COSTARD   She's too hard for you at pricks, sir. Challenge her to bowl.

BOYET   I fear too much rubbing. Goodnight, my good owl.

This is a dazzlingly virtuosic display of double-entendre in which we are invited to interpret the repeated phrase 'hit it', which would have already been familiar to the play's original audiences as the refrain of a bawdy popular song and dance, as 'succeed sexually' in parallel to the meaning 'hit the centre of the archery target'; in which the word 'mark' means the centre of both the target and the woman's anatomy; in which 'prick' means both 'bull's eye' and 'penis'; in which Boyet's words to Maria 'An if my hand be out, then belike your hand is in' refers both to skill in archery and to use of either the male or female hand in sexual play; and in which Costard's 'Then will she get the upshot by cleaving the pin' means that she will bring about an ejaculation by, as the Arden editor, with no false delicacy, puts it, 'holding fast to his penis'. Even 'owl' addressed to Costard might mean 'cuckold'.[2]

Although not all of this sexual wordplay is explicitly signalled in the dialogue, it becomes apparent by its accumulative effect; by the fact that some of the bawdy innuendos would already have been familiar through songs and proverbs; and retrospectively by Maria's rebuke 'Come, come, you talk greasily, your lips grow foul.' Even then the game is not over, as Costard says, 'She's too hard for you at pricks, sir. Challenge her to bowl,' to be answered with Boyet's 'I fear too much rubbing.' As Woudhuysen puts it, 'Boyet is thinking of masturbation.' It is interesting that these bawdy interchanges take place between persons of very diverse social status—two aristocratic ladies (though not the Princess), the lord Boyet, and the country swain Costard.

The sexual wordplay in this passage of *Love's Labour's Lost* implies close intimacy among the speakers, as in a women-only scene (3.4) in *Much Ado About Nothing* in which Hero, Margaret, and Ursula, to be soon joined by Beatrice, are preparing for Hero's wedding. They indulge in ribald wordplay on the theme of 'the heavier for a husband', which could refer equally to the weight of a man over the female body in intercourse and to the weight of pregnancy, and Beatrice, who complains that she is 'stuffed' because she has a cold, is teased with 'A maid and stuffed! There's goodly catching of cold.' Later in the play too Benedick jests sexually, even flirtatiously with Margaret while seeking her help in his wooing of Beatrice in terms reminiscent of the passage quoted earlier from *The Taming of the Shrew*:

> MARGARET   Will you then write me a sonnet in praise of my
> beauty?
> BENEDICK   In so high a style, Margaret, that no man living shall
> come over it, for in most comely truth, thou deservest it.
> MARGARET   To have no man come over me—why, shall I always
> keep below stairs?   (5.2.3–9)

'Come over' here presumably has the innocent primary sense of 'excel the sonnet in excellence', but Margaret interprets it sexually as 'cover' (or perhaps, even more lewdly, as 'ejaculate over'). 'To keep below stairs' means 'remain a servant', presumably here implying 'improve my social status through marrying'. Benedict's response suggests that Margaret is making a sexual joke:

> BENEDICK   Thy wit is as quick as the greyhound's mouth, it
> catches.

Greyhounds were used in hunting; 'catches' implies 'snatches quickly at'. I suspect unfathomable sexual undertones here.

> MARGARET   And yours as blunt as the fencer's foils, which hit but
> hurt not.

'Blunt' may imply 'impotent': a fencer's foils (with innuendo for 'penis') would be rendered incapable of penetrating.

> BENEDICK   A most manly wit, Margaret, it will not hurt a woman.
> And so I pray thee call Beatrice. I give thee the
> bucklers.

His penis ('wit') is 'manly' because it will please rather than hurt a woman. He gives up the game, surrendering the 'bucklers' ('a buckler was a small shield with a detachable spike screwed (sexual pun intended) into the centre'[3]) to Margaret.

> MARGARET   Give us the swords. We have bucklers of our own.

She caps this with a suggestion that women can protect their virtue by manipulating their limbs:

> BENEDICK   If you use them, Margaret, you must put in the pikes
> with a vice—and they are dangerous weapons for
> maids.

'Pikes' are spikes—more innuendo for penises; a 'vice' was a 'clamp used to screw an item into place'[4]; Benedick seems to be suggesting that if women protect themselves they will have to use force to get sexual pleasure; maybe 'vice' and 'pikes' imply 'dildos'.

> MARGARET   Well, I will call Beatrice to you, who I think hath legs.
> BENEDICK   And therefore will come.

Because Beatrice has legs she can walk ('come'), but also can open them to Benedick's penis.

Again we have a game of cumulative, and highly intelligent, sexual jesting, each participant feeding the other with cues. Here the files, swords, and pikes take the place of the tongue, and the buckler that of the tail, in *The Taming of the Shrew*. The punch line, as the RSC edition puts it with unusual tentativeness, uses 'come' 'with a possible [unsignalled] pun on [have an] "orgasm"', a sense not acknowledged by, e.g., the Arden editor but endorsed by Gordon Williams in his authoritative *Glossary of Shakespeare's Sexual Language*.[5]

There are many more examples of sexual wordplay than those that I have commented on here, and not all of it in comedies—*Romeo and Juliet* is full of it (see Chapter 6). There is some in *Henry V*, such as the French puns in Catherine's conversation with Alice, and even, in a poignant way, in the Hostess's account of Falstaff's death:

> Now I, to comfort him, bid him a should not think of God, I hoped there was no need to trouble himself with any such thoughts yet. So a bade me lay more clothes on his feet. I put my hand into the bed and felt them, and they were as cold as any stone. Then I felt to his knees, and so up'ard and up'ard, and all was as cold as any stone. (2.3.19–25)

It is an elegy for lost sensuality: the warmth that she has been accustomed to feel and to stimulate in and above Falstaff's thighs has all gone.

There are numerous sexual jests in *As You Like It*, on which I shall have more to say later, and in *Twelfth Night*. The heatedness of Shakespeare's sexual wordplay is a fascinating aspect of his psycho-sexual development in his dramas written up to around 1600, but as his career develops his use of sexual wordplay for comic purposes both dwindles and darkens. In *Measure for Measure*, *All's Well That Ends Well*, and *Pericles*, with its scenes set in a brothel, it serves a more darkly comic purpose than mere fun. Even in late plays there are still occasional flashes, as for example in *Antony and Cleopatra* when Charmian and Iras are jesting with the Soothsayer:

IRAS   Am I not an inch of fortune better than she?
CHARMIAN   Well, if you were but an inch of fortune better than I,
where would you choose it?
IRAS   Not in my husband's nose.   (1.2.52–5)

Only a slight vocal inflection is needed to convey that the improvement would be more valued in the husband's penis than in his nose.

In part the diminution in sexual jesting, and the fact that it becomes less light-hearted, more cynical and bitter in tone, is the result of changes of subject matter and of dramatic genre. Perhaps it also reflects changes in Shakespeare's approach to life, a deepening seriousness of purpose, a dwindling of youthful delight in exuberant wordplay, even in sex itself, as weightier matters come to the fore.

*

In addition to the fun of sexual wordplay let's discuss the dramatic fun that can be created out of situations of sexual desire. In the same way that much of the comedy of *Venus and Adonis* arises from the thwarting of Venus's desire for Adonis, so part of the fun—for the audience—of *The Taming of the Shrew* derives from Petruccio's refusal, after he has married Kate and they have arrived at his house in the country, to take her to bed to consummate their marriage; the situation is explicitly resolved in what is almost the play's last line: 'Come, Kate, we'll to bed.'⁶ It is a kind of sex strike, a reversal of the situation in Aristophanes's *Lysistrata*, where the women refuse to have sex with the men.

A more complex example of the fun that Shakespeare derives from the sexual chase is provided again by *Love's Labour's Lost*. Much of this play's comedy depends on demands made by desire—and by love—on ambitions to quell it. In the opening scene the King of Navarre and his three attendant lords are preparing to withdraw from the world and to form a 'little academe' in which 'The mind shall banquet, though the body pine.' The action that follows forms an examination of the tension in their lives between reason and instinct, wit and folly, private desire and public duty, and, most relevant here, between ambitions for celibacy and the desire for sexual fulfilment. The men's determination not to be 'seen to talk with a woman within the term of three years' is immediately challenged by the arrival on a diplomatic mission of the Princess of France with, predictably, three matching ladies.

Rhetorically, metrically, situationally, and in its plotting this is the most elaborately patterned of Shakespeare's plays. The patterning reaches its climax in the scene (4.3) in which each of the lords reveals that he has succumbed to desire. Biron, the most intelligent, and the one most conscious of the fragility of their aims, has already confessed his love for Rosaline and paid the clownish Costard for delivering a letter to her. He enters alone and speaks ruefully of his love. His later statement 'Like a demigod here sit I in the sky' (l.76) requires him to move to a higher level, perhaps by climbing a stage tree, as the King enters and, believing himself to be alone, delivers his love sonnet addressed to the Princess. With another level of comic irony, Biron then watches and comments in ironical asides as the King, concealed in a bush, watches Longueville, who also believes himself to be alone, read a love sonnet, this one addressed to Maria. Then all three watch as Dumaine, similarly deceived, reads his sonnet addressed to Katherine. After doing so he expresses the ironically redundant wish 'O, would the King, Biron, and Longueville | Were lovers too!' Each of the three overhearers is ignorant of the others' presence, and they reveal themselves one by one, each unaware that he has been overheard and sanctimoniously rebuking the other. 'I should blush, I know', says Longueville to Dumaine, 'To be o'erheard and taken napping so.' The King comes out of hiding and rebukes both of them: 'What will Biron say when that he shall hear | Faith so infringèd, which such zeal did swear?' (See Plate 4) The audience, of course, knows that Biron *has* heard this, and recognizes his hypocrisy when he steps forward, as he says, 'to whip hypocrisy', mocks each of the others, and complains of being betrayed:

I am betrayed by keeping company
With men like you, men of inconstancy.
When shall you see me write a thing in rhyme,
Or groan for Joan, or spend a minute's time
In pruning [preening] me? When shall you hear that I
Will praise a hand, a foot, a face, an eye,
A gait, a state, a brow, a breast, a waist,
A leg, a limb?

Biron does indeed seem to those on stage—though not to the audience—to be in an impregnable moral position when one of the play's rustic characters, Jaquenetta, arrives with the letter that turns out to be that in which he has declared his love to Rosaline. Acutely embarrassed, he tears it to pieces as soon as he has read it. Realizing that the game is up, and that he too is about to be exposed as a lover, he confesses his guilt. He, like all the others, is a human being, susceptible to sexual desire—'We cannot cross the cause why we were born'—but also to love.

In this more than in any of his earlier comedies Shakespeare portrays characters in whom desire can be contained within a love that encompasses both the physical and the ideal—as he will also do in *Romeo and Juliet*. Biron gives eloquent voice to this in his great speech beginning 'Have at you now, affection's men at arms.' Shakespeare took special pains over it, as we know from the accidental inclusion when it was first printed of a false start.[7] It is the parallel in the comedies of Juliet's 'Gallop apace, ye fiery-footed steeds' in the tragedies (see p. 162), though Biron lays more emphasis than Juliet on the idealized than on the physical aspects of love:

A lover's eyes will gaze an eagle's blind.
A lover's ear will hear the lowest sound
When the suspicious head of theft is stopped.
Love's feeling is more soft and sensible
Than are the tender horns of cockled snails.
Love's tongue proves dainty Bacchus gross in taste.

> For valour, is not love a Hercules,
> Still climbing trees in the Hesperides?
> Subtle as Sphinx, as sweet and musical
> As bright Apollo's lute strung with his hair;
> And when love speaks, the voice of all the gods
> Make heaven drowsy with the harmony.   (4.3.310–21)

This is a rapturous celebration of romantic love, which can include the sexual but which emphasizes the spiritual.

Shakespeare counterpoints this plot with the earthier goings-on of the country bumpkin Costard and the affected Spaniard Don Armado in their rivalry over the maid Jaquenetta. The lords have imposed their vows of chastity not only on themselves but also on those who serve them, but Costard, like Biron, knows that it 'is the simplicity of man to hearken after the flesh' (1.1.214–15). A preposterously phrased letter from Armado betrays to the King that Costard has been taken 'With a child of our grandmother Eve, a female, or for thy more sweet understanding, a woman.' Costard seeks to wriggle out of the proclaimed punishment of 'a year's imprisonment to be taken with a wench' by claiming first that Jaquenetta is not a wench but a damsel, then a virgin, then a maid, and on the King's saying 'This "maid" will not serve your turn, sir' gives in with the bawdy admission that 'This maid will serve my turn, sir.' The King sentences him to subjugate his desires by fasting for 'a week with bran and water'.

In the scene that immediately follows, we learn that Armado too is not merely tempted to break the King's commandment, but that the object of his desire is the very woman he has betrayed: 'I do love that country girl that I took in the park with the rational hind Costard.' And he declares his love when Constable Dull brings her in on her way to be punished. At this point her reaction to his declaration is not encouraging—indeed she positively mocks him:

ARMADO   I will visit thee at the lodge.
JAQUENETTA   That's hereby.

ARMADO	I know where it is situate.
JAQUENETTA	Lord, how wise you are!
ARMADO	I will tell thee wonders.
JAQUENETTA	With that face?
ARMADO	I love thee.
JAQUENETTA	So I heard you say.
ARMADO	And so farewell.
JAQUENETTA	Fair weather after you. (1.2.127–36)

Nevertheless he has his way with her, as we learn when, at the climax of the jollifications of the pageant of the Nine Worthies, Costard reveals before all the company that 'she is two months on her way…She's quick [pregnant]. The child brags in her belly already. 'Tis yours.' Almost simultaneously the ultimate realities of human existence break in on the artificialities and unrealities by which the play's characters have been seeking to govern their lives. Though mirth and mockery are resumed as Costard and Armado prepare to fight, all is stilled as news of a forthcoming birth is followed by news of a recent death. The information that the Princess's father, the King of France, is dead is conveyed wordlessly and simultaneously to both the characters and the audience, by the sombre appearance of the previously unknown messenger, Mercadé. (See Plate 5) 'The scene', as Biron remarks with an aptly theatrical metaphor, 'begins to cloud'. The fun of the sexual chase, fun of any kind, leaves the play as its characters take on a new seriousness, forced to adjust their relationships with each other. The men make awkward attempts to resume their wooing, but the time is out of joint. Like lovers in a medieval romance they must undergo tests to show that they are worthy. The King must go 'To some forlorn and naked hermitage | Remote from all the pleasures of the world.' Biron, at the end of his central speech on love, had asked 'who can sever love from charity?' Now Rosaline demands that if he is to win her love he must put his wit to charitable ends, turning from mockery to cheering the sick:

> You shall this twelvemonth term from day to day
> Visit the speechless sick and still converse
> With groaning wretches, and your task shall be
> To enforce the painèd impotent to smile.

It is the most conditional, and the most original, ending to any of Shakespeare's comedies, and Shakespeare draws attention to its originality as Biron, in a moment of alienation, says 'Our wooing doth not end like an old play.' 'Jack hath not Jill' (5.2.861)—'hath' in the double sense of 'possess' and 'have sexual congress with'—and the play ends with the songs of the cuckoo, which 'mocks married men', and the owl.

*

In *As You Like It* Shakespeare's handling of the fun of sex resembles that in *Love's Labour's Lost* but displays greater subtlety and an even more delicate touch. In many plays of his time the juxtaposition in main plot and subplot of high-born, aristocratic characters with others from a lower social plane, along with the assumption that the former are likely to be witty, sensitive, and romantic while their lowlier brethren are uneducated, crude in their sexual impulses, and down-to-earth is a dramatic convention to which Shakespeare by no means always subscribes but on which he plays frequent variations. The counterparts in *As You Like It* to Costard and Jaquenetta in *Love's Labour's Lost* are the clown Touchstone and the wench Audrey, though as usual with Shakespeare there is no simple equivalence. It is after all the high-bred but foolish Armado, not Costard, who gets Jaquenetta with child. Moreover in the later play Shakespeare complicates matters by portraying a wider range of attitudes towards sex and love, juxtaposing and contrasting them with great skill. As in *Love's Labour's Lost*, there are four pairs of lovers: Silvius and Phoebe, Touchstone and Audrey, Oliver and Celia, and Rosalind and Orlando, but they are more clearly differentiated than those in the earlier play. *As You Like It*, which is only lightly plotted, derives much of its dynamic from the relationships between these couples and their varying attitudes to love and sex.

Silvius and Phoebe come straight out of the Renaissance pastoral convention, deriving partly from Petrarch. Hundreds of Elizabethan lyrics, including some scattered through Shakespeare's main source for the play, Thomas Lodge's *Rosalynde*, depict the situation of the faithful, abject lover whose beloved is fair of face but hard of heart. Shakespeare replicates this situation with Silvius sighing upon a 'midnight pillow' for Phoebe, who scorns him. There is much gentle comedy in Silvius's idealization of Phoebe, and in Phoebe's falling in love with Rosalind in her disguise as Ganymede, but everything is on an elevated plane except when Rosalind seeks to persuade Phoebe to face up to the basic realities of love:

> ...mistress, know yourself; down on your knees
> And thank heaven, fasting, for a good man's love;
> For I must tell you friendly in your ear,
> Sell when you can. You are not for all markets.
> Cry the man mercy, love him, take his offer;
> Foul is most foul, being foul to be a scoffer.   (3.5.58–63)

But Rosalind-as-Ganymede's robustness has the unexpected and undesired effect of causing Phoebe to fall in love with her/him.

If Silvius and Phoebe's love is idealistic until Rosalind puts them under her spell, so that Jaques can commend Silvius 'to a long and well-deservèd bed', Touchstone's and Audrey's is basic. Touchstone has hardly met Audrey before he is looking for a parson, but he is without romantic illusions: 'As the ox hath his bow, sir, the horse his curb, and the falcon her bells, so man hath his desires; and as pigeons bill, so wedlock would be nibbling.' To some extent Touchstone's robust realism acts as a criticism of Silvius's moonishness, but it is itself criticized. He is clearly more intelligent than Audrey, which gives an edge of exploitativeness to his cynical admission that, like Richard III with Lady Anne, he will 'have her' but 'will not keep her long' (*Richard III*, 1.2.217). So when Jaques remonstrates with him that 'a man of his breeding' should not 'be married under a bush, like a beggar' by the hedge-priest Oliver Martext, Touchstone admits, 'I am not in the mind but I were better to be married of him than of another, for he is not like to marry me well, and not being well married, it will be a good excuse for me hereafter to leave my wife' (3.5.75–84). And at the conclusion of the play, Jaques consigns Touchstone 'to wrangling, for thy loving voyage | Is but for two months victualled.'

The dramatic perspective that Shakespeare adopts allows only limited development of the love affair of Celia and Oliver, but Touchstone's statement to Audrey 'We must be married, or we must live in bawdry' has its exact counterpart on another social plane in Rosalind's declaration that Celia and Oliver have 'made a pair of stairs to marriage, which they will climb incontinent, or else be incontinent before marriage.' (We have seen that Shakespeare's townsfolk were frequently arraigned for 'incontinency'.) It finds a parallel too, in a less explicit way, as the play approaches its climax when Orlando, lamenting 'How bitter a thing it is to look into happiness through another man's eyes', declares 'I can live no longer by thinking' (5.2.48). He needs the natural culmination of love, sexual fulfilment with the person he loves.

The principal love focus of this play is on Rosalind and Orlando. Rosalind sustains her disguise as the youth Ganymede far longer than the plot requires, but the unrealistically and artificially long-drawn-out game of courtship that they play creates the opportunity for a complex and sexually ambivalent exploration of the many faces of love. Rather as in *Twelfth Night, or What You Will*—the play's full title emphasizes its pervasive concern with desire, often unfulfilled—Orsino finds himself trembling on the verge of falling in love with Viola in her persona as the page Cesario, so Shakespeare shows us Orlando becoming confused between desire for an imaginary Rosalind and for the boy Ganymede whom the real Rosalind impersonates. It is an ambivalence that would have been enhanced when the real Rosalind was played by a boy, and that would have been signalled and emphasized by the use of the name 'Ganymede', a common term for a man's young male sexual partner. Its climax comes as Orlando daringly asks Aliena (Celia) to marry him to Rosalind/Ganymede: 'Come, sister, you shall be the priest and marry us' (4.1.116–17). What Aliena says is 'I cannot say the words', and this may well represent a moment of horror on her part at the request that she do something that in Elizabethan terms would represent a legal marriage between two persons of the same sex (as Orlando believes) enacted by the ceremony of hand-fasting (see p. 19). The play is rich in sexual ambiguities which may be explored by actors as well as critics:

> There is throughout this dialogue a rich suggestiveness of action which might be possible between the lines. There could be a significant and electrifying pause after Orlando's 'Pray thee, marry us' before Celia's own, usually deflating, comic response, 'I cannot say the words.' The fact that Orlando is given the standard Anglican prayer book response of 'I will' can make this episode as serious or playful as the actors or director choose.[8]

Is Orlando feeling desire for the woman behind the disguise or for the boy as whom she is disguised? Or even for the actor who plays him?

The amount of sexual wordplay, or badinage, in As You Like is a matter of dispute. This play does not have set pieces of signalled bawdy such as I have discussed in The Taming of the Shrew and Love's Labour's Lost. There are occasional unambiguously bawdy ripostes, as when Rosalind says, 'I prithee, take the cork out of thy mouth, that I may drink thy tidings,' provoking Celia's 'So you may put a man in your belly.' There are, predictably in a play that takes place largely in a forest, a number of 'horn' jokes. There are also passages in which modern scholars have, rightly or wrongly, discerned 'deep' bawdy that is not signalled but which depends on the hearer taking words which could have an innocent sense as sexual allusions of a coded nature, which is apparent to listeners with a sophisticated alertness to sexual innuendo.

An example comes as Ganymede is teasing Orlando. 'What would you say to me now an I were your very, very Rosalind?'

ORLANDO	I would kiss before I spoke.
ROSALIND AS GANYMEDE	Nay, you were better speak first, and when you were gravelled for lack of matter you might take occasion to kiss. Very good orators, when they are out, they will spit; and for lovers, lacking—God warr'nt us—matter, the cleanliest shift is to kiss.
ORLANDO	How if the kiss be denied?
ROSALIND AS GANYMEDE	Then she puts you to entreaty, and there begins new matter.
ORLANDO	Who could be out, being before his beloved mistress?
ROSALIND	Marry, that should you if I were your mistress, or I should think my honesty ranker than my wit.
ORLANDO	What, of my suit?
ROSALIND	Not out of your apparel, and yet out of your suit. (4.1.65–81)

There is no suggestion of bawdy in this dialogue in the notes to, for example, H. J. Oliver's New Penguin edition of 1968 or Agnes Latham's second Arden, of 1975. Yet the passage is not entirely clear unless some degree of bawdy is assumed. Were the editors exercising self-censorship, or did they really not perceive it? Alan Brissenden, in his Oxford edition of 1993, sees bawdy only in the word 'wit', which he interprets as 'the sexual organs', and devotes an appendix to demonstrating this sense of the word in other writings of the period. Juliet Dusinberre's 3rd Arden, of 2006, is similarly restrained. But 'God warr'nt us' is an apology which should raise the alert that what follows may need excuse; some recent scholars have variously glossed 'matter' as 'semen', and following from this 'out' as 'inability to ejaculate', 'honesty' as 'chastity' (a common sense of the word), and, like Brissenden, 'wit' as 'sexual organ'.

There is, however, an alternative set of interpretations. Gordon Williams, in his *Glossary*, defines 'out' not as 'inability to ejaculate' but as 'denied vaginal entry'. From this he goes on to interpret Rosalind's 'that should you if I were your mistress, or I should think my honesty ranker than my wit' as 'I should deny you entry if I were your beloved.' Rosalind, Williams suggests, 'turns [Orlando's] words "out of my suit"' to mean that 'she will not admit him naked, "out of your apparel"'. So we are left with the possibility that some members of Shakespeare's first audiences saw no bawdy in the passage, that others found one set of indecent meanings, while other audience members found something quite different to snigger over. How rich is Shakespeare's imagination that it can give rise to such variety of interpretation!

I close this chapter with a look at the most farcical of Shakespeare's comedies, *The Merry Wives of Windsor*. The fun of this play does not derive to any great extent from sexual wordplay. There are occasional passages of mild bawdy, but it comes to the fore only in Mistress Quickly's misunderstandings of the Latin that the schoolmaster, Sir Hugh Evans, is trying to inculcate in the schoolboy William—surely Shakespeare's self-projection of his younger self:

EVANS	What is your genitive case plural, William?
WILLIAM	Genitive case?
EVANS	Ay.
WILLIAM	*Genitivo: 'horum, harum, horum.'*
MISTRESS QUICKLY	Vengeance of Jenny's case [sexual organ]! Fie on her! Never name her, child, if she be a whore.
EVANS	For shame, 'oman!
MISTRESS QUICKLY	You do ill to teach the child such words. He teaches him to hick and to hack [copulate], which they'll do fast enough of themselves, and to call 'whorum'. Fie upon you! (4.1. 52–62)

Ostensibly, *The Merry Wives of Windsor* derives much of its fun from the sexual chase, but in fact the motives that drive Falstaff in his double pursuit of Mistresses Ford and Page are financial, not sexual. This is made clear early on when Falstaff, apparently deluded into the belief that both women are burning with desire for him, says of the former, 'Now, the report goes, she has all the rule of her husband's purse', and of the latter, 'She bears the purse too. She is a region in Guiana, all gold and bounty' (1.3.47–62). The fact that he attempts to press his lecherous desires simultaneously upon the women even to the extent of addressing identical love letters to both of them emphasizes the mercenary nature of his pursuit as well as helping the audience to suspend moral judgement. It results also in the hilarious scene (2.1) in which the women discover and comment on the trick he is trying to play on them.

In another of the play's plots too, that of the wooing of Anne Page, the motives of two of her ostensible suitors, Abraham Slender and Dr Caius, have little if anything to do with either sexual desire or love. Slender, the most bashful and least confident of wooers, nervously wishes that he had his 'book of songs and sonnets here' with which to bolster his suit. Asked by Justice Shallow if he can 'love the maid', the best he can say is 'I will marry her, sir, at your request. But if there be no great love in the beginning, yet heaven may decrease'—a pre-dogberryism for 'increase'—'it upon better acquaintance' (1.1.225–8). Unsurprisingly, Slender has been portrayed in performance as gay; a witness of the Globe production in 2008 wrote

> William Belchambers threatened to steal the show on several occasions as an obviously gay Slender, who was more than happy to find he had ended up with a boy at the wedding, and who struggled to talk to Anne at all when left alone, completely out of his depth with a woman.[9]

Pressed by Anne to enter the house, Slender hesitates nervously on the threshold, claiming that he is not hungry, until Master Page urges him to do so.

Nor is it easy to see the absurdly self-centred Doctor Caius as a serious suitor. Love and true desire enter the play only with the appearance of the handsome and well-born, if impecunious, Master Fenton. Even he admits that 'I will confess thy father's wealth | Was the first motive that I wooed thee, Anne,' but he persuades her that 'wooing thee, I found thee of more value | Than stamps in gold or sums in sealèd bags' (3.4.13–16). No one familiar with the conventions of romantic comedy could doubt that he is the one who will succeed. Slender's standard argument in favour of arranged marriages—that the couple may come to love after marriage—will be countered at the end of the play when Fenton, in a powerful expression of the values of romantic love, says to Anne's parents:

> You would have married her, most shamefully,
> Where there was no proportion held in love.
> The truth is, she and I, long since contracted,
> Are now so sure that nothing can dissolve us.
> Th'offence is holy that she hath committed,
> And this deceit loses the name of craft,
> Of disobedience, or unduteous title,
> Since therein she doth evitate and shun
> A thousand irreligious cursèd hours
> Which forcèd marriage would have brought upon her.   (5.5.213–22)

Pre-eminently, the situational fun of this play derives from two plot strands, the first generated by the wives' revenge on Falstaff. The devices of Falstaff having to hide in a buck basket which is eventually unloaded, with him in it, into the Thames, then of his needing to be disguised as the Old Woman of Brentford (the only certain example in all Shakespeare's plays of a man cross-dressing as a woman), and climactically the trick played on him in Windsor Forest as, disguised as Herne the Hunter (with the cuckold's horns on his head), he is tormented by Mistress Quickly and a group of children disguised as fairies, are comic in themselves. But the fun derives no less from Falstaff's reactions to them than from the ingenuity of the tricks.

Taken purely on a plot level this play could be no more than a mechanical farce. It is given richness and depth both by Shakespeare's exploitation of the multiple ironies of the situations and by the dense, almost Dickensian particularity of the language in which they are clothed. Falstaff seems to relish his own discomfiture as he describes what happened to him:

> Have I lived to be carried in a basket like a barrow of butcher's offal, and to be thrown in the Thames? Well, if I be served such another trick, I'll have my brains ta'en out and buttered, and give them to a dog for a New Year's gift. 'Sblood, the rogues slighted me into the river with as little remorse as they would have drowned a blind bitch's puppies, fifteen i'th' litter! And you may know by my size that I have a kind of alacrity in sinking. If the bottom were as deep as hell, I should down. I had been drowned, but that the shore was shelvy and shallow—a death that I abhor, for the water swells a man, and what a thing should I have been when I had been swelled? By the Lord, a mountain of mummy!   (3.5.4–17)

The rich, warm humour of that passage derives from Falstaff's relaxed self-acceptance. It stands in extreme contrast to the frenzied near-hysteria of the self-deluded Master Ford in the second main situational thread of the play's comedy, that which derives from the ironies resulting from Master Ford's unjust suspicions of his wife's fidelity which culminate in his humiliation and his ultimate correction and forgiveness. In the tragedy *Othello*, the tragicomedy *The Winter's Tale*, and even the comedy *Much Ado About Nothing* (which has strong elements of tragicomedy), sexual jealousy is treated seriously. Here it is a theme for mirth. The comedy of Falstaff's second account of his near-drowning is greatly enhanced in performance by the fact that it is spoken to the jealous husband himself. As John Dennis, with perceptive awareness of the scene's acting potential, wrote in the preface to his adaptation of the play as *The Comical Gallant* (1702), it 'gives an occasion for a great Actor to shew himself. For all the while

Falstaff is making this relation *Ford*, at the same time that in dumb acting he shews a concern and a fellow-feeling to the Knight, shews a great deal of Joy and Satisfaction to the audience.' After Falstaff leaves for his date with Mistress Ford, Ford himself vows to take his revenge:

> Hum! Ha! Is this a vision? Is this is a dream? Do I sleep? Master Ford, awake! Awake, Master Ford! There's a hole made in your best coat, Master Ford. This 'tis to be married! This 'tis to have linen and buck baskets! Well, I will proclaim myself what I am. I will now take the lecher. He is at my house. He cannot scape me; 'tis impossible he should. He cannot creep into a halfpenny purse, nor into a pepperbox. But lest the devil that guides him should aid him, I will search impossible places. Though what I am I cannot avoid, yet to be what I would not shall not make me tame. If I have horns to make one mad, let the proverb go with me: I'll be horn-mad.   (3.5.128–end)

The later scene in which Ford searches the basket, wrongly thinking that Falstaff must again be concealed in it, followed by the comic bathos of 'Well, he's not here I seek for,' by Ford's beating Falstaff in his disguise as the Old Woman of Brentford, and by Ford's frenzied search of his house in the expectation of finding Falstaff concealed in it, expertly provide opportunities for robust physical comedy. And though Ford is at the centre of the play's most farcical episodes, the verse lines in which he asks his wife's forgiveness for his unjust suspicions of her fidelity, and pays tribute to her virtue, steer the play towards a romantic rather than a farcical conclusion:

> Pardon me, wife. Henceforth do what thou wilt.
> I rather will suspect the sun with cold
> Than thee with wantonness. Now doth thy honour stand,
> In him that was of late an heretic,
> As firm as faith.   (4.4.5–9)

And there is a final touch of sexual wordplay in the play's closing lines, also spoken by Ford:

> Let it be so, Sir John.
> To Master Brooke you yet shall hold your word,
> For he tonight *shall* lie with Mistress Ford.

*

In this chapter we have been concerned with the fun that Shakespeare portrays in his characters and creates for his audiences from sexual jesting and from comic situations arising from sexual desire. In the next chapter we'll continue with the theme of sexual desire but consider it in relation to the distinction, often difficult to make, between love and lust, and the tragic as well as comic consequences that desire can create.

5

Sexual Desire

I n writing about Shakespeare's poems and sonnets I have inevitably discussed sexual desire in a variety of its manifestations and artistic transformations. In *Venus and Adonis* the goddess's desire for an unresponsive mortal being becomes a source for high comedy laced with the pathos of frustration. In that poem's companion piece *The Rape of Lucrece*—the other panel of the diptych, as it were—lustful desire unredeemed by love, offering only momentary satisfaction in its fulfilment, results in tragedy. Tarquin's 'lust in action', to quote Sonnet 129, is indeed 'murd'rous, bloody, full of blame'. Much later in Shakespeare's career he was to recall Tarquin's rape in the context of murder in *Macbeth*:

> withered murder,
> Alarumed by his sentinel the wolf,
> Whose howl's his watch, thus with his stealthy pace,
> With Tarquin's ravishing strides, towards his design
> Moves like a ghost. (2.1.52–6)

The Sonnets run the gamut in their treatment of the varied manifestations of desire and love, idealized and lustful, joyful and self-hating,

115

accepting and tortured. As we saw in the case of Christopher Beeston, with his 'hundred wenches' (p. 28), some men of Shakespeare's time, far from feeling guilt, bragged of their lustful conquests. But others anguished over their falls from grace. Shakespeare's Sonnet 129, especially—quoted on p. 80—expresses the bitter self-contempt of one who castigates himself for having yielded to lust.

Our discussion of the fun of sex in the plays no less inevitably has drawn on situations motivated by sexual desire, whether directed to the consummation of true love, as with Beatrice and Benedick, Orlando and Rosalind, or to the more basic satisfaction of the pleasures of the flesh, as with Don Armado and Jaquenetta, Touchstone and Audrey. In this chapter we'll concentrate on Shakespeare's portrayals of sexual desire in relation to the distinction between love and lust. The distinction is not always easy to maintain. The word 'lust' originally meant simply 'pleasure' or 'delight', which could be experienced without sin in, for example, the virtuous exercise of the fundamental human (and animal) instinct of sexual desire for a particular person if it led to or was experienced within marriage directed towards procreation. As the preamble to the marriage service in the Book of Common Prayer puts it, marriage 'is not by any to be enterprised, nor taken in hand, unadvisedly, lightly, or wantonly, to satisfy men's carnal lusts and appetites, like brute beasts that have no understanding; but reverently, discreetly, advisedly, soberly, and in the fear of God'.

But the word 'love' also was (and is) commonly used of sexual desire in its purest sense, whereas 'lust' from an early stage in its history has been categorized as 'inordinate desire, especially sexual, leading to sin'—'carnal lusts', as the Book of Common Prayer puts it—and thus in opposition to 'love'. This sense prevails today. Traces of the word used with no sense of moral disapprobation are found in Shakespeare, but he much more commonly uses it of desire which is sinful because it seeks merely temporary self-gratification, or which, like attempts to rape, is criminally directed. Adjectives that Shakespeare uses with it include, for example, 'wanton', 'burning', 'shameful', 'monstrous', 'sweating', 'seducing', and 'black'.

In his romantic comedies, naturally enough, desire tends to be portrayed in an idealized fashion. Though lovers are motivated by desire, in the earlier of these plays its sexual basis is rarely made explicit. In his first play, for instance, *The Two Gentlemen of Verona*, the young men Valentine and Proteus are on the threshold of sexual experience. In the opening scene Valentine, who has not yet begun to love, affectionately castigates his friend Proteus for being 'a votary to fond desire', regarding it as a painful and foolish state of mind

> where scorn is bought with groans,
> Coy looks with heart-sore sighs, one fading moment's mirth
> With twenty watchful, weary, tedious nights.
> If haply won, perhaps a hapless gain;
> If lost, why then a grievous labour won;
> However, but a folly bought with wit,
> Or else a wit by folly vanquishèd.   (1.1.29–35)

(Valentine's understanding of 'desire' is Petrarchan; 'watchful, weary, tedious nights' are experienced also as a result of longing desire by the persona of Sonnet 27.) There is a hint in the phrases 'fading moment's mirth' and 'a hapless gain' of the transience of the pleasure of sexual satisfaction such as Tarquin experiences in *The Rape of Lucrece*, and as Shakespeare explores far more seriously in Sonnet 129 ('A bliss in proof and proved, a very woe'), but the tone, though rueful, is light-hearted.

While Proteus defends himself by claiming that 'doting love | Inhabits in the finest wits of all', he admits nevertheless that his loving desire for Julia has made a fool of him:

> I leave myself, my friends, and all, for love.
> Thou, Julia, thou hast metamorphosed[1] me,
> Made me neglect my studies, lose my time,

> War with good counsel, set the world at naught;
> Made wit with musing weak, heart sick with thought.   (1.1.65–9)

He is in exactly the situation of the young men in *Love's Labour's Lost* after the appearance of the ladies of France has eroded their plans to give up all worldly pursuits.

Julia too, having received a letter from Proteus, testifies to the folly of love:

> Fie, fie, how wayward is this foolish love
> That like a testy babe will scratch the nurse
> And presently, all humbled, kiss the rod.   (1.2.57–9)

Foolish it may be, but it has its pleasures, too, as Proteus says in lines which in their vernal imagery recall the most lyrical of Shakespeare's Sonnets:

> O, how this spring of love resembleth
> The uncertain glory of an April day,
> Which now shows all the beauty of the sun,
> And by and by a cloud takes all away.   (1.3.84–7)

Just as Proteus admits that Julia has 'metamorphosed' him, so, after Valentine has fallen in love with Silvia, his page, Speed, satirically listing the conventional marks of a lover, declares that his master is 'metamorphosed with a mistress' (2.1.29).

Darker tones are sounded when Proteus, having become his friend's rival in love, acknowledges that he no longer loves Julia and that his former 'zeal to Valentine is cold'. In a speech that lightly anticipates Angelo's self-castigation in *Measure for Measure* (2.2.168–92), he expresses his guilt for his 'three-fold perfidy'—to Julia, to Valentine, and to himself:

> To leave my Julia shall I be forsworn;
> To love fair Silvia shall I be forsworn;
> To wrong my friend I shall be much forsworn.   (2.6.1–3)

Suffering spreads from himself to the disguised Julia, poignantly expressed in her dialogue with the Host as she hears Proteus's serenade to Silvia (4.2); but desire remains on a non-sexualized, Platonic or Petrarchan plane, as in the non-Shakespearian sonnet sequences (see p. 46), until the final scene when Proteus, goaded beyond endurance by Silvia's expressions of hatred, her refusal of his suit, and her rebukes of his treatment of Julia, threatens to rape her:

> I'll woo you like a soldier, at arm's end,
> And love you 'gainst the nature of love: force ye
> .... I'll force ye yield to my desire. (5.4.57–9)[2]

Happily Proteus's evil designs are averted by Valentine's opportune intervention and, overcome by 'shame and guilt', he repents in the least plausible of Shakespeare's happy endings.

The yielding of love to lust in *The Two Gentlemen of Verona*, underdeveloped though it is, anticipates many other points in Shakespeare's writings where he wrestles with the problem of distinguishing between lustful and loving desire. In *Venus and Adonis* he was to write that

> Love comforteth, like sunshine after rain,
> But lust's effect is tempest after sun.
> Love's gentle spring doth always fresh remain;
> Lust's winter comes ere summer half be done.
> Love surfeits not; lust like a glutton dies.
> Love is all truth, lust full of forgèd lies. (ll. 799–804)

And *The Rape of Lucrece* forms an extended examination of the effects of lust without love.

In Shakespeare's early plays, however, the counterpart to *The Rape of Lucrece* is *Titus Andronicus*, where also loveless desire leads to brutal rape. This play appears to have been written around the same time as *The Rape of Lucrece*, published in 1594. The fact that these are the only two of Shakespeare's works in which rape actually occurs, although there are others in which it is threatened, might suggest that Shakespeare was preoccupied with the topic at this date. In view of current attempts to revive the idea that about one-third of the play was written not by Shakespeare but by George Peele,[3] it would be unwise to attempt to use it as evidence about Shakespeare's personal opinions. On the other hand it should not be ignored in an overall consideration of the Shakespearian corpus, and the virtually complete dissociation of sexual desire from love in *Titus Andronicus* makes the play impossible to overlook in a study of Shakespeare's portrayal of sexual desire.

Personal relationships in the play's early scenes are so superficial and shifting that it is difficult to believe that they are based on anything other than expediency. It is not always easy to be sure whether this is the result of deliberate design or of technical inadequacy on the part of the dramatist(s) which might cause them to treat their characters as puppets to be manipulated according to the demands of the plot rather than as simulacra of real people. There is a sequence of implausibilities as, for instance, Bassianus, having claimed that he loves Lavinia, makes no objection when the new emperor Saturninus declares that he will make her 'Rome's royal mistress, mistress of my heart', not because he loves her but because of his wish 'to advance [Titus's] name and honourable family' (1.1.238–41). Implausibility is compounded when, only a few minutes later, Saturninus describes the captive Tamora, Queen of the Goths, whom he has just encountered, as 'A goodly lady…, of the hue | That I would choose, were I to choose anew' and asks Lavinia if she has any objections to a change of their marital plans. At least he has the grace to thank her when she accommodatingly concurs.

There is another quick shift in direction as Bassianus, in defiance of Titus's wish to restore Lavinia to the Emperor—who, ungratefully describing her as 'a changing piece', makes it clear that he no longer wants her—belatedly claims Lavinia as his own and runs off with her, causing a scuffle in which Titus kills one of his own sons (1.1.287.1). After Saturninus takes Tamora, instead of Lavinia, to the Pantheon to 'consummate [their] spousal rites' he has the nerve to rebuke Bassianus for what he calls his 'rape' of Lavinia—'rape' here meaning 'snatching away', not 'sexual violation'. The latter meaning of the word comes closer as Tamora's sons Chiron and Demetrius quarrel over Lavinia—now a married woman—and, despite Chiron's claims to love her 'more than all the world', readily agree to Aaron's suggestion that they take advantage of the countryside's 'many unfrequented plots... | Fitted by kind for rape and villainy' to take turns to 'serve' their 'lust' and 'revel in Lavinia's treasury' (2.1.71 onwards). In other words what the brothers call love is no more than sexual desire at its most brutal.

Tamora's expressions of desire for Aaron are of a piece with her readiness to help him in his plan to enable her sons to 'make pillage of [Lavinia's] chastity | And wash their hands in Bassianus' blood.' The old motif of the cuckold's horns is taken up with grim humour when Bassianus and Lavinia show their awareness of Tamora's adultery: 'Jove shield your husband from his hounds today', says Lavinia, ''Tis pity they should take him for a stag.' Criminal rape comes closer with Tamora's incitement of her sons to kill Bassianus and to rape Lavinia: 'Drag hence her husband to some secret hole,' says Chiron, 'And make his dead trunk pillow to our lust.' And they carry her off with a line that I sometimes think Andrew Marvell may have recalled:

> Come, mistress, now perforce we will enjoy
> That nice-preservèd honesty of yours

says Chiron, anticipating Marvell's

> then worms shall try
> That long preserv'd virginity,
> And your quaint honour turn to dust,
> And into ashes all my lust.   ('To his Coy Mistress')

Lavinia's reappearance is described in one of the most horrifying stage directions in drama: *Enter the Empress' sons, Chiron and Demetrius, with Lavinia, her hands cut off and her tongue cut out, and ravished* (2.4.0.1–3). (See Plate 6)

Titus Andronicus, then, might be described as a study in the evil of sexual desire when it is violently divorced from love.

In later plays Shakespeare wrestles more creatively with human problems created by tensions between, on the one hand, raw sexual desire that seeks satisfaction only in the moment of gratification, as he explores it in Sonnet 129, and on the other hand sex as a natural and fruitful realization of virtuous and God-given desires which can find their fulfilment within a tenderly loving relationship on which the heavens may pour blessings. In two plays—*Measure for Measure* and *All's Well That Ends Well*—especially he sets up characters and situations that enable him to debate the issues of both self-control and control from outside the self that result from the tensions between lust and love. It is no denigration of Shakespeare's romantic comedies, from *The Two Gentlemen of Verona* to *Twelfth Night*, to say that after having written them he turned to a more earnest, morally self-conscious exploration of such issues. There is a sense in which each of Shakespeare's plays, however whole and perfect in itself, is also a prelude to, and a study for, others that lie ahead.[4]

In both *Measure for Measure* and *All's Well That Ends Well* Shakespeare creates and explores situations in which sexual desire leads to an impasse which can be resolved only by the conventional plot device of the bed trick, by which a man is tricked into having sex with a woman whom he does not desire and whom he believes to be other than she really is. In a sense this is the rape of the man by the woman as much as it would be if the woman had drugged the man into insensibility and then forced herself upon him. It is not forcible rape like that of Lavinia by Chiron and Demetrius; but it is rape all the same in that the man would not be having sex with this woman, might indeed (as is true at least in *All's Well That Ends Well*) view the prospect with no less repugnance than Lucrece views the advances of Tarquin, or Lavinia of Chiron and Demetrius (or, for that matter, than Adonis views those of Venus), if he knew her true identity.

But although both plays employ the same central device, each of them does so with the aim of exploring different moral and ethical issues. In *Measure for Measure* these centre on the State and the Church as agents of sexual control. In the opening scene the Duke, head of the state, temporarily abnegates authority to his deputy Angelo. Against this background Shakespeare sets up a delicately balanced sexual situation which will form the basis of his complex dramatic debate. The second, seriocomic scene, with its references to sexually transmitted diseases contracted under the bawd Mistress Overdone's roof, depicts a state that overflows with sexual corruption. The newly appointed Deputy has issued a proclamation by which all the bawdy 'houses in the suburbs of Vienna'—a thinly disguised London—'must be plucked down.'⁵ And the first victim of the new regime is Claudio, who has been 'arrested and carried to prison' where, as Overdone bluntly puts it, 'within these three days his head' is to be 'chopped off' for 'getting Madame Julietta with child' (1.2.59–71). But Juliet is no whore, and Claudio is no Christopher Beeston. He loves Juliet, she loves him, and, as we have seen (p. 19), he thinks of her as 'fast my wife'. They have entered into a contract which means that they are as close to being married as it was possible to get without the final blessing of the Church. They wished for this, too; but their virtuous intents have been thwarted by external circumstances and they have yielded to desire: Juliet is pregnant. The State, represented by the Duke's deputy, Angelo, whom Claudio characterizes as 'the demigod Authority', has revived a long disused law to impose on Claudio the sentence of death—a far more severe punishment than, as we have seen, was suffered by Shakespeare's fellow-townsman John Davis for a similar, real-life offence in 1625 (p. 18). Nevertheless Claudio admits that he has acted with 'too much liberty', and in a memorable image of rats ravenously swallowing that which will poison them, figures forth the concept that human beings are driven by their inherent natures to self-destructive actions:

> Our natures do pursue,
> Like rats that raven down their proper bane,
> A thirsty evil; and when we drink, we die.   (1.2.120–2)

At the other extreme, Claudio's sister, Isabella, is as close to having espoused the celibate life as it is possible to get: she is about to enter a cloister; when we first see her she is discussing with a nun the restraints placed upon the 'sisterhood, the votarists of Saint Clare' in which she has enrolled as a novice, and expressing her wish for even more strict restraints upon her liberty than those she has been told of.

Angelo, too, is characterized by the amoral libertine Lucio as a dedicated if secular celibate,

> a man whose blood
> Is very snow-broth; one who never feels
> The wanton stings and motions of the sense,
> But doth rebate and blunt his natural edge
> With profits of the mind, study, and fast.   (1.4.56–60)

(A more serious version of what the men in *Love's Labour's Lost* sought to become.) And Lucio, hoping that Isabella's self-evident virtue will move Angelo to compassion, urges her to plead directly with him for her brother's life. Angelo's right-hand man, Escalus, delicately suggests to Angelo that he himself may be subject to temptation, but Angelo maintains a rigorously legalistic stance:

> 'Tis one thing to be tempted, Escalus,
> Another thing to fall.   (2.1.17–18)

And, in words that will resonate in the play's last scene, he declares that if indeed he should offend as Claudio has, he should suffer the same punishment: 'Let mine own judgement pattern out my death.'

Although Shakespeare is deeply concerned to explore the moral complexities of the situations that he has set up, he is aware too both that he is writing an entertainment and that he needs to work on a broad canvas in order to give ample expression to as many sides of the question as possible. This is a play of debate, not a moral treatise. So in a largely comic scene in which we see the agents of the law prosecuting their case against the keepers and frequenters of bawdy houses, Mistress Overdone's servant Pompey Bum is allowed to suggest—as Thomas Nashe had (p. 31)—that bawdy houses serve a socially justifiable function in satisfying basic human needs. Responding to Escalus's condemnation of his trade as a bawd, he asks 'Does your worship mean to geld and spay all the youth of the city?' (2.1.220–1). And though Escalus is bound by the ties of duty and aware that lenience may encourage sin, his heart is with Claudio: 'Pardon is still the nurse of second woe. | But yet, poor Claudio!' The Provost, keeper of the prison who has the duty of overseeing Claudio's execution, also deplores Angelo's over-severity:

> Alas,
> He [Claudio] hath but as offended in a dream.
> All sects, all ages, smack of this vice; and he
> To die for't! (2.2.3–6)

Immediately before Isabella, accompanied by Lucio, arrives to speak for her brother to Angelo, the deputy's legalistic, unimaginative attitude is brilliantly illuminated by his choice of a single noun to refer to the 'groaning' Juliet: 'See you the *fornicatress* be removed' (2.2.23). So a person is reduced to a criminal label, like a tag dangling from her neck. Angelo's legalism pervades his early responses to Isabella, who needs all of Lucio's prompting to persist in her suit.

Whatever Lucio's faults, it is difficult for the audience not to admire this cheerful sinner's concern for Claudio's welfare as he urges Isabella on. She makes a powerful appeal through Christian religion:

> Why, all the souls that were were forfeit once,
> And He that might the vantage best have took
> Found out the remedy. (2.2.75–7)

Her reference is to Jesus' redemption of the human race through his own self-sacrifice. And she goes on to engage Angelo in a skilful theological debate, reaching great heights of eloquence until at last he admits in an aside 'She speaks, and 'tis such sense | That my sense breeds with it'—the second use of 'sense' here implying the onset of sexual desire. In modern productions the actor has been known to clutch his crotch at this point, or at his later words 'What's this? What's this?' to imply that Angelo is experiencing an erection. And as at last Isabella leaves, with an appointment to see him again the next day, he admits

> I am going that way to temptation,
> Where prayer is crossed.

The scene ends with Angelo's great speech of dawning self-recognition in which he acknowledges his temptation:

> Never could the strumpet,
> With all her double vigour—art and nature—
> Once stir my temper; but this virtuous maid
> Subdues me quite. Ever till now
> When men were fond, I smiled, and wondered how.

His second interview with Isabella portrays a man in an acute state of sexual tension. At first his discussion with her remains on a hypothetical level:

> Which had you rather: that the most just law
> Now took your brother's life, or, to redeem him,
> Give up your body to such sweet uncleanness
> As she that he hath stained? (2.4.52–5)

The give-away word there surely is 'sweetness': though he speaks of the sexual act as a 'staining' (implying 'with semen'), he is encouraging her to think that there might nevertheless be pleasure in the sin.

Slowly he comes to the point, asking her what she would do if there were no other way to save Claudio's life than for her to 'lay down the treasures of [her] body' to one who desired her. Her reply has been linked with stories of female saints 'who endured martyrdom rather than lose their virginity',[6] but is there also a touch of masochistic desire in what she says, hinted at by the references to stripping herself, to a bed, to 'longing', and to the blood-colour of 'rubies'?

> As much for my poor brother as myself.
> That is, were I under the terms of death,
> Th'impression of keen whips I'd wear as rubies,
> And strip myself to death as to a bed
> That longing have been sick for, ere I'd yield
> My body up to shame.   (2.4.99–104)

One of the play's editors reads this as a subconscious, or subtextual, revelation of desire: 'Unconsciously Isabella provokes Angelo's sadistic lust with the talk of rubies...strip...bed...longing.' Of 'longing' specifically he writes 'omission of the personal pronoun gives extra emphasis to this word, with its erotic connotation (something of which Isabella herself is not to be supposed to be conscious, but to which Shakespeare wishes to alert the audience'.[7] Certainly Shakespeare causes her to express herself with a more complex density of expression than is needed to convey her basic meaning.

From speaking in abstract, hypothetical terms Angelo slowly brings the discussion round to a specific proposition. Insultingly, perhaps, to one who is on the brink of choosing to live as a 'barren sister all [her] life' (as Theseus puts it in A Midsummer Night's Dream, 1.1.72), Angelo speaks of loss of virginity as 'putting on the destined livery'—very much as Donne writes of putting on 'perfection and a woman's name' in his sensual 'Epithalamion made at Lincoln's Inn'. And coming down at last to brass tacks Angelo declares, 'Plainly conceive, I love you.' The choice of the word 'conceive', where he might have said e.g. 'understand', is pointed.

Love or lust? How far away here are we from Tarquin's desire for Lucrece, or that of Chiron and Demetrius for Lavinia? If Isabella were to give way to Angelo at this point, would he not in effect be raping her? Certainly as he pursues his suit raw sexual desire appears to predominate over the tenderness of love such as that of Romeo for Juliet or Orlando for Rosalind. Isabella sees through him, and tries to capitalize on the situation by threatening to expose him unless he signs a pardon for her brother; but Angelo coldly asks, 'Who will believe thee, Isabel?' and acknowledges his sinfulness as he declares that he will give '[his] sensual race the rein' unless she yields up her 'body to [his] will'. As we have seen, the word 'will' could bear the secondary sense of 'penis'. If she refuses him, Claudio will not only die but will be tortured too: 'thy unkindness shall his death draw out | To ling'ring sufferance' (2.4.166–7).

At this point the play's focus shifts away from Angelo and his desire, to focus on Claudio and his fear of death—a measure of the ultimate seriousness of this play in comic form. Religion is still to the fore. The Duke in his disguise as a friar visits Claudio in prison and, though the young man still hopes for a reprieve, advises him, successfully at first, to prepare himself to die in the great *consolatio* 'Be absolute for death' (3.1.5). But no sooner has Claudio declared

> To sue to live, I find I seek to die,
> And, seeking death, find life. Let it come on

than sexual issues come to the fore again with the entrance of Isabella. Slowly, a little evasively, she breaks the news to her brother that she could save his life by yielding to Angelo's desires. She fears his reaction:

> O, I do fear thee, Claudio, and I quake
> Lest thou a feverous life shouldst entertain,
> And six or seven winters more respect
> Than a perpetual honour.   (3.1.72–5)

She is suggesting that even in the ordinary course of things Claudio could die within a few years, whereas her honourable reputation would last for ever. And when at last she comes out with it—'If I would yield him my virginity, | Thou might'st be freed!'—Claudio's first reaction is one of abhorrence: 'O heavens it cannot be!'...'Thou shalt not do't!' But slowly, in a dialogue that is as subtly nuanced in its modulations as a passage of Mozartian recitative, the life force makes its way to the surface.

> ISABELLA Be ready, Claudio, for your death tomorrow.
> CLAUDIO Yes. Has he affections in him
> That thus can make him bite the law by th'nose
> When he would force it? Sure it is no sin,
> Or of the deadly seven it is the least.
> ISABELLA Which is the least?
> CLAUDIO If it were damnable, he being so wise,
> Why would he for the momentary trick
> Be perdurably fined? O Isabel!
> ISABELLA What says my brother?
> CLAUDIO Death is a fearful thing.
> ISABELLA And shamèd life a hateful. (3.1.106–17)

And after the recitative we have the aria, Claudio's great counterweight to the Duke's *consolatio* beginning 'Ay, but to die and go we know not where.' After it he raises the theological question of whether a deed that appears in itself to be sinful can become a virtue if it is undertaken for good ends:

> What sin you do to save a brother's life,
> Nature dispenses with the deed so far
> That it becomes a virtue.

'Nature', we notice, not 'God' (but the name of the deity appears to have been censored out of this text, and anyway it would not have scanned). Isabella's response is interesting as a speech which can have disparate psychological resonances according to how it is delivered. It begins

> O, you beast!
> O faithless coward, O dishonoured wretch,
> Wilt thou be made a man out of my vice!

and ends

> Might but my bending down
> Reprieve thee from thy fate, it should proceed.
> I'll pray a thousand prayers for thy death,
> No word to save thee.

If it is spoken in measured tones it comes across as a cruelly cold-hearted and priggish condemnation of her brother. But its repeated exclamations would justify an interpretation more sympathetic to Isabella: that it is the hysterical, unreasoned outburst of a disillusioned, emotionally immature girl, frightened of the very idea of sex. How old is she? In the Elizabethan theatre she would have been played by a boy, which might favour the latter interpretation. But in any case her insistence that her brother should be willing to die to save her chastity—'More than our brother is our chastity' (2.4.185)—does not show her to be living a gospel of love.

The dialogue culminates in her declaration that it would be best for Claudio to die quickly. The plot has arrived at a stage at which it seems that its outcome must be tragic to either Claudio or Isabella. Then the Duke steps out of hiding, and enacts the role of Shakespeare the play plotter. This is the major turning point of the drama. After it the dominant medium of expression turns from verse to prose. The passion of intellectual debate recedes, the emotional temperature goes down, and the later part of the play comes to seem more morally didactic than psychologically probing. The Duke's role becomes peculiarly problematic. The amount of plotting that he must do in order to help Shakespeare bring the plot to a conclusion has a distancing effect, especially after the deeply absorbing action that precedes it.[8] The ease with which he takes on the role of friar lends colour to the fact that he has sometimes been presented in production as a saintly character, even as a Christ figure bearing a cross, and the ultimate benevolence of his intentions in the latter part of the play may support this. But he goes about it in a morally dubious manner. His manipulativeness, his assumption that he knows best what is good for everybody and even that he has the right to cause them pain as he attempts to bring it about, may repel. 'I will keep her ignorant of her good,' he says of Isabella when it seems likely that Claudio will be reprieved, 'To make her heavenly comforts of despair | When it is least expected.'⁹ Thanks a lot, she might have responded, and he proceeds to tell her that Claudio is dead. He attempts to justify his use of the bed trick with the words 'Craft against vice I must apply,' but it may seem both implausible and morally suspect that he should persuade Isabella to pretend to agree to sleep with Angelo even though the woman in the bed will actually be Mariana, Angelo's former fiancée whom he has jilted because she had the misfortune to lose her dowry, but who, improbably, loves him still.

The action has social implications. Modern audiences may find it disconcerting that in the latter part of the play the forced marriages of Angelo to Mariana and of Lucio to the punk Kate Keepdown should be used as a form of punishment. The Duke's confrontations with the drunken murderer Barnardine, who represents the sheer will to live, and with the slanderous rogue Lucio may seem emblematic of the never-ending struggle of Church and State with the unregenerate forces of unbridled sexuality and violence. Lucio, reiterating what we have already heard in the earlier part of the play, tells the Duke that it will be impossible to quell lechery 'till eating and drinking be put down' (3.1.366–7), and Barnardine, described as 'a man that apprehends death no more dreadfully but as a drunken sleep; careless, reckless, and fearless of what's past, present, or to come; insensible of mortality, and desperately mortal' (4.2.144–7), resolutely refuses to be put to death. The combined and related forces of sexuality and of desire for life exert themselves, and there is nothing that the Duke, whether as statesman or as Friar, can do about it.

The final stretch of action centres firmly on the Duke's plotting and becomes didactic as, almost like a puppeteer, he declares to Isabella that although she might be willing to pardon Angelo 'For Mariana's sake', yet

> The very mercy of the law cries out
> Most audible, even from his proper tongue,
> 'An Angelo for Claudio, death for death.'
> Haste still pays haste, and leisure answers leisure;
> Like doth quit like, and measure still for measure. (5.1.404–8)

'Even from his proper tongue' here must mean 'even against its—mercy's—appropriate language', that is to say, contrary to what would be expected of mercy. The primary reference is to Matthew's account of Jesus' Sermon on the Mount: 'Judge not, that ye be not judged. For with what judgment ye judge, ye shall be judged: and with what measure ye mete, it shall be measured to you again.'[10] This may not seem like Christian morality, but earlier in the Gospel Jesus has alluded to the doctrine of 'an eye for an eye, a tooth for a tooth', continuing 'But I say unto you, that ye resist not evil: but whosoever shall smite thee on the right cheek, turn to him the other also'[11] and 'Love your enemies, bless them that curse you, do good to them that hate you, and pray for them which despitefully use you, and persecute you.' In apparently adopting the revenge ethic, the Duke, no longer disguised as a representative of the Church, is testing Isabella, pretending to expect that she will behave to Angelo as he has behaved to her. He maintains the pretence even as Mariana implores Isabella to join her in begging for Angelo's forgiveness:

> Against all sense you do importune her.
> Should she kneel down in mercy of this fact [crime],
> Her brother's ghost his pavèd bed would break,
> And take her hence in horror. (5.1.430–3)

He makes the issue absolutely plain:

> He dies for Claudio's death.

And he waits for Isabella's response. When it comes it emblematizes the superiority of mercy over strict justice. And that, surely, *is* a Christian message.

The Duke's testing of Isabella is very much at the forefront of this long scene. The remainder of the action is curiously foreshortened. It is like a painting which, centring on one episode, portrays others more sketchily in a series of vignettes. In part this is due to the exigencies of the dramatic medium in which Shakespeare is working. If he had been writing a novel, he could have given each episode equal prominence; but drama demands concision even at the expense of psychological verisimilitude.

Self-consistent to the end, Angelo, who had asked that if he fell into temptation his 'own judgement' should 'pattern out [his] death' (p. 124), now declares that he craves 'death more willingly than mercy. | 'Tis my deserving, and I do entreat it.' His marriage and formal forgiveness are accomplished within a few lines. The reunion of Isabella with Claudio, returned from the dead, is underwritten—neither brother nor sister says a word as the Duke apportions rewards and punishments, pardoning Angelo and blessing his marriage to Mariana, condemning Lucio to marry his 'punk', and thanking his helpers. This is at the opposite extreme from the long, rapt duologue between another sister and the brother she had believed dead, Viola and Sebastian in *Twelfth Night, or What You Will* (5.1. 215–56).

Moreover Isabella says nothing for all the rest of the scene after her plea for Angelo's forgiveness, even though in the course of it she receives two separate proposals of marriage from the Duke. Textually there has been no hint of sexual attraction between them up to this point, though in production it is possible to hint subtextually at a developing relationship during their two previous private conversations. In Adrian Noble's production at Stratford in 1983, 'There was a sense of steadily ripening intimacy between [Isabella] and the Duke, and their final union came as no surprise.'[12] Nor does sexual desire figure conspicuously in the marriage of Angelo to Mariana, or at all in Lucio's to Kate Keepdown—on the contrary, he protests vigorously against it: 'Marrying a punk, my lord, is pressing to death, whipping, and hanging' (5.1.521–2). As the Duke makes his first proposal, Isabella is in a state of shock at the revelation that Claudio is alive, and he does not press his suit. Whether she should accept the second one wordlessly has become a theatrical crux since John Barton, in a 1970 Stratford production, had her stand looking puzzled in the centre of the stage as the other characters departed.

The close of the play brings it—just—within the category of comedy. Is the mutedly happy ending no more than a sacrifice to the conventions of the genre? Or does it represent Shakespeare's considered conclusion to the issues he has raised in the course of the action? Is the Duke's intended marriage to Isabella—whether we are to imagine it as happening after the play is over—a symbolic union of the forces of justice and mercy, of State and Church? Or is it, as seems most likely with Shakespeare, an interim answer, not exactly a shrugging off of the questions, but an acknowledgment that there are no final answers, and that it is more important to be open to moral problems than to think you can solve them?

*

Measure for Measure is often grouped with *All's Well That Ends Well* under the heading of 'problem plays'. A major difference between the two is that in the latter play sexual desire is portrayed very much from the woman's point of view. (This is true also of *As You Like It*, but there the tone is far lighter.) Whereas Isabella in *Measure for Measure* is desperate to preserve her virginity, Helen in *All's Well That Ends Well* spends much of the play trying to lose hers, and eventually succeeds through underhand means. *All's Well That Ends Well* is a love story that reaches at best only a fragile resolution, and one that must call into doubt the very genre of comedy to which it ostensibly belongs. It is packed full of ideas, a play in which behaviour is explicitly related to abstract concepts and in which moral conflicts are portrayed and explored. And the story, which derives from Boccaccio, is told in a broad range of linguistic styles including the jocular, the relatively naturalistic, the courtly, the highly stylized, the high poetical, and the oracular, sometimes in abrupt juxtaposition. Rhymed verse is often used with a distancing effect. The characterization is similarly varied, ranging from the artificial and conventional through to the psychologically naturalistic and penetrating.

Rather than including debates within its structure, as *Measure for Measure* does, *All's Well That Ends Well* is shot through with moral reflectiveness. It is constantly concerned with issues relating to the difference between inherited and acquired characteristics, and between human action and superhuman will, the extent to which human beings are playthings of fortune or are in command of their fate. To a large extent it does this through the portrayal of sexual desire centring on both a woman—Helen—and a man—Bertram, in that order.

The play opens with a parting: young Bertram, son of the widowed Countess of Roussillon, has been made a ward of court to the King of France, who is seriously ill of a fistula. This is an ulcer or abscess which may be situated near the genitals, though 'the text does not clearly locate the fistula, and the King's implication that the disease is properly owned by his heart suggests that Shakespeare was probably following his source, in which the fistula derives from a swelling on the King's breast'.[13] Bertram's very first speech looks forward to a crucial moment of the action in showing his awareness of the royal power over his future: 'I must attend his majesty's command, to whom I am now in ward, evermore in subjection.' He leaves behind him not only his mother but also her attendant gentlewoman, Helen, a 'poor physician's daughter' whose father, the Countess believes, would have been able to cure the King of his mortal illness were he still alive.

Helen's undisclosed love and desire for Bertram form the focus of the opening scene. Left alone on his departure she gives eloquent and idealized expression to her feelings: 'There is no living, none, | If Bertram be away.' But she fears he is far above her sphere:

> 'Twere all one
> That I should love a bright particular star
> And think to wed it. (1.1.84–6)

A rapid shift of tone which reveals a different side of Helen's character, and one that broadens our view of her sexuality, follows when the braggart soldier Paroles cheekily asks if she is 'meditating on virginity'. She is uninhibited in the ensuing discussion, in which Paroles provides racily expressed answers to her questions first as to how virginity may be preserved, and then of how it may be lost to a maid's 'own liking'. There is clear sexual innuendo in her question 'Is there no military policy how virgins might blow up men?' and in Paroles's reply 'Virginity being blown down, man will quicklier be blown up. Marry, in blowing him down again, with the breach yourselves made you lose your city.' Williams writes, 'Paroles turns this blowing up to mean the male orgasm, while "blowing down" = detumescence. But to achieve this, the girl must achieve her own explosion, thus confirming her womanly status.'[14] The braggart soldier Paroles has spoken in military terms, and Helen responds in the same: 'Man is enemy to virginity: how may we barricado it against him?' 'To speak on the part of virginity', says Paroles, 'is to accuse your mothers' (1.1.109–35).

Helen is clearly a young woman of mettle. She loves Bertram body and soul, she wants to lose her virginity to him, and for all her misgivings about her worthiness she hints at a means of creating a situation in which she may do so. Her hint comes in the context of a philosophical meditation written in rhymed couplets on the relationship between human will and divine providence:

> Our remedies oft in ourselves do lie
> Which we ascribe to heaven. The fated sky
> Gives us free scope, only doth backward pull
> Our slow designs when we ourselves are dull.

She takes comfort in the thought that she may accomplish her will by her own endeavours:

> Who ever strove
> To show her merit that did miss her love?

And we are given a clue to this physician's daughter's intentions by her reference to

> The King's disease—my project may deceive me,
> But my intents are fixed and will not leave me.

By putting the King heavily in her debt she will create a situation in which he will, she hopes, use his power to cause his ward to marry her. This is, as she will discover, very different from causing the young man to love her.

Shakespeare has made it clear that Helen's love and desire for Bertram are all-embracing. Rather as in *As You Like It* he counterpoints Rosalind's love for Orlando with the earthier relationship between Touchstone and Audrey—'wedlock would be nibbling'—so here he enhances Helen's seriousness by causing the Countess's 'clown', Lavatch—a kind of court jester—to express his desire to marry Isbel (a curious half-echo of Isabella) because 'My poor body, madam, requires it. I am driven on by the flesh.' Like Touchstone, he has no expectation that the marriage will last; indeed, he argues in a cynically riddling fashion that 'He that comforts my wife is the cherisher of my flesh and blood; he that cherishes my flesh and blood loves my flesh and blood; he that loves my flesh and blood is my friend; *ergo*, he that kisses my wife is my friend.' Later we will learn that he has gone off Isbel: 'I begin to love as an old man loves money: with no stomach' (3.2.15–16). But whereas Shakespeare draws Touchstone and Audrey into the pattern of the play, Lavatch's relations with Isbel remain peripheral to the action.

Helen's secret love for Bertram is apparent from her conversation with his mother in the opening scene, where she stresses that she loves both 'chastely' and with all humility. ('Chastely' here clearly does not imply 'non-sexually'.) So far we know little of the young man, but the depth of both Helen's and the Countess's love for him may predispose us, too, in his favour. Helen is a realist in that she hopes that her skills as a physician may help her to bring about the end that she desires, but she hopes too that Heaven will help her, expressing confidence that the skills she has derived from her father may be supplemented and 'sanctified | By th' luckiest stars in heaven' (1.3.243–4). This belief—is it in fortune or in God?—helps her to persuade the King to try to cure him. She is God's minister, and God will help the King through her. In overcoming the King's resistance she stresses the impersonal nature of her power:

> most it is presumption in us when
> The help of heaven we count the act of men.
> Dear sir, to my endeavours give consent.
> Of heaven, not me, make an experiment.

Is she perhaps overconfident that heaven is on her side? Her style becomes positively oracular as, as if she were indeed divinely inspired, she promises in incantatory, hypnotic, end-stopped couplets that

> The great'st grace lending grace,
> Ere twice the horses of the sun shall bring
> Their fiery coacher his diurnal ring,
> Ere twice in murk and occidental damp

138

Moist Hesperus hath quenched her sleepy lamp,
Or four-and-twenty times the pilot's glass
Hath told the thievish minutes how they pass,
What is infirm from your sound parts shall fly,
Health shall live free, and sickness freely die.   (2.1.160–8)

In the BBC television production directed by Elijah Moshinsky, Helen's healing of the King took on strongly sexual overtones. The director 'nudged Helena's healing of the King toward the sexual, as a return to potency', and Donald Sinden, playing the King, 'managed to make the scene an arousal of the King climaxed by his long, hard kiss'.[15]

Heavenly participation in Helen's ministrations is suggested too by the King's sense that she is the weak 'organ' of some powerful 'blessèd spirit' which may achieve the apparently impossible. As if in a folk or fairy tale in which a hero or heroine accepts that the penalty for not successfully performing a task on which they have embarked is death, Helen agrees that 'Not helping, death's my fee.' But her stipulation that if she is successful the King will allow her to choose a husband from among those over whom he has power is manipulative: he will compromise his honour if he fails to help her to fulfil her sexual desire.

Helen's success as a physician is marked by her joyful entrance with the King in a dance, and they sit for the parade of four young men from whom she is to make her choice.[16] The reactions of the attendant lord Lafeu as he supposes (mistakenly—presumably he can see but not hear what is going on) that the first two of them have rejected her puts forward the point of view that physical attraction alone should be an adequate criterion for acceptance in marriage:

Do they all deny her? An they were sons of mine I'd have them whipped,
or I would send them to th' Turk to be made eunuchs of.   (2.3.87–9)

—that is, to be castrated. When Helen comes to Bertram last, after rejecting the four other young bachelors whom the King has paraded before her, the play's title might lead us to expect that the fifth candidate is the one who will succeed. But Bertram's refusal turns the story from a fairy tale displaying Helen's wish-fulfilment to psychological reality:

> In such a business give me leave to use
> The help of mine own eyes.

A modern audience might well sympathize, feeling that he has the right to exercise his own powers of choice in so important a matter. And most members of Shakespeare's own audiences too, to whom forced marriages were no matter of course, may have felt the same. But the reason Bertram gives for rejecting her is unattractive:

> She had her breeding at my father's charge.
> A poor physician's daughter, my wife? Disdain
> Rather corrupt me ever.

This snobbishness provokes from the King a deeply serious and explicitly moralizing speech on the relationship between worldly rank and innate virtue. High-ranking persons may lack 'virtue', but good, even if it goes unrecognized, carries its own value along with it. So, he claims, Helen derives her honour from her own acts, not from her ancestors; her virtue and her person are the dowry that she brings to the match; the King 'can create the rest', giving her 'honour and wealth'.

Bertram remains obdurate; Helen tries to shrink into the background: 'That you are well restored, my lord, I'm glad. | Let the rest go.' But the King persists, declaring, 'My honour's at the stake,' and threatens Bertram with such pitiless revenge that the young man gives in, pretending that the King's raising of Helen to superior social status removes his obstacles to marrying her. 'Take her by the hand | And tell her she is thine,' says the King, but verbally Bertram agrees only to the first demand. 'I take her hand.' As the not entirely happy couple go to be married forthwith, Bertram petulantly declares to Paroles his determination not to consummate the marriage, an omission which would render it open to annulment: 'I will not bed her…I'll to the Tuscan wars and never bed her.' 'Wars is no strife | To the dark house and the detested wife.' His response to Helen as she tentatively, nervously hints at a request for a parting kiss, but is denied, is a subtle and psychologically plausible study in embarrassment:

> HELEN   Pray, sir, your pardon.
> BERTRAM   Well, what would you have?
> HELEN   Something, and scarce so much: nothing indeed.
>   I would not tell you what I would, my lord. Faith, yes;
>   Strangers and foes do sunder and not kiss.   (2.5.78–85)

Bertram evades her request with the words, presumably addressed to Paroles, 'I pray you, stay not, but in haste to horse.' But Helen is a determined young woman. Though she fails here, she will later get more than a kiss out of Bertram without his knowledge.

This situation has a clear relationship to that of *Venus and Adonis*, and here as in the poem the young man's resistance to the advances of a woman who is more sexually aware than himself hints at psychological reasons which may lie beyond his conscious understanding. Is he just immature, or does he have the right to reject a woman simply because he despises her rank? At the age of seventeen Shakespeare's patron the Earl of Southampton, who was ward to Lord Burleigh, faced an enormous fine and his influential guardian's serious displeasure for refusing to marry Burleigh's granddaughter, Lady Elizabeth Vere, simply, it would seem, because she did not attract him and in any case he—like Bertram—did not want to marry. This was three years before Shakespeare's dedication to him of *Venus and Adonis*. But a few years later Southampton made the Queen furious by seducing Lady Elizabeth Vernon, whom he later married. Had his sexuality fluctuated in the mean time, or did he simply resist an arranged match while waiting for the right woman to come along? It is not impossible that Shakespeare had these real-life events in mind as he wrote *All's Well That Ends Well*.

The turning point of the play comes in the letter which the Countess receives from her son informing her of his marriage and of his refusal to consummate it: 'I have wedded her, not bedded her, and sworn to make the "not" eternal' (3.2.21–2). Helen, too, has received from Bertram a letter which bears a riddling message: 'When thou canst get the ring upon my finger, which never shall come off, and show me a child begotten of thy body that I am father to, then call me husband; but in such a "then" I write a "never".' As often in Shakespeare, 'ring' has vaginal connotations, though they are not made explicit here. The remainder of the action will concern itself with the unfolding of Bertram's riddle.

He comes into focus in the play's concern with sexual desire as the action shifts to Italy and to the company of a well-born but impoverished old woman, like the Countess a widow, and her household. His refusal to bed his wife has clearly not been due to any lack of libidinal energy. He is all too anxious to take the virginity of another woman, Diana (significantly, the name of the goddess of chastity). The household know not only of Bertram's valiant exploits in the wars, but also of how he has behaved to Helen, and it is the Widow who hints that Helen might substitute for Diana in a sexual assignation: 'This young maid might do her | A shrewd turn if she pleased.' Helen is duplicitous in her agreement with this suggestion, arranging that Diana will nominally consent to go to bed with Bertram and—reminding us of Bertram's riddle—that before making arrangements to do so the girl will make it a condition that he gives up to her a ring

> That downward hath succeeded in his house
> From son to son some four or five descents
> Since the first father wore it.   (3.7.23–5)

And Helen will reward Diana handsomely for doing so.

Thus the bed trick is set up, and Shakespeare, as if to deflect our possible disapproval of Helen's part in it, causes her to defend its morality in riddlingly paradoxical terms characteristic of this play:

> Let us essay our plot, which if it speed
> Is wicked meaning in a lawful deed
> And lawful meaning in a wicked act,
> Where both not sin, and yet a sinful fact.   (3.7.44–7)

This idea that a deed that would normally be considered sinful may be justified by the end to which it is directed had also been expressed by the Duke in *Measure for Measure* (see p. 129):

> What sin you do to save a brother's life,
> Nature dispenses with the deed so far
> That it becomes a virtue.

Is Shakespeare attempting to evade the moral implications of his plotting, conning us into approval of a dubious action, or is he, more subtly, inviting us to see his speakers as characters with an exceptional degree of moral awareness?

The argument that Bertram uses with Diana in favour of giving up her virginity is the same as that which Paroles had put before Helen in the opening scene: 'now you should be as your mother was | When your sweet self was got.' But Diana has an answer to this: 'No. | My mother did but duty; such, my lord, | As you owe to your wife.' He defends himself on the implausible grounds that his marriage was forced whereas he loves Diana 'By love's own sweet constraint, and will for ever | Do thee all rights of service.' In response to his protestations of undying love she asks him to give her his ring, and on his claiming that he has no right to do so since it is 'an honour 'longing to our house, | Bequeathèd down from many ancestors' argues that the same is no less true of her chastity. And Bertram, desperate in desire, gives her the ring. She demands that after penetrating her he shall stay in the darkness of her bed for no longer than an hour, and without speaking. She will explain her reasons for this when the ring is given back. In the meantime

> on your finger in the night I'll put
> Another ring that, what in time proceeds,
> May token to the future our past deeds. (4.2.62–4)

'Finger' clearly implies 'penis', and the vaginal significance of the ring is becoming clearer, but once more the tone is riddling and oracular, as if Diana were possessed of a supernatural power deriving perhaps from her virginity, and resembling that which had enabled Helen to cure the King. And Shakespeare builds in from Diana, too, as from Helen and the Duke (in *Measure for Measure*) a rhymed defence of the morality of her actions:

> in this disguise I think't no sin
> To cozen him that would unjustly win. (4.2.76–7)

Morality is the keynote of the following scene, too, in which the Lords Dumaine, who function mainly as commentators, express disapproval of Bertram's behaviour, and report the belief that Helen has died of grief. But their moralizing is not without compassion:

> The web of our life is of a mingled yarn, good and ill together. Our
> virtues would be proud if our faults whipped them not, and our crimes
> would despair if they were not cherished by their virtues. (4.3.74–7)

The false report of Helen's death leads into the play's last movement, in which, with a new contortion of the plot, we learn that the old courtier Lafeu has persuaded the King that the (supposedly) newly widowered Bertram would make a good husband for his daughter, Maudlin. An arranged marriage is in the air again; it is natural for the audience to wonder if history is going to repeat itself; indeed Bertram declares himself penitent and willing to marry Maudlin, even having the nerve to claim that his refusal of Helen was the result of his love for the girl. He betrays himself when he hands to Lafeu the ring that the King had given to Helen, and goes through a mounting series of lies as he tries to deny it. His twists and turns of caddishness as he denies his promises to Diana, accusing her of having been 'a common gamester to the camp' and claiming that she 'angled' for him, deserve nothing but contempt. It becomes clear that Diana's oracular utterances as she is called to give evidence and seeks to do so without revealing her part in the bed trick can be resolved only by an apparent resurrection characteristic of romance stories such as Shakespeare employs at all stages of his career, and especially like that of the supposedly dead Claudio in *Measure for Measure*: the appearance of the still living Helen. When that happens, as in that play, the moment is far from being a romantic climax. Bertram's sudden and total volte-face in his response to Helen's statement that "Tis but the shadow of a wife you see, | The name and not the thing'— 'Both, both. O, pardon'—leaves much to the actor. He is likely to kneel as Isabella does as she asks pardon for Angelo. But though the moment can be impressive and moving, it is unlikely to make us feel that heaven has effected through Helen a moral cure of Bertram equivalent to her physical cure of the King. When Helen, pointing out that she has fulfilled the conditions by which Bertram had said he would accept her, declares herself pregnant it is, if anything, her generosity that we admire, Bertram who should be grateful. Yet his response to her claim to have fulfilled the conditions he laid upon her is itself conditional:

> If she, my liege, can make me know this clearly
> I'll love her dearly, ever ever dearly.

But so is her offer to renounce him:

> If it appear not plain and prove untrue,
> Deadly divorce step between me and you.

The King's invitation to Diana to choose herself a husband is one that the whole of the previous action shows that she ought to think hard indeed about before accepting.

The effect of a play does not depend simply on what happens. But it is worth remarking that at the end of *All's Well That Ends Well* we have a pregnant Helen who has tried twice, once successfully, to trick Bertram into having sex with her against his will and whose unborn baby is the product of a trick played on its father, now offering to resume relations with the husband who has previously and ignominiously rejected her; Bertram undergoing instant conversion at the sight of her and conditionally offering to resume his husbandly duties despite all that has gone before; Lafeu's daughter, Maudlin (who does not appear), left in the wings after the King had told her father that he would marry her to Bertram, who accepted her; and Diana told that the King will pay her dowry if she chooses herself a husband, as Helen had. The King's last, also conditional words both to those on stage and to the audience belie the assurance of the play's title. To the first he says

> All yet seems well; and if it end so meet,
> The bitter past, more welcome is the sweet.

And to us:

> All is well ended if this suit be won:
> That you express content...

'*Seems* well' indeed.

*

I have discussed attempted rape in *The Two Gentlemen of Verona* and actual rape in *Titus Andronicus*, and I have suggested that the bed trick in both *Measure for Measure* and *All's Well That Ends Well* represents a kind of rape by a woman of a man. There are other plays of Shakespeare in which lust leads not to actual but to attempted or imagined rape. It is part of the back-story of *The Tempest*, and a theme of the brothel scenes in *Pericles*, and in *Cymbeline* Cloten, in a far subtler study of the psychopathology of lust than that in *Titus Andronicus*, horrifyingly imagines his violation of Innogen:

With that [her husband Posthumus's] suit upon my back will I ravish her—first kill him, and in her eyes; there shall she see my valour, which will then be a torment to her contempt. He on the ground, my speech of insultment ended on his dead body, and when my lust hath dined—which, as I say, to vex her I will execute in the clothes that she so praised—to the court I'll knock her back, foot her home again. She hath despised me rejoicingly, and I'll be merry in my revenge.   (3.5.137–44)

A chilling word, 'merry', in this context. Rape is the ultimate consequence of lust, the very opposite of love. Yet the physical act is identical.

6

Sex and Love in
Romeo and Juliet

*R*omeo and Juliet deserves a chapter to itself because of its status as one of the greatest love stories of the world, a play in which romantic love reaches sexual fulfilment against high odds but in which the lovers themselves are destroyed by inimical forces of fate and society. Romantic though it is, it is also one of the bawdiest of Shakespeare's plays, riddled with sexual puns, double meanings, and bawdy innuendo. The text has often been expurgated in school editions and for both the stage and the screen. Its length causes it often to be shortened in theatrical performance by several hundred lines, sometimes—though less frequently in modern times than in the past—by the omission of bawdy, which in any case is often made obscure for us by the passage of time. Even in scholarly editions editors have often evaded frankness in their explanatory notes, hinting at the presence of innuendo rather than spelling it out. The actor Roger Allam once played Mercutio, who has, as he writes, to speak 'a string of extremely explicit jokes'. He goes on to remark that 'Brian Gibbons, the Arden editor, uses the somewhat understated phrase "with a bawdy quibble" to indicate this. It made us laugh very much in rehearsals. We invented a pastiche Elizabethan song called "with a bawdy quibble" which was sung in cod

PLATE 1 'A woman's face with nature's own hand painted' (Sonnet 20): this portrait of the Earl of Southampton, dating from around the time that Shakespeare dedicated poems to him, was thought to represent a woman, Lady Norton, until 2002.

PLATE 2 This portrait by an unknown artist of John Donne, lover, poet, and later, priest, is believed to have been painted around 1595, when he was twenty-three years old.

PLATE 3 'I have my wish in that I joy thy sight' (*Edward II*, 1.1. 150): Ian McKellen as Edward II and James Lawrenson as Gaveston in the Prospect Theatre Company's touring production of Marlowe's tragedy, 1969.

PLATE 4 'I am betrayed by keeping company / With men like you' (*Love's Labour's Lost*, 4.3.177–8), directed by Gregory Doran, Royal Shakespeare Company, Stratford-upon-Avon, 2008: David Tennant (Biron) overlooks Tom Davey as Longueville, Edward Bennett as Ferdinand and Sam Alexander as Dumaine.

PLATE 5 'the news I bring / Is heavy in my tongue' (*Love's Labour's Lost*, 5.2.711–12), directed by Terry Hands, Royal Shakespeare Theatre, Stratford-upon-Avon, 1990: (from left to right): Carol Royle as the Princess of France, Simon Russell Beale as Ferdinand, Griffith Jones as Mercadé, and David Killick as Boyet.

PLATE 6 'She hath no tongue to call nor hands to wash' (*Titus Andronicus*, 2.4.7), directed by Peter Brook, Shakespeare Memorial Theatre, Stratford-upon-Avon, 1955: Kevin Miles as Chiron, Vivien Leigh as Lavinia, and Lee Montague as Demetrius. Coloured silk ribbons represented Lavinia's blood.

PLATE 7 'Wilt thou be gone?' (*Romeo and Juliet*, 3.5.1), directed by Ron Daniels, Royal Shakespeare Theatre, Stratford-upon-Avon, 1980: Judy Buxton as Juliet, Anton Lesser as Romeo. Modern staging allows for more naturalistic presen-tation than would have been possible when Juliet was acted by a boy.

PLATE 8 'You go not till I set you up a glass / Where you may see the inmost part of you.' (*Hamlet*, 3.4. 19–20): Royal Shakespeare Company, directed by Buzz Goodbody, The Other Place, 1975: Hamlet (Ben Kingsley) and Gertrude (Mikel Lambert). Casting of a relatively young actor as Hamlet's mother increases the scene's sexual tension.

PLATE 9 'In kissing, do you render or receive?' (*Troilus and Cressida*, 4.6.37), directed by Howard Davies, Royal Shakespeare Theatre, Stratford-upon-Avon, 1985: (background) Alan Rickman (Achilles); (foreground), left to right, Mark Dignam (Nestor), Patroclus (Hilton McRae), Juliet Stevenson (Cressida), Officer (Hugh Simon). The Greek leaders force their attentions on an initially reluctant Cressida.

PLATE 10 'Hold off the earth a while, / Till I have caught her once more in mine arms' (*Hamlet*, 5.1.245–6): Royal Shakespeare Company, 1970, directed by Trevor Nunn: Hamlet (Alan Howard) catches up the dead Ophelia (Helen Mirren) in his arms.

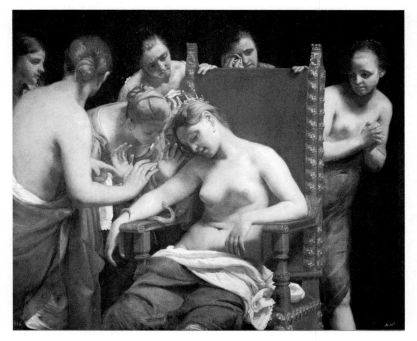

PLATE 11 'Now boast thee, death, in thy possession lies / A lass unparalleled' (*Antony and Cleopatra*, 5. 2. 309–10) 'The Death of Cleopatra', an oil painting by Guido Cagnacci (1601–1663) showing more grieving waiting women than are present in Shakespeare's play.

PLATE 12 'Let me twine / Mine arms about that body' (*Coriolanus*, 4.5.107–8): Royal Shakespeare Company, 1972, directed by Trevor Nunn: Aufidius (Ian Hogg) and Coriolanus (Patrick Stewart) engage in a love/hate embrace.

PLATE 13 (*Next page*) 'A fish, he smells like a fish; a very ancient and fish-like smell' (*The Tempest*, 2.2.25–6): National Theatre Company, directed by Peter Hall, 1988, Tony Haygarth (Caliban), Tim Pigott-Smith (Trinculo).

PLATE 14 'Will you stay no longer, nor will you not that I go with you?' (*Twelfth Night*, 22.1.1–2). Royal Shakespeare Company, 2001, directed by Lindsay Posner: Sebastian (Ben Meyjes) makes to leave Antonio's (Joseph Mydell) bed; the staging mirrors the production's implication of a lesbian relationship between Viola and Olivia.

operatic tones to the guitar. It made us laugh even more.'[1] Actors will often attempt to help the audience to see the point of sexual references by illustrating them with lewd gestures or even through the use of props. An inflatable banana figured in a production given by the Hull Truck Company.[2] There is also a story about an eighteenth-century actress who involuntarily added to the play's bawdy:

There being a fight and scuffle in this play, between the House of Capulet, and the House of Paris; Mrs Holden acting his wife, entered in a hurry, crying, 'O my dear Count!' She inadvertently left out, 'O', in the pronunciation of the word 'Count!', giving it a vehement accent, put the house into such a laughter, that London Bridge at low-water was silence to it.[3]

Shakespeare's sources were in no way responsible for the bawdy of *Romeo and Juliet*. In writing the play he made extensive use of the 3000-line-long poem, *The Tragical History of Romeus and Juliet*, by Arthur Brooke, who died young in a shipwreck in 1563 a year after his poem first appeared in print.[4] Brooke's prefatory address to the reader is heavily moralistic and strongly anti-Roman Catholic. He claims that he wrote his poem

to describe unto thee a couple of unfortunate lovers, thralling themselves to unhonest desire, neglecting the authority and advice of parents and friends, conferring their principal counsels with drunken gossips, and superstitious friars—the naturally fit instruments of unchastity—attempting all adventures of peril for the attaining of their wished lust, using auricular confession—the key of whoredom and treason—for furtherance of their purpose, abusing the honourable name of lawful marriage, to cloak the shame of stolen contracts, and finally by all means of unhonest life hasting to most unhappy death.[5]

Brooke excuses himself for telling his readers so unpleasant a tale by claiming that he intends 'to raise in them an hateful loathing of so filthy beastliness'.[6]

In fact the poem that follows is so different from his description of it that one might reasonably wonder if it relates to the same work. Was it perhaps written by someone other than the author? *Romeus and Juliet* portrays both the lovers and their friends the nurse and the friar in a largely sympathetic light. The poem's language is unmitigatedly chaste, and the lovers are motivated entirely by love, not by what the Preface calls 'wished lust'. All the bawdy language of Shakespeare's play is spoken either by characters whom he has added to Brooke's story, such as the servants in the opening scene, or by others whom he has greatly developed, most notably Mercutio and the Nurse. And the bawdy is entirely integral to his artistic purposes, an essential part of the design of an exceptionally carefully designed and highly patterned play.

Shakespeare's Prologue offers a brief summary of the play's action, in this resembling the 'Argument' of Brooke's poem, though without adopting a moralistic tone; also like Brooke, Shakespeare casts his prefatory remarks in the form of a sonnet, a poetic form whose conventions pervade the play. His Prologue is entirely decorous, but it is interesting that he speaks of the feud that divides the houses of Montague and Capulet in terms of the lovers' sexual engendering: 'From *forth the fatal loins* of these two foes | A pair of star-crossed lovers take their life.' From the start the lovers are associated with the sexual act.

The opening scene consciously presents two opposing attitudes to love, and does so in the contrasting media of prose and verse. The colloquial, punning dialogue of the servants, Samson and Gregory, takes us straight into the world of Shakespeare's early comedies, with characters like Lance and Speed in *The Two Gentlemen of Verona*, or the Dromio twins in *The Comedy of Errors*. These are randy young men, boasting of their virility and of their endowments—'I will show myself a tyrant,' says Samson; 'when I have fought with the men I will be civil with the maids.—I will cut off their heads.'

GREGORY The heads of the maids?
SAMSON Ay, the heads of the maids, or their maidenheads, take it
in what sense thou wilt.

GREGORY   They must take it in sense that feel it.

SAMSON   Me they shall feel while I am able to stand, and 'tis
known I am a pretty piece of flesh.   (1.1.20–8)

The bawdy quibbles are obvious: 'take' could mean 'receive sexually',[7]
'stand', as we have seen, is often used in the sense of 'have an erection',
and it is clear which piece of his flesh Samson is alluding to.[8] The bawdy
continues as Gregory says 'Draw thy tool,' to which Samson replies,
'My naked weapon is out.' His penis is a weapon: the association of sex
with violence is part of the pattern of the scene.

    The play has begun with sex without love, and it is to continue with
love without sex. The dialogue moves into verse as the Prince rebukes
the brawling factions, and the way is paved for the entrance of Romeo
by a lengthy account of his melancholy withdrawal from daylight and
life. When he enters, his well-wishing friend Benvolio discovers 'what
sadness lengthens Romeo's hours'—he is in love, but 'Out of her favour
where [he is] in love' (1.1.160–5). Expatiating on his condition Romeo
reveals that his beloved is impervious to his suit. Again we are in the
world of the early comedies, but this time with their romantic side.
Romeo's beloved—we learn later that she is named Rosaline—is

>   too fair, too wise, wisely too fair,
> To merit bliss by making me despair.   (1.1.218–19)

'Holy fair and wise' is Silvia in *The Two Gentlemen of Verona*.

    But we are also in the closely related world of Shakespeare's Sonnets,
and, through them, in touch with the conventions of Elizabethan, and
Petrarchan, love poetry, in which the beloved is routinely unattain-
able. Romeo's first love, Rosaline, will 'not be hit | With Cupid's arrow;
she hath Dian's wit, | And, in strong proof of chastity well armed, |
From love's weak childish bow she lives unharmed.... O, she is rich in
beauty, only poor | That when she dies, with beauty dies her store'
(1.1.205–13). The theme is common, especially in Shakespeare's Sonnets
where for example a beloved is told that, unless he has a child,

> Thy unused beauty must be tombed with thee,
> Which usèd, lives th'executor to be.   (Sonnet 4)

But there is, as usual with Shakespeare, an original twist to his use of the convention in that the poet of the Sonnets is here addressing a young man, whereas Romeo is speaking of a woman.

Benvolio urges Romeo to seek a way forward, to look elsewhere in the hope of finding someone more responsive to his wooing: 'Be ruled by me; forget to think of her' (1.1.222). But at present Romeo cannot conceive that anyone could surpass Rosaline's beauty:

> Show me a mistress that is passing fair,
> What doth her beauty serve but as a note
> Where I may read who passed that passing fair?
> Farewell, thou canst not teach me to forget.   (1.2.231–4)

The next scene is again concerned with virginity, but this time with the idea that it may sooner or later be broached. Count Paris is a suitor to Old Capulet's as-yet-unnamed daughter, whose father, however, thinks that she is too young to be married—'She hath not seen the change of fourteen years' (1.2.9). It is unusual for Shakespeare to be anything like as precise as this about his characters' ages. We even know the exact date of Juliet's birth—31 July—she is named after the month. And it is curious that Shakespeare makes Juliet so early a teenager, only just, we must suppose, pubertal. It is especially curious since in Brooke's poem Juliet's father says that she is 'not yet full 16 years' (l. 1860), and that even so he thinks her 'too young to be a bride'—even though in the play importunate Paris says of Juliet 'Younger than she are happy mothers made' (1.2.12). Shakespeare is making a dramatic contrast between the generations—both Lord Montague and Old Capulet are portrayed as far older men than we might expect in view of the age of their children, and their conversation insists on their being past the age of love. (If anyone ever is.) Is it perhaps also a little curious that at around the time we believe Shakespeare wrote the play—1596—he himself had a daughter aged 13—Susanna was born in 1583?

The next time we see Romeo he is more sanguine and is willing to go to a party at the house of 'The great rich Capulet' where, Benvolio tells him, he will be able to compare Rosaline with other beauties who may make him change his mind about her. But Romeo, speaking of his love as 'the devout religion' of his eye, finds this inconceivable:

> One fairer than my love!—the all-seeing sun
> Ne'er saw her match since first the world begun.   (1.2.94)

As attention shifts to the Capulet household we are introduced to Juliet's Nurse, and it is significant that her very first words refer to her sexuality: 'Now, by my maidenhead at twelve years old', she swears (1.3.2), implying that she had lost her virginity by the time she reached Juliet's age. As we have seen, in Shakespeare's society twelve was the minimum age at which girls could legally be married.

The Nurse, we soon discover, is a woman close to nature. She talks of breast-feeding the infant Juliet 'under the dovehouse wall', of the nipple of her dug, she compares a bump on the two-year-old Juliet's brow to 'a young cock'rel's stone'—testicle—and she revels in recollections of her late husband's bawdy joke:

> even the day before, she broke her brow,
> And then my husband—God be with his soul,
> A was a merry man!—took up the child.
> 'Yea', quoth he, 'dost thou fall upon thy face?
> Thou wilt fall backward when thou hast more wit,
> Wilt thou not, Jule?' And, by my halidam,
> The pretty wretch left crying and said 'Ay!'   (1.3.40–6)

This kind of anecdote is liable to raise embarrassed blushes in an adolescent cheek, but clearly the Nurse is an old family retainer whose eccentricities are at least tolerated, perhaps enjoyed. Is Juliet old enough to be embarrassed, or does she respond to the old woman's jocularities with amused tolerance? The performer must decide, but Shakespeare is stressing Juliet's liminality, the fact that she is poised on the brink of womanhood when she may indeed enjoy falling backward to receive her lover's embraces. The Nurse, like the servants in the opening scene, stresses physicality: 'Women grow by men.' But Juliet is modest and obedient to her mother's will:

> I'll look to like, if looking liking move;
> But no more deep will I endart mine eye
> Than your consent gives strength to make it fly.   (1.3.99–101)

Irrepressibly, the Nurse sustains her theme, urging Juliet towards maturity:

> Go, girl; seek happy nights to happy days.   (1.3.107)

As for Romeo, we know that he is on his way to the Capulets' party, but Shakespeare delays his arrival to allow for an episode in which he is shown with his male friends. He is still melancholy, and Mercutio makes fun of him in language as redolent with bawdy quibbles as the Nurse's, or that of the servants in the opening scene. Mercutio's is high-class wit, but it still associates sex with violence:

> If love be rough with you, be rough with love.
> Prick love for pricking, and you beat love down.   (1.4.27–8)

—that is, quell your erection.

It is, however, one of the paradoxes of the play that Shakespeare gives Mercutio a long speech that seems to suggest in him an imaginative and poetic delicacy that might seem totally at odds with his coarse attitude to sex. The Queen Mab speech takes us unexpectedly into the world of *A Midsummer Night's Dream* as Mercutio recounts his dream of 'the fairies' midwife' who travels in a chariot made of 'an empty hazelnut' as she 'gallops night by night' provoking pleasing dreams in the brains of as wide a range of subjects as Shakespeare was later to portray in Jaques's speech of the Seven Ages of Man, in *As You Like It*. It is not easy to integrate this fantasy into a concept of Mercutio's role or into the overall design of the play, except perhaps that it ends with lines that take us back to what the Nurse's husband had said of Juliet:

> This is the hag, when maids lie on their backs,
> That presses them and learns them first to bear,
> Making them women of good carriage.[9]
> This is she—

And he is apparently so carried away by his own eloquence that Romeo has to stop him in his tracks:

> Peace, peace, Mercutio, peace!
> Thou talk'st of nothing.   (1.4.92–6)

We may recall that 'nothing' could be used of both the male and the female sexual organs.

We have been told that Rosaline was to be among those invited to the party, and although she has no lines to speak at any point in the play, some directors have brought her on stage as a silent presence in that scene. But the text provides no justification for this, and as soon as Romeo sees Juliet he speaks of her in the lines of rapturous lyricism beginning 'O, she doth teach the torches to burn bright!' (1.5.43), which make the terms in which he had previously spoken of Rosaline seem merely conventional. A few years previously Marlowe's Tamburlaine had addressed Zenocrate, 'the loveliest maid alive', as

> The only paragon of Tamburlaine,
> Whose eyes are brighter than the lamps of heaven,
> And speech more pleasant than sweet harmony,
> That with thy looks canst clear the darkened sky
> And calm the rage of thund'ring Jupiter.   (Part One, 3.3)

Juliet's eyes are bright too, 'her eye in heaven | Would through the airy region stream so bright | That birds would sing and think it were not night' (2.1.62–4). Shakespeare writes with all the stops out, outrivalling Marlowe to produce the most eloquent love poetry that had yet graced the English stage.

Romeo's vision of his new love idealizes her: 'touching hers' he will 'make blessèd [his] rude hand'. And all thoughts of his previous love leave his mind:

> Did my heart love till now? Forswear it, sight,
> For I ne'er saw true beauty till this night.   (1.5.51–2)

When Romeo first addresses Juliet his expression of desire is cloaked in religious imagery. She is a shrine which his lips approach as 'two blushing pilgrims'. Even so, they seek a kiss, and Juliet, sustaining the religious imagery, holds Romeo off with playful delicacy by pointing out that pilgrims greet by clasping hands rather than by kissing lips. He continues his sophistical arguments, and though Juliet continues to protest she not only accepts his kiss but enjoys it—'You kiss by th' book', she tells him (1.5.109).

Shakespeare's casting of this dialogue into sonnet form is a brilliant device. Its stylization sets the lovers' first conversation off from the surrounding bustle of the dance, creating an enclosed, private world in which time moves gently forward towards a coupling of lovers as well as of rhymes. Recalling the conventions of Petrarchan love associated with the sonnet form, it also denies them in its movement from avoidance to acceptance of physicality. Having kissed, the lovers embark on another sonnet, but after they have completed its first four lines they are brought back to the real world by a call from the Nurse, the first of a series of interruptions by her at crucial points which form part of the play's pattern (the others are at 2.1.178, 3.2.31, and 3.5.37).

The play's second Chorus—also written in the form of a sonnet— reminds us that Romeo's love for Rosaline is gone—'Now old desire doth in his deathbed lie'—but his friends don't know this, and in the next scene Mercutio is still teasing him about Rosaline, and in grossly physical terms which reach a climax as he imagines that the absent Romeo will

> sit under a medlar tree
> And wish his mistress were that kind of fruit
> As maids call medlars when they laugh alone.
> O Romeo, that she were, O that she were
> An open-arse, and thou a popp'rin'-pear. (2.1.34–8)

'Open-arse' is a dialect word for the ripe fruit of the medlar tree, known in French as *'fruit de trou de cul'*—open-arse fruit—which is not ripe until it is rotten. Interestingly the word does not occur in any of the early texts of the play. When *Romeo and Juliet* first appeared in print, in the corrupt text of 1597, the passage substituted a euphemism, 'open Et caetera', in an early example of censorship. When this edition was reprinted in 1599, apparently from a different manuscript, the type-setter printed 'open, or', which modern editors interpret as a misreading of 'open ars'; this is also printed in the 1623 Folio. Not until Richard Hosley's edition of 1957 was what is now generally regarded as the true reading restored.[10] An 'open-arse' is often said to resemble an open vagina, but this may be an evasion of an implication that Mercutio is accusing Romeo of wishing to take Rosaline anally.

Mercutio's cynical attitude to women and to love, revealed at its most brutal here, has given rise to elaborative stage business and to speculation about his own sexuality. Roger Allam writes that 'Mercutio seems everywhere obsessed with destroying Romeo's romantic view of love, and always speaks of women crudely and reductively in terms of sex.'[11] In a Stratford production by Terry Hands in 1973 the actor playing Mercutio 'constantly carried a grotesque, coarse-featured life-size female doll, upon which he vented a sado-masochistic sexual loathing'.[12] 'During the "invocation" scene'—the one I am now discussing—'he publicly dismembered the doll, lending a grotesque and disturbing violence to his feverish joking at Rosaline's expense.'

Is there any subtextual significance to all this? An actor, needing to imagine a fully rounded personality, is naturally liable to extrapolate information not directly provided by the text. There is, Allam suggests, 'confusion around the sexuality of [Mercutio's] relationship with Romeo'.[13] Some actors—and critics too—have gone so far as to indicate, by one means or another, homosexual desire for Romeo on Mercutio's part. So for example the critic Paul Hammond writes that

When Romeo's infatuation with Juliet removes him from the company of his male friends, led by Mercutio, they mock him in bawdy punning which seeks to re-establish a comfortable male subculture. Their puns show a particular interest in Romeo's 'prick' which will be 'beat…down' and his 'spirit' (that is, erect penis[14]) which Mercutio tries to 'raise up'. When Mercutio imagines Juliet as a medlar he chooses the fruit's dialect name and says: 'O that she were | An open-arse and thou a poperin pear', simultaneously evoking both vaginal intercourse and sodomy. His subsequent teasing of Romeo after what he imagines to have been Romeo's night of sexual activity with Rosaline is full of punning references to Romeo's penis, and he offers to give Romeo an affectionate nibble on the ear for a particularly good jest.[15] Homosocial play includes homoerotic play.[16]

And some actors have translated such interpretations into stage business of a more or less explicit kind. We are told, for instance, that Adrian Schiller, in Michael Boyd's 2000 RSC production, 'sat astride the prostrate Romeo and moved his pelvis over his friend's on [the words] "making them women of good carriage"'.[17]

Sex between the lines like this has extended too to heterosexual relationships in the play. Whereas Juliet's father, Old Capulet, gives every sign of being past sexual activity, his wife is, if we are to take literally her statement that she was Juliet's mother 'much upon these years | That you are now a maid' (1.3.74–5), only about twenty-eight years old. Directors and actors between them have frequently portrayed her as being in love with Tybalt,[18] whose death she will mourn in what may seem to be extravagant terms—still, he is her nephew. Niamh Cusack, who played Juliet in Michael Bogdanov's Stratford production in 1986, wrote confidently of 'the ill-concealed affair Lady Capulet is having with Tybalt'.[19] She has even been shown as having a sexual relationship with Paris, even though she is pressing Juliet to marry him.

All this sex between the lines may seem gratuitous, but in a German production it helped to provide an emblematic crystallization of the play's distinctions between lust and love: 'Paris and Lady Capulet embraced lasciviously downstage while upstage, in another world, Romeo and Juliet nakedly but chastely wrapped their arms round each other.'[20] (So far as I know no production so far has portrayed Lady Capulet as being in love with both Tybalt and Paris, either consecutively or simultaneously.) Sex between the lines has extended in production to a lesbian desire for Juliet on the part of the Nurse,[21] and critics have suggested that Old Capulet's rage with Juliet on her refusal to marry Paris is the result of concealed incestuous desire on his part. This is taking subtext to extremes. Interpretations like these can be neither proved nor disproved.

Mercutio's grossness forms a vivid contrast with the idealization of the 'balcony' scene which immediately follows it. Romeo's tender invocation of Juliet casts her as the sun which has eclipsed the moon, Rosaline:

> But soft, what light through yonder window breaks?
> It is the east, and Juliet is the sun.
> Arise, fair sun, and kill the envious moon,
> Who is already sick and pale with grief
> That thou, her maid, art far more fair than she.   (2.1.44–8)

(Incidentally, surely Juliet should be visible to Romeo at the beginning of this speech, not half way through it, as in many productions and editions—she *is* the light that he sees.) The chaste goddess the moon—Diana—wears 'a vestal livery' which 'is but sick and green'—greensickness was an illness associated with virginity—but, he says, 'none but fools do wear it'. He is looking forward to the consummation of his love, but when he addresses Juliet it is in the tenderest of terms, as far away as we can get from Mercutio's reductiveness. Again using religious imagery, he speaks of her as a 'bright angel' whose 'eye in heaven'

> Would through the airy region stream so bright
> That birds would sing and think it were not night.   (2.1.62–4)

And Juliet idealizes Romeo similarly as the 'god of [her] idolatry'. Theirs is, as Juliet says, 'a true-love passion', not a 'light love', and the intensity of Romeo's passion is only intensified by the danger of death that overshadows it. Although Juliet fears that their contract is 'too rash, too unadvised, too sudden',

> Too like the lightning which doth cease to be
> Ere one can say it lightens,

even so she sees that their 'bud of love | May prove a beauteous flower when next we meet' (2.1.160–4). Their conversation is interrupted by the second of the Nurse's series of unwanted calls, but the lovers do not part before Juliet has insisted that she will 'follow him...throughout the world' only if his 'bent of love' is honourable, and his purpose marriage. Romeo says farewell with 'Sleep dwell upon thine eyes, peace in thy breast.' He wishes that he 'were sleep and peace, so sweet to rest'—words whose sense echoes the Nurse's earlier advice to Juliet to 'seek happy nights to happy days', but does so in a totally different tone. Like Adonis in Shakespeare's poem, Romeo knows that

> Love comforteth, like sunshine after rain,
> But lust's effect is tempest after sun.   (*Venus and Adonis*, ll. 799–800)

Lascivious and loving approaches to sex can find expression in similar terms, however different may be the feelings that lie behind them.

Obedient to his love's request, the impetuous Romeo rushes off to his friend Friar Laurence to ask him to marry them that very day. The storm clouds of danger appear on the horizon as we learn on the following morning that Tybalt has sent a challenge to Montague's house, and Mercutio continues to mock Romeo's lovesickness, believing that it is still for Rosaline. Characteristically, Shakespeare drags in a reference to Petrarch: 'Now is he for the numbers that Petrarch flowed in,' says Mercutio (2.3.36–7), making a direct link for knowledgeable members of the audience with the literary tradition on which Shakespeare has been drawing. (He does exactly the same thing in *Titus Andronicus* when a copy of Ovid's *Metamorphoses*, an important source for the play, is actually brought on stage: 4.1.42.) Mercutio continues his bawdy teasing with, first, his reference to 'drivelling love' which is 'like a great natural that runs lolling up and down to hide his bauble in a hole', and then in his conversation with the Nurse when, asked the time of day, he says that 'the bawdy hand of the dial is now upon the prick of noon' (2.3.104–5).

This point in the play brings together for the first time its two chief representatives of unabashed sexuality, each of them standing in the same essential relationship to each of the play's lovers. Mercutio sees the Nurse as 'a bawd' and she speaks of him as a 'saucy merchant' full of 'ropery'—an unusual word which appears to mean lewd language. After she has learnt of Romeo's marriage plans, she praises him to Juliet in physical terms: 'his leg excels all men's, and for a hand and a foot and a body, though they be not to be talked on, yet they are past compare' (2.4.40–2). And again she talks knowingly of sexual activity: 'you shall bear the burden soon at night'.

The tone of the play undergoes a decisive change with Mercutio's death from a blow dealt from under Romeo's would-be protective arm, soon followed by Tybalt's death at Romeo's hands and by Romeo's banishment. Thus far it might almost have been going to be a romantic comedy; from now onwards, a tragic conclusion is inevitable. As Romeo says, 'This but begins the woe other [day]s must end' (3.1.120).

Juliet knows nothing of all this when we see her looking forward to her marriage, and doing so in terms which suggest that she has matured with extraordinary rapidity from the girl who, in terms of the play's time scale, only a day or two earlier was speaking of marriage as 'an honour that [she] dreamt not of'. Now she looks forward to it, and to her sexual initiation, with passionate and impatient rapture. At the start of her speech Shakespeare—as often in the play—picks up an image from Brooke's poem, but here he brings it forward from Brooke's description of the marriage night to Juliet's anticipation of its delights; 'The hastiness of Phoebus' steeds in great despite they blame', says Brooke, which Shakespeare transforms into 'Gallop apace, you fiery-footed steeds, | Towards Phoebus' lodging.' And Juliet goes on:

> Spread thy close curtain, love-performing night,
> That runaways' eyes may wink, and Romeo
> Leap to these arms untalked of and unseen.   (3.2.1–6)

She wishes to 'lose a winning match', and Shakespeare makes her emphasize that in doing so both she and Romeo will lose their virginity: the match is 'Played for a pair of stainless maidenhoods'. The consummation will be fully sexual, but 'True love acted', since it is hallowed by the sacrament of marriage, will be 'simple modesty'.

For the audience Juliet's anticipative rapture is overshadowed by the knowledge that Romeo lies under sentence of banishment, and this news comes to Juliet in another of the Nurse's interruptions when Shakespeare daringly plays with the audience's and with Juliet's emotions by causing the Nurse to appear to be saying that Romeo has died while actually talking of Tybalt's death. When the truth comes out, after a highly artificial series of rhetorical elaborations difficult to make clear to the audience, it is scarcely less unwelcome to Juliet than if Romeo had actually been killed:

> 'Romeo is banishèd'—to speak that word
> Is father, mother, Tybalt, Romeo, Juliet,
> All slain, all dead. 'Romeo is banishèd'—
> There is no end, no limit, measure, bound,
> In that word's death. No words can that woe sound.   (3.2.122–6)

Now, despite the Nurse's preparations for the consummation of their marriage, the new bride fears that 'death, not Romeo' will 'take [her] maidenhead'.

Romeo's following scene with the Friar, in which he too learns that he has been banished, forms both a stylistic and a narrative counterpart to Juliet's with the Nurse. Again he speaks of his love for her in religious terms: even so low a form of life as carrion flies

> may seize
> On the white wonder of dear Juliet's hand,
> And steal immortal blessing from her lips,
> Who, even in pure and vestal modesty,
> Still blush, as thinking their own kisses sin.   (3.3.35–9)

And the patterning of the scene is completed with the entrance of the Nurse to tell Romeo of Juliet's anguish. It takes a fifty-line speech from the Friar to persuade Romeo that it may be possible

> To blaze your marriage, reconcile your friends,
> Beg pardon of the Prince, and call thee back
> With twenty hundred thousand times more joy
> Than thou went'st forth in lamentation.   (3.3.150–3)

After Tybalt's death Romeo had expressed the fear that Juliet's 'beauty hath made me effeminate' (3.1.114), and now both the Nurse and the Friar repeatedly call his manhood into question, raising issues of appropriate masculine behaviour: 'Stand up, stand up, stand an you be a man,' says the Nurse, with possible bawdy play on the word 'stand'; and the Friar asks

Art thou a man? Thy form cries out thou art.
Thy tears are womanish....
Unseemly woman in a seeming man,
.....Thy noble shape is but a form of wax,
Digressing from the valour of a man.

It is remarkable that just as the play turns irrevocably towards tragedy after Mercutio's death, so the language of sexuality dwindles and disappears from the following scene onwards, after Juliet's 'Gallop apace' speech, in which she looks forward to her marriage bed. Sex, love, and marriage still impel the action, but except for a couple of remarks from Lady Capulet and the Nurse about Juliet's imagined wedding night with Paris,[22] I find no clear use of comic bawdy in the rest of the play.

Arthur Brooke, writing a narrative intended to be read, is able to offer a more explicit description of the consummation of the marriage than Shakespeare, writing for performance on the visually chaste Elizabethan stage, can give. And although Brooke stresses the purity of Romeo's and Juliet's married love, he describes their love-making in martial terms:

And now the virgin's fort hath warlike Romeus got,
In which as yet no breech was made by force of cannon shot,
And now in ease he doth possess the hopèd place.
How glad was he, speak you that may your lovers' parts
    embrace.   (11. 921–4)

What Shakespeare gives us in place of this is the beautiful scene in which the newly married couple part after their one night of love, an episode which draws on a common topos of European literature, the dawn parting.[23] (See Plate 7.) The entirely chaste way in which Shakespeare presents the bedroom scene is particularly understandable in the Elizabethan theatre, where Juliet was played by a boy, but it is also in keeping with his idealization of the relationship. Later ages have modified it. The Victorians uneasily introduced a few visual suggestions of what had been going on; a famous Juliet of the late nineteenth century, Helena Modjeska, who was of Polish origin but worked mainly in America, wrote disapprovingly of 'such naturalistic details as a disarranged four-poster bed, of the turning of a key in a locked door at the Nurse's entrance, or Romeo's lacing his jerkin, and a dishevelled Juliet in a *crepe de chine* nightgown.'[24] Anything beyond the merest hint of sexual activity would have been unthinkable, or at least illegal, on the English stage until the abolition of the Lord Chamberlain's powers of censorship in 1968. Since then, however, on both stage and film, various degrees of nudity have assisted audiences' imaginations; Zeffirelli's film 'created something of a sensation by showing Romeo's bare buttocks and a glimpse of Juliet's breasts',[25] while on stage Adrian Noble opened the scene with the lovers apparently naked and in bed. Michael Bogdanov gave a comic twist to the action, making Romeo and Juliet genuinely quarrel over whether the bird they are hearing is 'the nightingale and not the lark' (no ornithologists they), or raising a laugh by the hasty way in which Romeo pulls on his trousers.[26]

As he lets down his rope ladder he asks only for 'One kiss, and I'll descend.' Arrangements for Juliet's planned marriage to Paris are conducted in a seemly manner, and though Paris is politely and properly expressive of his wish to hurry forward the marriage day—'I would that Thursday were tomorrow'—he shows none of the sexual ardour with which Romeo had pursued his suit.

Characteristically, the Nurse is totally pragmatic in her attitude to the proposed match with Paris. Romeo is banished, so the only sensible thing for Juliet to do is to look elsewhere. She should be glad that her parents have provided so attractive a substitute. The Nurse praises Paris's physique just as previously she had praised Romeo's. 'O, he's a lovely gentleman! | Romeo's a dishclout to him.' In bed, she seems to imply, one handsome young man is as good as another. For Juliet, this is betrayal, an extreme of treachery which ends her relationship with the Nurse and leaves her alone. 'Ancient damnation! O most wicked fiend!…Go, counsellor! | Thou and my bosom henceforth shall be twain' (3.5.235–6). I have seen productions—such as a Stratford one in 1967 with Elizabeth Spriggs as the Nurse—in which she was portrayed at this point as secretly sympathetic with her charge, dissembling her true feelings either out of deference to the wishes of her employers or because she truly feels that, however sorry she may be for Juliet, acceptance of Paris is the only sensible way forward. This is, I think, sentimental. However lovable the Nurse may be in performance, her imagination is seriously limited, and her attitude to love and sex—like that of many of Shakespeare's contemporaries—is symptomatic of this. The same is true of Mercutio, and as the lovers grow in understanding of the relationship between love and sexuality, so they outgrow their former companions, who become redundant to the scheme of the play. This surely is why Shakespeare kills off Mercutio and why the Nurse fades out of the action after the scene of mourning for her supposedly dead mistress.

As the play approaches its tragic conclusion the association of crude, loveless sex with violence which had permeated the early scenes becomes crystallized in the notion of death as a sexual violator, a rapist. The image of orgasm as a 'little death' was commonplace. Over Juliet's supposed corpse her father, believing her to be still a virgin, tells Paris that

> …the night before thy wedding day
> Hath death lain with thy wife. See, there she lies,
> Flower as she was, deflowerèd by him.
> Death is my son-in-law, death is my heir.
> My daughter he hath wedded.   (4.4.62–6)

Similarly Romeo in the tomb asks if he should believe

> That unsubstantial death is amorous,
> And that the lean abhorrèd monster keeps
> Thee here in dark to be his paramour.   (5.3.103–5)

But the kiss that Romeo gives Juliet as he poisons himself is a 'right-eous' one. Juliet too kisses Romeo just before she dies, and one does not have to be a Freudian analyst to see phallic imagery in Juliet's apos-trophe to Romeo's dagger as she prepares to stab herself:

> O happy dagger,
> This is thy sheath! There rust, and let me die.   (5.3.168–9)

'Happy' here is an ambivalent word. The dagger is happy—both fortu-nately available and productive of happiness—for Juliet in that it will bring her the death that she seeks; it may also be seen as happy in itself in that it penetrates her like a lover. This is a liebestod, a love/death in which the bitterness of death is mitigated by the sense of a union for these star-crossed lovers who can no longer find it in life.[27] It is miti-gated too by the reconciliation that it brings about between the lovers' families. In the play's concluding speeches the Friar emphasizes, for the sake of the grieving onlookers, including Juliet's parents and Romeo's father, who do not know that Romeo and Juliet were married, that Romeo 'was husband to that Juliet', and that Juliet was 'Romeo's faithful wife'.[28] In the end the play becomes an elegy for wedded love, a condition in which sex, while it is important, is subsumed in celebra-tion of a spiritual as well as physical unity.

Romeo and Juliet is a self-consciously and elaborately literary play which draws on a full repertoire of rhetorical devices in a manner that makes it not always easy to read or to act. In it Shakespeare deploys his mastery of language to differentiate character with virtuosic skill. And behind it lies a structure of ideas that makes it a landmark in his portrayal and implicit discussion of sex and love.

7

Sexual Jealousy

Jealousy, says the biblical Song of Solomon, 'is cruel as the grave: the coals thereof are coals of fire, which hath a most vehement flame.'[1] A closed, obsessive state of mind, it can seem comic to the detached observer while being acutely painful to the sufferer. Shakespeare uses it as the basis for farcical comedy in *The Merry Wives of Windsor* (see p. 112), but portrays it more sympathetically in other plays, most notably *Much Ado About Nothing, Othello, Troilus and Cressida,* and *The Winter's Tale.* In both the first of these and in *Othello* the jealousy, which is unjustified, is deliberately set up by a malevolent plotter, and in each play there is no fully developed investigation of motives for the plotting beyond a generalized sense of ill will. This has led actors and critics to seek subtextual motives, including sexual ones, for the deceit.

In *Much Ado About Nothing* Shakespeare experiments with comic form in subordinating what is technically the main plot, the deception of Claudio by Don John and his henchman Borachio into believing that Hero has been unfaithful to him on the eve of their marriage, to the story of the plot to cause Benedick and Beatrice to fall in love with each other. It is Don John who, along with Borachio, engineers the situation that provokes Claudio into sexual jealousy; and Don John is little more than a plot mechanism, a two-dimensional malcontent, out of sorts with himself and the rest of the world.

As with Edmond in *King Lear*, Shakespeare draws on dramatic convention in making the villain a bastard, 'a walking impersonation of the way in which illegitimate sexual activity can produce social malcontents'.[2] There are hints as to the cause of his melancholy. He has been defeated in battle by his brother Don Pedro, and he gives two reasons for disliking Pedro's friend and right-hand man Claudio. One is envy of his military success: he sees the youth as a 'young start-up' who has 'all the glory of my overthrow'. There is a hint too that he envies Claudio his youthful good looks—at least it is easy to read his description of him as 'the most exquisite Claudio' as an envious sneer. It is on this basis that actors, including for instance Richard Pasco in Ronald Eyre's 1971 Stratford production, seeking psychological reality in a type character, have suggested a subtext that Don John's malevolence to the youth is motivated by frustrated sexual desire for him—an interpretation which has also been applied to Iago, in *Othello*. Don John has also, however, been shown as harbouring desire for Hero.[3]

There is a false trail early in the play: Claudio is shown to be callowly suspicious when, knowing that Don Pedro has undertaken to woo Hero on his behalf, he overhears a conversation which causes him to jump to the conclusion that in fact Pedro seeks her for himself:

> 'Tis certain so, the Prince woos for himself.
> Friendship is constant in all other things
> Save in the office and affairs of love.   (2.1.164–6)

He is soon disabused of his error, but his gullibility in falling into it so easily prepares us for the more serious deception that is to follow.

Some directors of stage productions, and Kenneth Branagh in his film version of 1993, have shown the episode in which Claudio is

deceived into thinking that he sees Hero 'talk with a ruffian'—
Borachio—'at her chamber window', and is told that she 'Confessed
the vile encounters they have had | A thousand times in secret'
(4.1.92–4). Shakespeare, perhaps wisely, merely reports it, saving its
consequences for the climactic scene in the church at which Claudio
repudiates Hero at the altar. He has been deceived by false appearances, and Shakespeare makes much of the discrepancy between
seeming and reality in the dialogues that follow. Cruelly returning
Hero to her father Leonato, who has just given her away as a bride,
Claudio expatiates on the theme with glib sententiousness:

> Give not this rotten orange to your friend.
> She's but the sign and semblance of her honour.
> Behold how like a maid she blushes here!
> O, what authority and show of truth
> Can cunning sin cover itself withal!

Speaking of her 'outward shows' he alleges that 'She knows the heat
of a luxurious [lecherous] bed' (3.5.32–41). Leonato's desperate attempt
to save the situation by implying that Claudio can be forgiven if he
has had premarital sex with Hero would have come as no surprise to
Elizabethans such as those we have encountered among the Stratford
records, but Claudio denies it with another outburst against 'seeming',
which anticipates Hamlet's 'I know not "seems"' (*Hamlet*, 1.2.76).
Claudio claims to be able to discern the reality that lies behind Hero's
maidenly blushes. Shakespeare depicts his state of mind in regular
blank verse speeches of a formal kind. He utters more sententious
commonplaces:

> O, what authority and show of truth
> Can cunning sin cover itself withal!   (4.1.35–6)

He draws in an artificially literary fashion on classical references,
contrasting Hero's appearance of being as chaste as the goddess Diana

with what he sees as her raging libidinousness parallel to that of
Venus:

> You seem to me as Dian in her orb,
> As chaste as is the bud ere it be blown
> But you are more intemperate in your blood
> Than Venus or those pampered animals
> That rage in savage sensuality.   (4.1.57–61)

(The Arden3 editor, citing examples from *Othello* and *King Lear*,
suggests that the animals are pet monkeys, or 'well-fed horses', known
for lasciviousness.[4])

Like characters in other plays when faced with a situation that
totally violates their sense of expectation—for example Egeon in *The
Comedy of Errors* when his son fails to recognize him (5.1.309–20), or
Troilus when faced with evidence of Cressida's faithlessness
(5.2.140–63), or King Lear when his daughters behave in a way that
contradicts all he expects of them (1.4.208–12)—Claudio questions
his sense of his own and the onlookers' identity:

> Leonato, stand I here?
> Is this the Prince? Is this the Prince's brother?
> Is this face Hero's? Are our eyes our own?   (3.5.70–72)

And he expounds the paradoxes of the situation:

> But fare thee well, most foul, most fair, farewell
> Thou pure impiety and impious purity.   (3.5.103–4)

Claudio's convictions infect both Don Pedro, who feels himself 'dishon-
oured, that have gone about | To link my dear friend to a common
stale', and Leonato, who wonders if he is dreaming and wishes both
himself and Hero dead, the latter in a lengthy speech of humiliation
and rebuke (4.1.121–44).

But not everyone subscribes to Claudio's interpretation of Hero's
reactions to the accusations that have been brought against her.

Benedick proclaims himself 'attired in wonder' and Beatrice is entirely disbelieving: 'O, on my soul, my cousin is belied' (4.1.147). Most significantly, the Friar, who been observing quietly, has drawn entirely independent conclusions from the appearances with which he has been presented. Shakespeare, it might be said, is dramatizing the manner in which interpretation of appearances may result in diametrically opposed interpretations of reality.

It may be significant that the one who sees the truth should be a man of the church. The Friar is an experienced man, confident that his 'age', his 'reverence', 'calling', and 'divinity' bear witness to the correctness of his perception that Hero is innocent. And under the Friar's influence Benedick discerns that the deviser of the plot is 'John the bastard, | Whose spirit toils in frame of villainies.' (This is the first time that he has been identified in the play's dialogue as a bastard, but evidence of speech prefixes and stage directions shows that Shakespeare thought of him as this from the start.) It is the Friar who devises the scheme of hiding Hero away under the pretence that she is dead until Claudio can be convinced of her innocence, and this is successfully brought about. Though Claudio, like many of Shakespeare's real-life contemporaries, performs a solemn act of penitence in church, he remains a silly ass and a cad to the end, and his agreement to marry the veiled figure of Hero under the belief that she is Leonato's niece 'were she an Ethiope' suggests that he has learnt nothing from his experiences.

There is one important respect which puts Claudio's jealousy into a different category from the other instances that I shall discuss in this chapter. It is, we might say, jealousy before the fact: he himself has not slept with Hero; indeed so far as we know he, like her, is sexually inexperienced. Perhaps this helps to account for a certain distancing of Shakespeare's portrayal of the passion of jealousy in this play. There is a textbook quality to it, an intellectuality of presentation as if Shakespeare were writing from observation rather than from experience. It is a far cry from Claudio's self-consciously sententious and well-balanced alliteration and use of paradox in 'But fare thee well, most foul, most fair, farewell | Thou pure impiety and impious purity' (4.1.103–4) to the self-lacerations in jealousy of Troilus, the anguished incoherence of Othello, and the tortured introspection of Leontes. Whether this difference can be attributed to the demands of genre, to developments in Shakespeare's dramatic technique, or to a deepening of his personal experience can only be a matter for personal judgement.

*

As in *Romeo and Juliet*, Shakespeare opens *Othello*, a tragedy of true love, with images of lust. Even before we learn that Roderigo desires Desdemona, Iago, abetted by Roderigo, is maligning the newly married Othello to his father-in-law Brabanzio with grossly reductive images of bestial sexuality, characterizing Othello as 'an old black ram' who 'Is tupping your white ewe' and as 'a Barbary horse' who is 'covering' the old man's daughter. The couple, he declares, 'are now making the beast with two backs'. Roderigo joins in, speaking of 'the gross clasps of a lascivious Moor', and Brabanzio, asking how Desdemona has 'got out'—as if, like Shylock with Jessica in *The Merchant of Venice*, he had shut her up to keep her away from possible suitors—speaks of her elopement as a 'treason of the blood' effected by 'charms | By which the property of youth and maidhood | May be abused' (1.1.171–5). And when he first confronts Othello it is with a reference to 'the sooty bosom | Of such a thing as thou' and with accusations that Othello is 'a practiser | Of arts inhibited' who has 'enchanted' Desdemona, binding her 'in chains of magic', deluding her 'with foul charms', abusing 'her delicate youth with drugs or minerals | That weakens motion' (1.2.71–6). He repeats these accusations to the Duke in the scene before the Senate when he precisely echoes the words that Shylock is reported to have spoken on hearing of Jessica's elopement: 'My daughter!...O, my daughter!' (*The Merchant of Venice*, 2.8.15; *Othello* 1.3.59). The notion of supernatural, magical influences causing people to behave against their natural character is one that will recur throughout the play in, for example, references to the 'magic in the web' of Othello's handkerchief and to Iago as a 'devil'.

Othello directly rebuts, indeed gently mocks such charges in his address to the Senate, scorning the very idea that he has used 'drugs,...charms...conjuration and...mighty magic' in his courtship (1.3.91–2). The First Senator raises the tone with his suggestion that Othello's wooing may have been effected 'by request and such fair question | As soul to soul affordeth', and the idea that Othello's and Desdemona's love is a true union of souls is established in the speeches that the pair make to the Senate.

Unlike Romeo and Juliet, these are not young people encountering each other for the first time. Desdemona is young enough to be still under her father's care, but Othello is a mature man, apparently in his middle years; they are, already—though only just—married to each other when we first see them; and they both make public declarations of the genuineness of their love in convincing enough terms to persuade the Duke of its reality—'this tale would win my daughter, too'. Desdemona is confident—ironically so in view of what happens later—that she can see Othello's 'visage in his mind'.

That their love is physical as well as spiritual is made explicit when Desdemona asks to be allowed to accompany Othello on his military journey:

> if I be left behind,
> A moth of peace, and he go to the war,
> The rites for why I love him are bereft me.

The word 'rites' here can be heard as 'rights'; Desdemona uses a word associated with religion to speak of her 'rights' to sexual fulfilment. But in supporting her request Othello is at pains to emphasize that he does so not simply out of physical desire:

> I therefor beg it not
> To please the palate of my appetite,
> Nor to comply with heat—the young affects
> In me defunct—and proper satisfaction,
> But to be free and bounteous to her mind.

And the Duke gives his blessing to the union in saying to Brabanzio

> And, noble signor,
> If virtue no delighted beauty lack,
> Your son-in-law is far more fair than black.

The spirituality in Othello's love finds expression in a number of uses of the word 'soul'. Arriving in Cyprus he greets Desdemona with the words 'O my soul's joy', and decrees that

> My soul hath her content so absolute
> That not another comfort like to this
> Succeeds in unknown fate

and Desdemona calls upon 'the heavens' to increase their joys.

In the discussion of *Romeo and Juliet* I suggested that the reductive attitude towards sex initiated by the servants in the opening scene and carried forward principally through the figures of Mercutio and the Nurse dwindles, or is internalized, after Mercutio's death. The young lovers transcend it and die unsullied by it. But in *Othello* this attitude is carried throughout the play in the figure of Iago, and results in the destruction of Othello's love and in his corruption. Like Don John in *Much Ado About Nothing*, Iago acts, it would seem, out of what Coleridge famously called 'the motive-hunting of a motiveless malignity';[5] and whether any textual or subtextual motives for his actions can legitimately be identified has been endlessly debated. He himself puts reasons forward—but can we believe him, and are they self-contradictory? Repeatedly declaring his hatred of the Moor he says that it results from Othello's choice of Cassio, not Iago, as his lieutenant

(1.1.8–32), that it is rumoured, and that he suspects, that Othello has slept with Iago's wife, Emilia (1.3.379–80, 2.1.294–5), and that he himself loves Desdemona, 'not out of absolute lust...But partly led to diet my revenge | For that I do suspect the lusty Moor | Hath leapt into my seat' (2.1.290–5). Emilia herself refers to his suspicions of her (4.2.149–51). But none of these potential motives seems either dominant or adequate enough to explain the absoluteness of his evil.

As with Don John, actors have sometimes looked for subtextual motives that may not be apparent even to Iago himself, and, also as with Don John, have been known to locate it in homoerotic desire for one of the play's characters. Bruce Smith remarks that 'Latent homosexuality has become virtually a cliché in how twentieth-century actors interpret the part.'[6] This maybe something of an exaggeration, though the idea goes at least as far back as Tyrone Guthrie's production, of 1938, in which Laurence Olivier played Iago and Ralph Richardson Othello, at a time when Freudian interpretations of Shakespeare were particularly popular. Olivier and the director interviewed Freud's disciple and biographer Ernest Jones, who told them of his belief that Iago's jealousy came about 'not because he envied Othello's [?] position, not because he was in love with Desdemona, but because he himself possessed a subconscious affection for the Moor, the homosexual foundation of which he did not understand'. Olivier's attempt to put this interpretation into practice had only limited success: 'the audience and reviewers...failed to understand it, even when Olivier in the first few performances, responded to Richardson's simulated fit by falling on the ground beside him and simulating an orgasm'.[7] His Othello, too, failed to understand it. Olivier said that in rehearsal, 'losing all control of myself, I flung my arms round Ralph's neck and kissed him. Whereat Ralph, more in sorrow than in anger, sort of patted me and said, "Dear fellow, dear boy", much more pitying me for having lost control of myself than despising me for being a very bad actor.'[8] And when Sir Ben Kingsley played Othello in Stratford in 1985, 'after Othello's suicide David Suchet's Iago threw himself on the body and had to be dragged away. In the context of that production, the moment was interpreted as confirmation of Iago's homosexuality.'⁹

Iago speaks the most homoerotically charged lines in the whole of Shakespeare when, attempting to substantiate his imputation of Cassio's adultery with Desdemona, he claims to have shared Cassio's bed (not an unusual occurrence in Shakespeare's time, as we have seen):

> In sleep I heard him say 'Sweet Desdemona,
> Let us be wary, let us hide our loves',
> And then, sir, would he grip and wring my hand,
> Cry 'O, sweet creature!', then kiss me hard,
> As if he plucked up kisses by the roots,
> That grew upon my lips, lay his leg o'er my thigh,
> And sigh, and kiss, and then cry 'Cursèd fate,
> That gave thee to the Moor!'   (3.3.423–30)

The detail with which Iago relates his fantasy may suggest that he enjoys it. It may seem surprising, even revealing, that he should claim to have allowed matters to go as far as he says they did without trying to put an end to it all; but of course the episode is of his own invention, the product of his diseased mind. He is poisoning Othello's imagination with thoughts of his wife in bed with another man, while also raising images of homoerotic activity. It is also possible, as in Oliver Parker's film in which Kenneth Branagh played Iago, to suggest that Iago is attracted to Roderigo, who has a dependent relationship with him.¹⁰

In *Othello*, as in *Much Ado About Nothing*, Shakespeare makes much of the discrepancy between appearances and reality, but in the tragedy the initial deception, though externally engineered, is brought about not by the staging of an event that purports directly to provide evidence of infidelity but from within the victim's own mind by a process of psychological corruption.

A preliminary hint of the manner in which the construction of human identity depends on the attitude of mind of the beholder is provided in the discrepant comments of Iago and Cassio on Desdemona as she and Othello leave for bed after Othello has arrived in Cyprus. Iago says that they are leaving early because Othello 'hath not yet made wanton the night with her, and she is sport for Jove'. (There is inconsistency about whether or not the marriage has been consummated before this point.) Cassio responds with guarded respect: 'She's a most exquisite lady.' But Iago persists in lewdness: 'And I'll warrant her full of game.' Still Cassio remains respectful: 'Indeed, she's a most fresh and delicate creature.' Iago is not to be deterred: 'What an eye she has! Methinks it sounds a parley to provocation.' Cassio has reservations: 'An inviting eye, and yet, methinks, right modest.' Iago is still lubricious: 'And when she speaks, is it not an alarum to love?' Cassio's praise continues to be generalized: 'She is indeed perfection.' Iago fires a parting shot: 'Well, happiness to their sheets', before luring Cassio into drunkenness—an episode which, significantly, Shakespeare added to the story he took from Cinthio.

This episode too is premonitory in an emblematic manner. Othello's condemnation of the brawl that results from Cassio's drunkenness serves as a symbol of that control over unruly passions that he takes pride in exercising but which will soon be eroded. It is paradoxical that the terms in which he expresses his condemnation of what has happened associate this black man with the forces of Christianity opposed to barbarism:

> Are we turned Turks, and to ourselves do that
> Which heaven hath forbid the Ottomites?
> For Christian shame, put by this barbarous brawl.   (2.3.163–5)

Furthermore the episode provides a basis for Desdemona's pleas to Othello for Cassio's forgiveness which will be her undoing. And in his penitence, Cassio speaks a brief sermon on temperance which provides both a moral gloss on the significance of what he has done and, more importantly, an epitomizing image for the course of the moral and spiritual journey that Othello is to undergo under Iago's influence:

> O God, that men should put an enemy in their mouths to steal away their brains! That we should with joy, pleasance, revel, and applause transform ourselves into beasts!...To be now a sensible man, by and by a fool, and presently a beast! O, strange! Every inordinate cup is unblessed, and the ingredient is a devil.   (2.3.283–6, 298–301)

Othello's enemy will enter by the ears not by the mouth—'I'll pour this pestilence into his ear,' says Iago—and Othello too will be transformed by Iago's poison from a sensible man to a fool, and then to a beast. Whether he finally reverts to being a sensible man is one of the major critical questions about the play.

Though, notoriously, Iago seems 'honest' to every character in the play until the denouement—'I never knew a Florentine more kind and honest,' says Cassio as Iago is plotting his downfall—his villainy is constantly apparent to the audience, revealed in the soliloquies in which he confides in us. He tells us exactly what he is about:

> Whiles this honest fool [Cassio]
> Plies Desdemona to repair his fortune,
> And she for him pleads strongly to the Moor,
> I'll pour this pestilence into his ear:
> That she repeals him for her body's lust,
> And by how much she strives to do him good
> She shall undo her credit with the Moor.   (2.3.344–50)

And he proceeds to do so.

In *Much Ado About Nothing* Claudio had been instantly convinced by the deception played upon him. After witnessing what he was tricked into believing to be evidence of Hero's infidelity, he went away 'enraged, swore he would meet her as he was appointed next morning at the temple, and there, before the whole congregation, shame her with what he saw o'ernight, and send her home again without a husband' (3.3.152–6). He was an instant victim of false appearances. In *Othello*, however, Shakespeare portrays an insidious process of mental corruption brought about by Iago's moral seduction. Iago's destructive cynicism consistently equates love with lust. He implicitly admits to villainy—'And what's he then that says I play the villain?'—'How am I then a villain?'—and even speaks of himself as a devil, drawing on the traditional imagery of devils as black which is responsible for many of the paradoxes of this play in which the black Othello initially belies his appearance:

> Divinity of hell:
> When devils will the blackest sins put on,
> They do suggest at first with heavenly shows.   (2.3.341–3)

Shakespeare causes Iago to accomplish his corruption in a single long scene (3.3), which is essentially a conversation between the two men broken by the episode in which Emilia picks up and gives to Iago the handkerchief that Othello has dropped and that is to play a crucial part in the action. The scene is a virtuoso piece of dramatic craftsmanship which portrays a no less brilliant feat of psychological seduction. Detaching Othello's affections from Desdemona, Iago attaches them to himself. It is this that may fuel theories of a sexual relationship between the two men. The last words of the scene, Iago's 'I am your own for ever' addressed to Othello, sound like a declaration of dedication in marriage.

The first drop of poison to enter Othello's ear is Iago's simple words 'Ha! I like not that' (3.3.33) as Cassio takes his leave of Desdemona and Emilia, stealing away 'guilty-like' according to Iago. Desdemona naively contributes to her own downfall in continuing to press Cassio's suit, but as she leaves, Othello expresses love for her—again using the word 'soul'—in words of terrible irony:

Excellent wretch! Perdition catch my soul
But I do love thee, and when I love thee not,
Chaos is come again.   (3.3.91–3)

As with Claudio, Shakespeare draws on commonplaces about 'seeming':

IAGO   Men should be what they seem,
        Or those that be not, would they might seem none.
OTHELLO Certain, men should be what they seem.   (3.3.131–3)

And Iago plays with this idea in pointing to Desdemona's having deceived her father with false seeming in her elopement with Othello.

Othello, knowing for all his gullibility that appearances may deceive, demands 'ocular proof' of Iago's insinuations. Like Claudio, he questions the evidence of his own senses: 'By the world, | I think my wife be honest, and think she is not. | I think that thou art just, and think thou art not.' Iago feeds his imagination with gross and bestial images of Desdemona in the sexual act with Cassio: 'Would you, the supervisor, grossly gape on, | Behold her topped?' 'Were they as prime as goats, as hot as monkeys, | As salt as wolves in pride.' And then he launches into his fantasy about the sleeping Cassio making love to Iago in the belief that he is Desdemona (see p. 177).

Othello's reactions are far more violent than Claudio's—'I'll tear her all to pieces.' 'Yield up, O love, thy crown and hearted throne | To tyrannous hate!' 'O, blood, blood, blood!' And at the end of the scene he and Iago kneel to enact the grotesque ritual in which Othello swears revenge and Iago dedicates himself to his service in a kind of mock-marriage with the words 'I am your own for ever!'

The withdrawal from Othello of his sense of his own identity is symbolized in his language by the descent from the sublimely eloquent verse of

> Farewell the tranquil mind, farewell content,
> Farewell the plumèd troops and the big wars
> That makes ambition virtue!...   (3.3.353–5)

to the incoherent prose of 'Pish! Noses, ears, and lips! Is't possible?
Confess? Handkerchief? O devil!' (4.1.40–2) in which Cassio, not
Iago, is the devil. And the descent is symbolized in his behaviour by
the literal descent from the upright posture of the dignified
commander to the ignominious falling down in a trance in which
Iago can exult over him. Perdition has caught his soul, and chaos is
come again.

Shakespeare's portrayal of the women in the play shows a deliberate patterning of female attitudes to sex and to sexual morality.
There are three women, and they occupy discrete levels along the
scale. Cassio's mistress, Bianca (ironically, the name means 'white'), is
described in the Folio list of characters, though not in the text itself, as
a 'courtesan', a word which could mean anything from a courtier's
mistress to a prostitute. Iago—not the most reliable witness—despises
her as 'A hussy that by selling her desires | Buys herself bread and
cloth' (4.1.93–4), and the respectably married Emilia regards her as a
strumpet, though Bianca herself claims to be 'no strumpet, but of life
as honest | As you that thus abuse me' (5.1.123–4). She certainly occu-
pies the lowest rank in the play's feminine hierarchy.

Emilia comes higher up the scale, while not reaching the standards
of morality and modesty enunciated by her mistress, who abhors even
to speak the word 'whore' (4.2.166). The most explicit discussion of
female sexual morality comes in the meditative episode between
Emilia and Desdemona in which Desdemona sings the 'song of willow'
that will not go from her mind as she prepares for bed after the terrible
scene in which Othello has treated her like a whore in a brothel with
Emilia as the doorkeeper. The 'poor soul' in the song has 'called [her]
love false love', to which he retorted, 'If I court more women, you'll
couch with more men.' The virtuous Desdemona is incredulous that

women could 'abuse their husbands | In such gross kind'; she herself would not do so 'for all the world'. Emilia takes a less idealistic attitude:

> Marry, I would not do such a thing for a joint ring, nor for measures of lawn, nor for gowns, petticoats, nor caps, nor any petty exhibition; but for all the whole world? Ud's pity, who would not make her husband a cuckold to make him a monarch? I should venture purgatory for 't. (4.3.71–6)

Then, responding to Desdemona's repeated expressions of disbelief, Emilia launches into a vehement claim that women should have equal sexual rights with men in a speech that seems well ahead of its time and which indeed appears to be one of Shakespeare's afterthoughts since it appears only in the revised Folio text of 1623, not in the 1622 quarto. It is 'their husbands' faults', she says, 'If wives do fall.'

> Say that they slack their duties,
> And pour our treasures into foreign laps,
> Or else break out in peevish[11] jealousies,
> Throwing restraint upon us; or say they strike us,
> Or scant our former having in despite:
> Why, we have galls; and though we have some grace,
> Yet have we some revenge. (4.3.85–92)

Women have 'affections, / Desires for sport, and frailty, as men have', and if men are tempted to stray, they can only expect their wives to do so too.

As this passionate speech is not particularly applicable to Emilia's situation it has something of the quality of a manifesto, as if Shakespeare felt compelled to speak out for women's rights. But it provokes from Desdemona the declaration of a superior moral stance, a prayer that she may not 'pick bad from bad, but by bad mend'. Shakespeare leaves us in no doubt about the purity of her motives. She is an exemplar of that married chastity of which he writes in 'The Phoenix and Turtle'. And if Emilia is less idealistic in her attitude to sexual morality, she rises to moral greatness in the final scene with her passionate defence of her mistress, her vehement denunciation of her husband, and her determination to die by Desdemona's side.

What of Othello in the final scenes? After he has recovered from the fit induced by Iago's taunting he sees himself as a man transformed to a beast, in the way that Cassio has said drunkenness can 'transform ourselves into beasts': 'A hornèd man's a monster and a beast,' says Othello (4.1.60). Does he, in the closing episode, remain a beast or does he recover his manly stature? A. C. Bradley, writing in 1904, eloquently expressed the favourable point of view: 'pity itself vanishes, and love and admiration alone remain, in the majestic dignity and sovereign ascendancy of the close. Chaos has come and gone; and the Othello of the Council-chamber and the quay of Cyprus has returned, or a greater and nobler Othello still.'[12] This opinion can be supported by the horror that Othello expresses at what he has done even before he knows that Desdemona is innocent:

> O insupportable, O heavy hour!
> Methinks it should be now a huge eclipse
> Of sun and moon, and that th'affrighted globe
> Should yawn at alteration. (5.2.107–10)

The intensity of his remorse when he knows the truth is awesome in its vision of purgatorial suffering:

> Whip me, ye devils,
> From the possession of this heavenly sight,
> Blow me about in winds, roast me in sulphur,
> Wash me in steep-down gulfs of liquid fire! (5.2.284–7)

And in his last big speech he recovers something of the eloquence with which he had addressed the Senators of Venice.

Other critics, perhaps reacting against Bradley, have rejected the concept of an Othello whose suicide redeems him. T. S. Eliot, in an essay published in 1927, famously remarked that he had 'never read a more terrible exposure of human weakness—of universal human weakness—than the last great speech of Othello…What Othello seems to me to be doing in making this speech is cheering himself up.'[13] The discrepancy of interpretation that the play permits reflects the difficulty of distinguishing between seeming and truth experienced by its characters.

*

Sexual infidelity lies at the very centre of *Troilus and Cressida*. Indeed the Prologue announces it as the principal theme of the play's action: the Greeks have sailed 'To ransack Troy, within whose strong immures | The ravished [abducted] Helen, Menelaus' queen, | With wanton Paris sleeps—and that's the quarrel.' Later the scurrilous Thersites will express this more pungently as 'All the argument is a whore and a cuckold' (2.3.71; 'argument' has a specifically literary and dramatic sense as a digest of a plot). Helen appears in only one scene (3.1), where she is shown as so irredeemably silly that it is easy for us to agree with Hector in the debate scene in the Trojan camp: 'Brother, she is not worth what she doth cost | The holding.' And the mad prophetess Cassandra warns of the likely consequences of continuing the fight:

> Cry, Trojans, cry! Ah Helen, and ah woe!
> Cry, cry 'Troy burns!'—or else let Helen go. (2.2.110–11)

But Troilus defends Helen as 'a Grecian queen, whose youth and freshness | Wrinkles Apollo's and makes stale the morning.' To him, 'she is a pearl | Whose price hath launched above a thousand ships | And turned crowned kings to merchants' (2.2.77–82). Hector himself is finally persuaded that it is right not to return her to her husband, which would bring an end to the war, and Troilus applauds the decision since 'She is a theme of honour and renown, | A spur to valiant and magnanimous deeds.' Her husband, Menelaus, is a rueful figure whose occasional appearances seem designed mainly to provide the occasion for gibes about cuckolds and horns. Finally he and Paris engage in single but wordless combat, but their personal dispute remains unresolved.

Menelaus's jealousy forms only a small part of the play's sexual content, which centres primarily on the love between the Trojans Troilus and Cressida. The interaction between love and war is made explicit in the opening lines of the play proper, spoken by Troilus himself:

> Call here my varlet. I'll unarm again.
> Why should I war without the walls of Troy
> That find such cruel battle here within?   (1.1.1–3)

His love for Cressida is presented in relentlessly physical terms. Her uncle Pandarus, he claims, pours Cressida's 'eyes, her hair, her cheek, her gait, her voice' into 'the open ulcer of [his] heart'. Her 'bed is India', she 'a pearl'. And she herself speaks bawdily with her uncle, jesting about defending her belly and about receiving a blow which may 'swell past hiding'. She sees a thousand times more in Troilus than Pandarus expressed, but speaks of her wooing strategy in terms which reveal an almost cynical detachment about the tactics of love, emphasized by the rhyming couplets in which they are couched:

> Yet hold I off. Women are angels, wooing;
> Things won are done. Joy's soul lies in the doing.
> That she beloved knows naught that knows not this:
> Men price the thing ungained more than it is.
> That she was never yet that ever knew
> Love got so sweet as when desire did sue.
> Therefore this maxim out of love I teach:
> Achievement is command; ungained, beseech.
> Then though my heart's contents firm love doth bear,
> Nothing of that shall from mine eyes appear.   (1.2.282–91)

Troilus's love for Cressida is presented as an overwhelming, almost destructive passion which virtually deprives him of his senses, making him 'giddy' with desire. He wants to 'wallow in the lily beds' of the Elysian fields, and he imagines losing his sense of identity in orgasmic rapture in carnal terms:

> What will it be
> When that the wat'ry palates taste indeed
> Love's thrice-repurèd nectar? Death, I fear me,
> Swooning destruction, or some joy too fine,
> Too subtle-potent, tuned too sharp in sweetness
> For the capacity of my ruder powers.   (3.2.16–23)

What is going on linguistically in these densely packed lines? 'Palates taste', the reading of both the quarto and the Folio texts ('pallats taste'), is often emended to 'palate tastes', but the Oxford *Textual Companion* notes 'Not only might *pallats* be used figuratively here for "senses", but it could literally mean both their palates, and might even play on the sense…"small bed" [pallets].' But if 'palates' is taken in the most obvious literal sense it implies the physical sensation within the lovers' mouths as they taste—what? Each other's saliva? The Cambridge editor, Anthony Dawson, accepts the emendation and explains as 'The mouth watering in anticipation'; he defines 'love's thrice repurèd nectar' as 'the elixir of love', without saying what that is. 'Nectar' was the liquor of the gods; Williams (*Dictionary*) shows that it could be used of a 'genital emission', saying that Shakespeare is recalling 'the Neo-Platonic banquet of sense…as Troilus fears that his first experience with Cressida will involve "some joy too fine…For the capacity of my ruder powers".' The 'parallel with thrice-decocted [heated up three times, distilled] blood insists on the seminal nature of the nectar'. If the emendation is correct, 'palate' could refer to Cressida's moist vagina, and 'nectar' to Troilus's semen. Or might it be a reference to *fellatio*?[14] In any case this is surely Shakespeare's most direct attempt to convey the physical sensation of the act of love—a far cry from the idealization of Romeo.

When Cressida comes to Troilus, guided by Pandarus (3.2), she does so with a nervous excitement which may be genuine but could be a playing out of the tactic of feigned reluctance that she spoke of in her soliloquy. Troilus speaks knowingly of the 'monstruosity in love' 'that the will is infinite and the execution confined; that the desire is boundless and the act a slave to limit', and Cressida responds in no less knowing terms: 'They say all lovers swear more performance than they are able, and yet reserve an ability that they never perform.' And she reverts to an admission of self-conscious tactics of wooing as she says that she has loved Troilus for many months but played hard to get.

> though I loved you well, I wooed you not—
> And yet, good faith, I wished myself a man,
> Or that we women had men's privilege
> Of speaking first. (3.2.123–6)

She reverts to coyness as Troilus kisses her, but the scene ends with the extraordinary and profoundly ironical litany of mutual dedication in which Troilus declares that after-ages will see him as an everlasting model of the true lover, Cressida that if she is ever false to him her name will become a byword for treachery in love, and Pandarus that if either is false to the other, 'all pitiful goers-between' shall be called 'to the world's end after [his] name': 'Let all constant men be Troiluses, all false women Cressids, and all brokers-between panders.' As of course they are (or were).

And so to bed.

The next we see of the lovers is in the dawn-parting scene (4.2), which has obvious parallels with that in *Romeo and Juliet*. Their union is consummated; Cressida vacillates between concern that Troilus should leave before they are detected and desire that he should 'tarry'. 'You men will never tarry,' she says, with a knowingness that seems to belie Pandarus's subsequent assumption that she has only just lost her virginity. And she repeats the idea that she might have been wise to play harder to get: 'I might have still held off, | And then you would have tarried.' Minutes later Aeneas enters with the dire news that she is to be sent to join her renegade father in the Grecian camps in exchange for the Trojan Antenor. This provokes from her a passionate declaration of love for Troilus:

> Time, force, and death
> Do to this body what extremity you can,
> But the strong base and building of my love
> Is as the very centre of the earth,
> Drawing all things to it. (4.3.27–31)

Troilus is no less passionate in speaking of her:

> Cressid, I love thee in so strained a purity
> That the blest gods, as angry with my fancy—
> More bright in zeal than the devotion which
> Cold lips blow to their deities—take thee from me. (4.5.23–6)

And Pandarus, the third member of the trio who pledged their eternal reputations on their constancy, joins in the lamentations. Shakespeare is laying on the irony with a trowel.

Before they part the lovers exchange love tokens, but already Troilus is showing signs of anticipative jealousy, warning Cressida that 'sometimes we are devils to ourselves'—as Iago was a devil to Othello— 'When we will tempt the frailty of our powers' (4.5.95–6).

The Greek to whom Troilus hands Cressida over is Diomedes, who is to become her lover; with added irony he accepts her with the courtly greeting 'to Diomed | You shall be mistress, and command him wholly' (4.5.119–20); this disturbs Troilus, who perhaps hears a double meaning in 'mistress'. As Cressida enters the Greek camp each of the leaders insists on kissing her. (See Plate 9) Her reactions to this scene have become an interpretative crux.[15] It used to be assumed that she acquiesced readily; this was supported by Ulysses's denigratory comment:

> Fie, fie upon her!
> There's language in her eye, her cheek, her lip;
> Nay, her foot speaks. Her wanton spirits look out
> At every joint and motive [motion] of her body.
> O these encounterers so glib of tongue,
> That give accosting welcome ere it comes,
> And wide unclasp the tables of their thoughts
> To every ticklish reader, set them down
> For sluttish spoils of opportunity
> And daughters of the game.   (4.6.59–64)

More recently performers and critics influenced by feminist thought have portrayed the kisses as forced upon her, even in a kind of gang-rape, ascribing Ulysses's views to patriarchal prejudice. However the episode is interpreted, Cressida's eventual yielding to Diomedes is undeniable, and provides the occasion for one of Shakespeare's most complex experiments in dramatic perspective. (There is something of a precedent in *The Two Gentlemen of Verona*, where Julia and the Host overhear Proteus's serenade to Silvia, 4.2.25–70.) This is the love scene between Cressida and Diomedes in which, not without remorse, she presents him with the sleeve that Troilus had given her as a love token, a scene observed and commented upon by Troilus and Ulysses and, independently, by the scurrilous Thersites. Towards the end of the scene, having given way to Diomedes's seductive powers, she, like Hamlet before her, laments woman's and her own frailty, again in the distancing couplets by which Shakespeare signals what is virtually a choric comment:

> Ah, poor our sex! This fault in us I find:
> The error of our eye directs our mind.
> What error leads must err. O then conclude:
> Minds swayed by eyes are full of turpitude.   (5.2.111–14)

The outcome in Troilus is an anguished philosophical examination of the instability of the human personality. 'Injurious Time', as he has called it—which also Cressida has invoked, and which is the theme of one of Ulysses's most thoughtful speeches (3.3.139–184)—has transformed Cressida into someone who seems entirely different from what she was, even though she still inhabits the same body:

> This is and is not Cressid ...
> Instance, O instance, strong as Pluto's gates:
> Cressid is mine, tied with the bonds of heaven.
> Instance, O instance, strong as heaven itself:
> The bonds of heaven are slipped, dissolved, and loosed,
> And with another knot, five-finger-tied,
> The fractions of her faith, orts [remnants] of her love,
> The fragments, scraps, the bits and greasy relics
> Of her o'er-eaten faith, are bound to Diomed.   (5.2.146, 149–63)

Bitter though he is, he still loves Cressida:

> as much as I do Cressid love,
> So much by weight hate I her Diomed.

Does the 'poor girl', as Pandarus calls her, retain affection for him? She sends him a letter, but we never know what it says. The disillusioned lover tears it up and throws it to the winds:

> My love with words and errors still she feeds,
> But edifies another with her deeds.   (5.3.114–15)

He fights with reckless abandon in the play's climactic battle, engaging Diomedes—who wins his horse—in single combat. But both remain alive. In their dispute, as in that between Paris and Menelaus, there is no tragic resolution.

Whereas the accused women in *Much Ado About Nothing*, *Othello*, and *The Winter's Tale* are innocent, Cressida is not. There is no need of a Don John or an Iago to trick Troilus into unjustified jealousy. In the figure of Thersites, however, the cast list includes a similarly cynical, sexually disillusioned commentator who, standing on the edge of the action, counterpoints any tendency to idealism that others may express about both love and war with the expression of a bitterly reductive, sometimes comically deflating attitude towards the Greeks and himself, and indeed to all experience. From his first words, when he wishes a plague of boils upon Agamemnon, his language is riddled with allusions to disease, especially to venereal disease—'the Neapolitan bone-ache'—and its symptoms. No one, including himself—'a rascal, a scurvy railing knave, a very filthy rogue'—is immune from the lashings of his tongue: 'Nothing but lechery!', he snarls; 'All incontinent varlets!' (5.1.95).

This exceptionally time-conscious play, which tells the story of the first great event in the recorded history of the world, finally lurches forward into Shakespeare's own time with an oblique reference to the brothels of the south bank of London—where also the theatres were situated—and to the prostitutes who worked in them, the 'geese of Winchester'.[16] It ends bleakly with a total breaking of its time barrier from Pandarus, the character who, along with Thersites, has provided most of its comedy but who is now reduced to the 'pitiful goer-between' that he had prophesied he would become if Troilus and Cressida were unfaithful to each other. Riddled with venereal disease and cursed by Troilus, he steps forward, still in the guise of an entertainer, to address his 'Brethren and sisters of the hold-door trade'—fellow panders—bequeathing them nothing but his diseases. Through him Shakespeare speaks directly to his fellow-Londoners.

*

In *Othello* Emilia, responding to Desdemona's statement that she never gave her husband cause to be jealous, says

> …jealous souls will not be answered so.
> They are not ever jealous for the cause,
> But jealous for they're jealous. It is a monster
> Begot upon itself, born on itself.   (3.4.156–9)

She is entirely wrong about Othello, maybe because of her ignorance that her husband, Iago, is the 'monster' who has bred jealousy within him. Her words are far more applicable to Leontes, in *The Winter's Tale*, whose jealousy does indeed seem to be self-generated. When we see him at the opening of the play he is apparently a happily married man. Admittedly some actors, including John Gielgud in a 1951 production by Peter Brook, have tried to show him as jealous from the start, but this requires a quantity of acting between the lines which is more than the text should be asked to bear. Leontes's jealousy comes suddenly upon him in an episode which demonstrates even more acutely than with Claudio the danger that false interpretation of appearances may result in a disastrous distortion of reality. Maybe the insistence with which the pregnant Hermione presses their visitor Polixenes to extend his stay in Sicily, which has already lasted nine months—a significant period—resembles Desdemona's overzealousness on pleading with Othello on behalf of Cassio, even though she tries to reassure Leontes: 'Yet, good deed, Leontes, | I love thee not a jar o'th' clock behind | What lady she her lord' (1.2.42–4). And maybe Polixenes speaks tactlessly about the intensity of the childhood friendship between himself and Leontes. But Polixenes makes clear that their relationship changed when, with the onset of puberty, 'stronger blood' reared their 'weak spirits'—a way, presumably, of saying that sexual impulses caused them to turn to women.

The first words Leontes speaks that might suggest that the monster jealousy is rearing itself in his mind come when Hermione tells him that Polixenes has agreed to extend his stay: 'At my request he would not' (1.2.89): but he goes on to praise his wife's success. There is irony in the intensity with which he and Hermione speak of their love only moments before jealousy makes itself visible in Leontes's interior monologue, in which indeed he speaks of it as a sickness—'I have *tremor cordis* on me. My heart dances, | But not for joy, not joy' (1.112–13). Antony Sher, playing the role at Stratford, consulted a psychiatrist who diagnosed the character as suffering from a clinically recognized condition known as 'morbid jealousy' or 'psychotic jealousy'.[17]

There must be an opposition between what we see—Hermione's innocent taking Polixenes by the hand, and her cheerful conversation with him—and the false construction that Leontes puts upon it as he speaks of their 'paddling palms and pinching fingers'. This episode is not easy to stage convincingly. Trevor Nunn, in a 1969 production at Stratford, resorted to the use of a sudden change of lighting in which Hermione and Polixenes acted out the lasciviousness that Leontes ascribes to them while reverting to innocuousness at the end of his speech as the lighting changed back. In his distress Leontes turns to his son, Mamillius, speaking in terms that the audience, let alone the boy, may find difficult to understand about his belief that 'women will say anything'. His state of mind is portrayed as fanatical, self-consuming, incapable of admitting the possibility of error. His vision of his wife's adultery and its effect on him finds expression in one of the most notoriously obscure passages in the entire canon, so much so that Stephen Orgel has even suggested that its very unintelligibility is intentional[18]:

> Affection, thy intention stabs the centre.
> Thou dost make possible things not so held,
> Communicat'st with dreams—how can this be?—
> With what's unreal thou coactive art,
> And fellow'st nothing.   (1.2.140–4)

The idea that Leontes's state of mind is akin to a bad dream emanating from the unconscious mind is to be taken up later when he says sarcastically but all too truly to Hermione, 'Your actions are my "dreams", | You had a bastard by Polixenes, | And I but dreamed it' (3.2.81–3). Like Othello he lives in a self-induced world of grotesque, obscene imaginings. In this interior world of delusion, as in those of the tricked Claudio and of Othello, every gesture is bound to be misinterpreted.

Leontes fears ridicule:

> Go play, boy, play. Thy mother plays, and I
> Play too; but so disgraced a part, whose issue
> Will hiss me to my grave. Contempt and clamour
> Will be my knell.   (1.2.188–91)

In words that appear designed to create discomfort in the minds of couples standing in the theatre's yard, he imagines other men in situations similar to that in which he believes himself to be:

> …many a man there is, even at this present,
> Now, while I speak this, holds his wife by th'arm,
> That little thinks she has been sluiced in's absence,
> And his pond fished by his next neighbour, by
> Sir Smile, his neighbour.   (1.2.193–7)

He appears to comfort himself with the thought that he is not alone in cuckoldom:

> Should all despair
> That have revolted wives, the tenth of mankind
> Would hang themselves.   (1.2.199–201)

He ascribes the plague of cuckoldry to 'a bawdy planet', and (echoing Helen in her conversation with Paroles in *All's Well That Ends Well* (see p. 136)) conceives that there is 'no barricado for a belly', which will 'let in the enemy | With bag and baggage'. His delusions extend to denial of the integrity of the faithful Camillo, whose incredulous rebuke causes Leontes to descend vertiginously down a spiral of paranoia in a speech that takes us into the lowest depths of what Camillo will call his 'diseased opinion':

> Is whispering nothing?
> Is leaning cheek to cheek? Is meeting noses?
> Kissing with inside lip? Stopping the career
> Of laughter with a sigh?—a note infallible
> Of breaking honesty. Horsing foot on foot?

> Skulking in corners? Wishing clocks more swift,
> Hours minutes, noon midnight? And all eyes
> Blind with the pin and web [an eye disease] but theirs, theirs only,
> That would unseen be wicked? Is this nothing?
> Why then the world and all that's in't is nothing,
> The covering sky is nothing, Bohemia nothing,
> My wife is nothing, nor nothing have these nothings
> If this be nothing.   (1.2.286–98)

Here Leontes begins by imagining what happens when the supposed lovers are together, but then, with 'Wishing clocks more swift?', when they are apart. And 'nothing', which could mean 'of no value', shades into the sense of 'vagina'—his wife is reduced to no more than her sexuality.

Such self-absorption induces detachment in those who witness it. Camillo is incredulous, and when Leontes commits his wife to prison the courtier Antigonus and his strong-minded wife, Paulina, actively ridicule him. The effect of their incredulity resembles that created by the presence of Beatrice and Benedick in the church scene of *Much Ado About Nothing*, helping the play to remain on the comic side of imminent tragedy.

The unhappiness that Leontes feels as a result of his paranoia—'Nor night nor day, no rest!' (2.3.1)—may hint at subconscious awareness of guilt, and there is a symbolical relationship between his growing mental sickness, which causes the abandonment of his new-born daughter on a sea coast where man-eating bears prowl, and the illness that afflicts his son, though Leontes ascribes it (accurately in one sense) to the 'dishonour of his mother' (2.3.13). The destructive, self-punitive power of his jealousy is confirmed in the scene of Hermione's trial when, immediately following Leontes's blasphemous denial of the accuracy of the oracle's declaration that she is innocent, news arrives that their son is dead. Just as, in *King Lear*, Gloucester's false view of his sons is cured at the moment he is blinded (see p. 208), so the shock of the boy's death at last brings Leontes to his senses.

> Apollo's angry, and the heavens themselves
> Do strike at my injustice.

And as, in *Much Ado About Nothing*, Hero falls to the ground, apparently dead, at the moment of her accusation, so here Hermione swoons in apparent death on hearing of Mamillius's death. This is a turning point in the play, one that marks its shift in genre from potential tragedy to tragicomedy.

Like Claudio, Leontes does penance in a chapel: 'Once a day I'll visit | The chapel where they [Hermione and Mamillius] lie, and tears shed there | Shall be my recreation' (3.2.237–9). But the time scheme of this play is such that after Leontes's jealousy has burned itself out, he endures a far longer period of penance than Claudio in *Much Ado About Nothing*. The intensity of his suffering is greater, and so is that of his reward, as what he believes to be Hermione's statue comes to life.

The changes in Shakespeare's portrayals of jealousy from *Much Ado About Nothing* to the later plays discussed in this chapter show his increasing awareness of, or at least ability to depict, the corrosive passion whether, as with Claudio and Leontes, it derives from foolish misinterpretation of the truth, from a gullible susceptibility to external influence as with Othello, or from genuine sexual betrayal such as Cressida's of Troilus. As in some of Shakespeare's Sonnets it results in mistrust of the self and of external reality, a terrible sense of emotional instability which may seem risible to onlookers but which causes appalling anguish to the sufferer.

8

Sex and Experience

In this chapter we will consider three tragedies which, though very different from each other, are linked by their concern, in part or whole, with men and women of long sexual experience. In each play, too, adultery is a common factor.

Hamlet is transgenerational. Its sexual interest derives mainly from the central character's relationships with a younger and an older woman: Ophelia, daughter of Denmark's senior statesman, Polonius, and Hamlet's mother, Queen Gertrude. The engine that drives the play is a crime committed in part for sexual reasons; and the engine that drives Hamlet himself to seek revenge for this crime relates to his own complex sexuality. Shakespeare's intense portrayal of Hamlet's inner life sets him apart from all the play's other characters. To a unique extent, we see the action through his eyes and experience it through his sensibility, especially but not only in his soliloquies. And he himself is conscious of a deeper level of response, a thinner-skinned susceptibility to emotional experience, than those around him. He is a raw nerve in the thick-skinned court of Denmark.

Hamlet's relationships with both Gertrude and Ophelia are tortured. He is the outsider who cannot accept his mother's 'o'er-hasty marriage'

(2.2.57), as she herself calls it, to his father's brother. Whereas members of the court join in felicitating the couple, Hamlet, still in mourning dress, continues to think of his father's funeral. Left alone, he speaks bitterly of the speed with which his mother married her late husband's brother, and recalls the combination of tender love and sexual passion in her relationship with his father, who was 'so loving to my mother | That he might not beteem the winds of heaven | Visit her face too roughly'...she 'would hang on him | As if increase of appetite had grown | By what it fed on.' Is there already a hint of misogynistic, or perverse, disapproval of her 'appetite'? And he dwells sibilantly on the physical details of her coupling with her new husband with what might seem like unhealthy particularity: 'O most wicked speed, to post | With such dexterity to incestuous sheets!' The sheets are 'incestuous' because she was Claudius's sister-in-law, so their union is contrary to ecclesiastical law of Shakespeare's time; but there is something neurotic in Hamlet's insistent visualization of her rushing into bed with Claudius.

His sufferings are increased by his father's Ghost's revelation that the court has been tricked into thinking he died as a result of being stung by a serpent, whereas in fact 'the serpent' 'now wears his crown'. And the Ghost's description of Claudius as 'that incestuous, that adulterous beast', along with the idea that he had the power to seduce 'The will of my most seeming-virtuous queen' 'to his shameful lust' suggests that Claudius and Gertrude were lovers—which would have been adulterous as well as incestuous—before old Hamlet's murder. The Ghost contrasts his love and marital fidelity—'whose love was of that dignity | That it went hand-in-hand even with the vow | I made to her in marriage'— with the lust that would 'sate itself in a celestial bed, | And prey on garbage'. And he implores Hamlet not to allow 'the royal bed of Denmark' to 'be | A couch for luxury and damnèd incest.' That word again.

There is a strong implicit contrast between the virtuous relationship of old Hamlet and Gertrude, and that between Gertrude and her new husband. This finds expression in a number of misogynistic remarks about feminine faithlessness. In his first soliloquy, while deploring his mother's speedy re-marriage, Hamlet expresses disillusionment with womankind in general—'frailty, thy name is woman'. This attitude of mind sours his relationship with Ophelia, giving Gertrude and Claudius cause to set up a situation in which they may assess whether disappointed love, rather than their marriage, is the primary cause of his strange behaviour. But in response to Polonius's generalized comment on hypocrisy Claudius betrays his consciousness of guilt to the audience: 'How smart a lash that speech doth give my conscience. | The harlot's cheek, beautied with plast'ring art, | Is not more ugly to the thing that helps it | Than is my deed to my most painted word' (3.1.52–5). Cosmetics and harlotry are recurrent images in the play for 'female duplicity'.[1] Claudius admits that it cannot be love for Ophelia that lies behind Hamlet's distraction after Hamlet's confrontation with Ophelia, which Claudius and Polonius overhear and in which Hamlet declares, 'Those that are married already—all but one—shall live.' Hamlet speaks again of incest: 'th'incestuous pleasure of his bed'—as he makes his way to his mother's room to task her with her offences. He has ample reason to deplore what has happened, but when he reaches his mother's closet he taxes her with her sins in language so impassioned that it passes well beyond the boundaries of rationality (See Plate 8). He is not so much arguing with her as haranguing her in a manner that reveals more of himself than of her. His refusal to admit that Gertrude may still feel sexual desire projects on to her his own repressions: 'You cannot call it love, for at your age | The heyday in the blood is tame' (3.4.67–8). He is kidding himself. Shakespeare cannot have believed this; nor, clearly, does Hamlet, since he later urges his mother to 'assume a virtue if you have it not'. And again he visualizes her in sexual congress with a particularity that bespeaks obsession rather than judicial detachment:

> Nay, but to live
> In the rank sweat of an enseamèd bed,
> Stewed in corruption, honeying and making love
> Over the nasty sty—   (3.4.81–4)

What he says is even fuller of sexual reference than may appear on the surface: 'rank' means 'lustful' and 'enseamèd' implies 'sexually soiled', so the phrase 'is a disgusted evocation of soiled bed-linen', 'stewed' means 'seethed in sexuality', 'honey' can allude to semen, and a 'sty' was 'a habitation for whores'.[2] The intensity of Hamlet's self-flagellation as he lashes himself into even further hatred of Claudius, his spirits, as Gertrude puts it, wildly peeping at his eyes, and his hair standing on end—not something that the actor can be expected to portray literally—is such that it conjures up in his mind a vision of his father's Ghost—though we see it, his mother does not. And he returns to the charge in response to his mother's 'What shall I do?' in a curiously contorted piece of syntax where the use of the double negative seems designed to allow himself the perverse indulgence once again of graphically envisaging what he seeks to deplore, and by speaking of it in grossly reductive terms:

> Not this, by no means, that I bid you do:
> Let the bloat King tempt you again to bed,
> Pinch wanton on your cheek, call you his mouse,
> And let him for a pair of reechy kisses,
> Or paddling in your neck with his damned fingers,
> Make you to ravel all this matter out,
> That I essentially am not in madness,
> But mad in craft.   (3.4.165–72)

Shakespeare counterpoints his depiction of Hamlet's involvement with his mother's inner life with his relationship with Ophelia and her family. Early in the play (1.3) we learn that Hamlet has been showing 'favour' to Ophelia. Laertes gives her a brotherly warning: as a prince Hamlet is not his own man, 'for on his choice depends | The sanity and health of the whole state.' (It all sounds very modern.) Laertes implores his sister not to open her 'chaste treasure' 'To his unmastered importunity' with a long-windedness which, we may soon gather, is inherited from their father. Ophelia promises to do as he says while being spirited enough to tell him not to preach at her while committing similar sins himself:

> Do not, as some ungracious pastors do,
> Show me the steep and thorny way to heaven
> Whilst like a puffed and reckless libertine
> Himself the primrose path of dalliance treads
> And recks not his own rede.³   (1.3.47–51)

(Maybe the reference to the misdemeanours of 'ungracious pastors'—priests lacking the grace of God—would have rung a bell with contemporary audiences.) Up to this point Ophelia seems entirely well balanced in her attitude towards her princely suitor.

After Laertes has departed their father takes up the theme and presses Ophelia into revealing that Hamlet has indeed 'importuned me with love | In honourable fashion' and 'given countenance to his speech… | With all the vows of heaven.' Her worldly father warns her against taking Hamlet's protestations at face value. We learn later that his worldliness extends to his attitude towards his son, who serves as a foil to Hamlet, a kind of representation of an *homme moyen sensuel*, more straightforward in his responses to life's challenges than the neurotic Hamlet. Speaking of the enquiries that his messenger Reynaldo may make of fellow Danes about the lad's behaviour in Paris, Polonius is willing to allow 'such wanton, wild, and usual slips | As are companions noted and most known | To youth and liberty', says that Reynaldo may go so far as to suggest that Laertes practises 'drabbing', and countenances the possibility that the informant may say '"I saw him enter such a house of sale", | Videlicet, a brothel, or so forth.' In this respect Laertes's easy-going sexuality and experience serve as a counterpoint to Hamlet's inhibited behaviour. At the end of the scene, after Polonius advises her not to believe Hamlet's 'vows' and commands her not to waste any more time in talking to the Prince, she says simply, 'I shall obey, my lord.' So far there is nothing in the text to suggest that she will find this difficult.

In the meantime, Hamlet has had his transformational encounter with his father's Ghost—'Something have you heard | Of Hamlet's transformation', Claudius will say to Rosencrantz and Guildenstern (2.2.4–5), and Gertrude speaks of her 'too-much changèd son' (2.2.36). Immediately after Reynaldo has left comes Ophelia's frightened account of how 'Lord Hamlet' had come to her as she was sewing in her chamber looking as if he been 'loosèd out of hell'. This corresponds to his declaration to Horatio that he would 'put an antic disposition on'. She tells her father that she had returned her lover's letters and 'denied | His access' to her. Are we to take it that he has started feigning madness, or that he genuinely is, as Polonius infers, mad for her love? Or could it be something in between? Polonius tells the King and Queen of his belief, but Gertrude is more sceptical: 'I doubt it is no other but the main— | His father's death and our o'er-hasty marriage.' Polonius actually quotes one of Hamlet's letters to Ophelia, addressed 'To the celestial and my soul's idol', mentioning her 'excellent white bosom', and including the brief poem beginning 'Doubt thou the stars are fire'. It says little for Hamlet's poetical talents, but we are given no reason to believe that Polonius has made it up. The most natural interpretation of it all, it seems, is that Hamlet had indeed been courting Ophelia, that she had welcomed his approaches but repressed her feelings in obedience to her father, and that Hamlet's encounter with the Ghost had thrown him into so distracted a state of imbalance between his consciousness of a duty to revenge and his desire for Ophelia that it has rendered him catatonic.

Hamlet's next encounter with Ophelia (3.1) is set up as a way of testing whether—as Polonius is all too ready to believe—it is indeed love for her that is responsible for his strange behaviour, but during it he denies that he ever loved her, denigrates himself as an 'arrant knave' and consigns her to a nunnery—for Shakespeare's audiences the word may have had overtones of a brothel (see pp. 2–3). Claudius's judgement is that though what Hamlet spoke 'lacked form a little', it was 'not like madness', nor was it the result of love—a judgement that Polonius is reluctant to believe. The King's decision to send Hamlet to England on a diplomatic mission shows him to be astute enough to realize that Hamlet's state of mind, whatever its exact cause, bodes danger to himself. The only emotional relationship in which Hamlet finds stability is with Horatio, the 'man | That is not passion's slave', whom he will 'wear in [his] heart's core, ay, in [his] heart of heart'. Horatio makes no verbal response.

As Hamlet waits for the play within the play to start, his hyperactive state of mind is revealed by his bawdy remarks to Ophelia (3.2.107 onwards). His suggestion that, in her response to his offer to lie in her lap, she might have thought he meant 'country matters' has no meaning unless as a deliberate dragging in of the pun on 'cunt'—said by Schmidt, in his *Shakespeare Lexicon* first published in 1874, to be 'an obscure passage' that is 'thought by some to be an allusion to a certain French word of a similar sound'. In fact the word, which is of Germanic origin, is recorded in English as early as c.1230, in the name of a street in Oxford—'Gropecuntlane'—and Shakespeare's contemporary Florio 'uses it freely'.[4] The sexual suggestiveness of a 'thing' that may lie between a maid's legs is similarly demonstrative of Hamlet's nervous tension.

The attribution to Laertes of sexual laxity had contrasted with Hamlet's honourable treatment of Ophelia. When, following her father's killing by Hamlet, we see her mad (4.5), we understand that however close Hamlet had come to the borders of sanity, he had never completely crossed them. 'Her speech is nothing', says Horatio before she appears, and the inconsequentiality of what she says bears him out. Yet it is revealing. Her speeches and snatches of song relate partly to her dead father: 'He is dead and gone, lady.' She sings of a lover who enters the chamber of a maiden who is no longer a virgin when he leaves. 'Young men will do't if they come to it, | By Cock, they are to blame.' Her repressed sexuality comes to the surface with the relaxation of inhibitions induced by insanity. There is no direct reference to Hamlet, but clearly her state of mind has been induced by the tensions of her relationship with him. Whether we should assume from it that he had in fact 'come to it' with her is left unsaid.

Almost immediately after the mad Ophelia leaves, the reactions of Polonius's other child, Laertes, to his father's death similarly serve as a foil to Hamlet. Hamlet had taken elaborate measures to satisfy himself about the identity of his father's murderer, and bitterly deplored his own inability to commit himself to a course of instant revenge. Laertes, on the other hand, jumps impetuously to the wrong conclusion about the identity of *his* father's killer and seeks revenge instantly and at whatever cost to himself. His dramatic encounter with Claudius in which the King reveals that it was Hamlet who killed Polonius enlists Laertes as his ally in seeking revenge on Hamlet.

The Prince has recovered his emotional stability on returning to Denmark, but it is to be put to the test again in the graveyard scene (5.1), a masterly piece of dramatic construction in which Hamlet moves from graveside contemplation of the skull of a man he had known a quarter of a century ago, to awareness of a funeral procession for an unknown corpse, to the revelation that it is the body of a suicide, and finally, on hearing Laertes's outburst of grief for his dead sister combined with a curse on the very Hamlet who is overhearing him, to the realization that it is Ophelia who is to be buried (See Plate 10). Now at last his inhibitions are overcome and his true feelings for the woman he had rejected find full expression in the passionate cry over her corpse in which at last he speaks to people around him with the emotional honesty that previously, in his soliloquies, he had reserved for us, the audience:

> What is he whose grief
> Bears such an emphasis, whose phrase of sorrow
> Conjures the wand'ring stars and makes them stand
> Like wonder-wounded hearers? This is I,
> Hamlet the Dane.   (5.1.250–3)

He has unpacked his heart with words in an affirmation at once of love, of personal identity, and of kingship. His new-found sense of identity enables him also, when the opportunity arises, to take his revenge on Claudius as by a reflex action. And he does so with a final reference to incest:

> Here, thou incestuous, murd'rous, damnèd Dane,
> Drink off this potion.

*

Though sexuality is not foremost among the issues that Shakespeare confronts in *King Lear*, the play's opening lines introduce us to a bastard and to his father who makes light of his son's adulterous begetting. Introducing Edmond to the Earl of Kent, the Earl of Gloucester admits, 'I have so often blushed to acknowledge him that now I am brazed to't.' And he boasts that Edmond's mother was 'fair, there was good sport at his making, and the whoreson must be acknowledged'. Kent politely expresses admiration of Edmond: 'I cannot wish the fault undone, the issue of it being so proper' (1.1.8–17).

This passage sets in train a thread of allusions to sexual issues which underpins the drama at many points. Edmond is, however, at the centre of the only strand of plot that involves sexual intrigue. Speaking in soliloquy, he raises the question of why society should regard him as 'base' when his 'dimensions are as well compact, | My mind as generous, and my shape as true | As honest madam's issue?' Indeed he boasts that his engendering was the result of a far more passionate encounter 'Than doth within a dull, stale, tirèd bed | Go to th'creating a whole tribe of fops | Got 'tween a sleep and wake.' Implicitly this criticizes the manhood of his legitimate brother, Edgar. And in words that may evoke the familiar pun on 'stand' he declares 'I grow, I prosper. | Now gods, stand up for bastards!' (1.2.6–22).

Edmond's question is reasonable. Is there any necessary connection between the legitimacy of a man's birth and his personality? Like Iago in *Othello*, Edmond is supremely a rationalist. Shakespeare makes this very clear in contrasting him with his superstitious father who believes that 'These late eclipses in the sun and moon portend no good to us,' and elaborates the theme at length. After he departs, Edmond mocks his belief in astrology: 'I should have been that I am had the maidenliest star in the firmament twinkled on my bastardizing' (1.2.128–30). Specifically he ridicules the idea that 'planetary influence' may determine whether men are adulterers, which could be responsible for his being 'rough and lecherous'. (He does not deny that he is.) Cold reason motivates his sexual relationships. Goneril desires an adulterous liaison with him, and he encourages her: 'Yours in the ranks of death,' he responds to her advances (4.2.25). And when Edgar kills Oswald he finds a letter from Goneril to Edmond inciting him to 'cut off' her husband.

Regan also desires Edmond. She tells the steward Oswald that she and Edmond 'have talked', and that he is 'more convenient' for her hand than for Goneril's. But when Regan asks him if he loves her sister he claims that he does so only 'In honoured love' (5.1.9). He weighs up the options with cold detachment:

> To both these sisters have I sworn my love,
> Each jealous of the other as the stung
> Are of the adder. Which of them shall I take?—
> Both?—one?—or neither? Neither can be enjoyed
> If both remain alive. To take the widow
> Exasperates, makes mad, her sister Goneril,
> And hardly shall I carry out my side,
> Her husband being alive.   (5.1.46–53)

After the battle in which Lear and Cordelia are taken prisoner, Goneril and Regan squabble over Edmond: Regan declares that she creates him

her 'lord and master'. Unsurprisingly both her husband, Albany, and
Goneril object, and Albany has Edmond arrested on a charge of high
treason. It is after this that Edmond confronts his brother in a tourna-
ment, and Edgar, chivalrously exchanging charity with the vanquished
Edmond, declares that 'The gods are just, and of our pleasant vices |
Make instruments to plague us.' And, drawing a moral with an explicitness rare in Shakespeare, he says of their father 'The dark and vicious
place where thee he got | Cost him his eyes' (5.3.161–4). The 'place' is that
where Gloucester had the adulterous 'good sport' (1.1.22) that went to the
making of the bastard Edmond, and has been countered by the 'sport' in
which Regan and Cornwall had tied him to the stake like a bear, and
gouged out his eyes. So the flippancy with which Gloucester had spoken
of his adultery in the play's opening lines is seen as meeting retribution.

Shakespeare has not yet done with Edmond. As an anonymous
Gentleman brings news both that Goneril is dead and that she has
poisoned Regan, Edmond, knowing he is dying, speaks of their rela-
tionship: 'I was contracted to them both; all three | Now marry in an
instant.' Seeing the women's bodies, he says 'Yet Edmond was beloved. |
The one the other poisoned for my sake, | And after slew herself'
(5.3.203–4, 215–17). Kenneth Muir, in the Arden2 edition, described
this as a 'brilliant stroke', revealing 'that Edmund's career of crime was
caused by his feeling that he was not loved'.[5] This may be an over-
sentimental reading between the lines. But Shakespeare then causes
Edmond to display a compassion that seems, as he himself says, to be
entirely foreign to his nature.

> I pant for life. Some good I mean to do,
> Despite of mine own nature. Quickly send,
> Be brief in it, to th' castle; for my writ
> Is on the life of Lear and on Cordelia.

Is this a blatant betrayal of character consistency made purely to
further the plot? Or does it reveal a plausible if previously unsuspected

side to Edmond's character? Edgar has beaten him in combat, and Edmond appears to have accepted the moral judgement that such a victory was supposed to indicate. His brother has treated him with charity, telling him of his own suffering and of their father's death. This may have had a softening influence on Edmond: he has said, 'This speech of yours hath moved me, | And shall perchance do good.' (His delay in following up this presentiment has fatal consequences for Cordelia.) But Albany dismisses the news of his death with 'That's but a trifle here' (5.3.271).

Bastardy resulting from adultery remains a preoccupation of the play. The Fool's snatches of song include warnings against lechery:

> Leave thy drink and thy whore,
> And keep in-a-door,
> And thou shalt have more
> Than two tens to a score.   (1.4.123–6)

Later, struggling to understand how Regan might not have been glad to see him, Lear has said

> If thou shouldst not be glad
> I would divorce me from thy mother's shrine,
> Sepulchring an adultress.   (2.2.302–4)

Only bastardy (like Edmond's), he thinks, could explain the unnaturalness of his daughter's behaviour. And, addressing the blind Gloucester in his madness, he attempts, in a topsy-turvy reversal of conventional morality, to justify adultery on the grounds that the adulterously begotten Edmond has, he believes, behaved kindly to his father:

> I pardon that man's life. What was thy cause?
> Adultery? Thou shalt not die. Die for adultery!
> No, the wren goes to't, and the small gilded fly
> Does lecher in my sight. Let copulation thrive,
> For Gloucester's bastard son

> Was kinder to his father than my daughters
> Got 'tween the lawful sheets.   (4.5.109–15)

From this, Lear launches into a savage diatribe against female sexuality, ironically advocating 'luxury' (lechery) because, he say, he lacks soldiers, and satirically addressing 'simpering dame[s]' who affect virtue while practising promiscuity:

> Down from the waist
> They're centaurs, though women all above.
> But to the girdle do the gods inherit;
> Beneath is all the fiend's. There's hell, there's darkness,
> there is the sulphurous pit, burning, scalding, stench, consumption.

This equating of the pox-infected vagina with all the horrors of a hell imagined as vividly as in the paintings of Hieronymus Bosch is a terrible measure of the imbalance in Lear's mind. It is as obsessive, and as ultimately reductive, as Hamlet's involuntary imaginings of his mother in the act of sex. But Lear's whole crazy argument is undermined by the fact that he is wrong about 'Gloucester's bastard son'. It is the legitimate Edgar who has remained loyal to his father, Edmond who has betrayed him.

*

Edmond's adultery with Goneril and Regan is small scale and sordid compared with the grand passion of Antony and Cleopatra. Their love affair, adulterous too on Antony's side, is nevertheless the stuff of legend, and was already so to the play's original audiences. Shakespeare presents it on the largest possible scale. The action shuttles back and forth between sensual Egypt and austere Rome, pleasure-loving Antony contrasts with the stiff-backed Octavius Caesar, the grand courtesan Cleopatra with the pallid Octavia. The Egyptian court is one in which, says Antony, 'There's not a minute of our lives should stretch | Without some pleasure now' (1.1.48–9). Enobarbus describes Cleopatra on her barge in terms of the utmost sensuality, of music, perfumes, and extravagance of personal display. Preoccupied with the pursuit of all kinds of pleasure, this is a supremely materialistic, self-indulgent society of feasting, drinking, and sex. The Queen's maids, Charmian and Iras, jest bawdily with the Soothsayer about the length of their lovers' penises: 'if you were but an inch of fortune better than I, where would you choose it?—Not in my husband's nose' (1.2.53–5)—lovers' potency is set off against the impotent yearnings of eunuchs who can only dream of what Venus did with Mars (1.5.18). Even language is imagined as sexually active, as Cleopatra instructs a messenger 'Ram thou thy fruitful tidings in mine ears, | That long time have been barren' (2.5.24–5). Censorious Octavius Caesar speaks of Antony giving up 'a kingdom for a mirth' and 'reel[ing] the streets at noon' (1.4.18, 20), he is an 'amorous surfeiter' and 'ne'er lust wearied' (2.1.33, 38), he with eleven others feasts on 'Eight wild boars roasted whole at a breakfast' (2.2.186), and calls for 'conquering wine' to steep his senses 'In soft and delicate Lethe' (2.7.104–5). It would scarcely be unreasonable to present Antony, like Sir Toby Belch, in a permanent state of at least half-drunkenness.

But that would be too censorious. This is not a moralistic play. One of Shakespeare's great achievements in it is to see the action from multiple perspectives, as if through a series of lenses. Even more remarkably, he contrives also to show coexisting but conflicting states of mind within the protagonists themselves. The play's opening speech presents an outsider's view of Antony as a mature, long-experienced world conqueror who has dwindled into a sex machine, 'the bellows and the fan | To cool a gipsy's lust'. His passion, says Philo, is no more than 'dotage', Queen Cleopatra a lustful 'gipsy' and a 'strumpet'.

Antony, on the contrary, sees himself as being in the grip of a love that is beyond all limit, one that could be measured only by the creation of 'new heaven, new earth' (1.1.17). He defies conventional morality. That his passion is adulterous is immediately made clear by Cleopatra's allusion to Antony's wife, Fulvia; and his protestations of the transcendence of his love for Cleopatra draw from her a sceptical aside:

'Excellent falsehood! | Why did he marry Fulvia and not love her?' Her duplicity is immediately apparent. She will, she says, 'seem the fool' she is not. And Antony's private acknowledgement of the justice of Philo's criticism, that, held in 'strong Egyptian fetters', he is indeed in danger of losing himself in 'dotage' (1.2.109–10), gives a double edge to his amorous protestations. His sense of shame at the hold that Cleopatra exerts over him is at times as strong as the self-disgust of the persona of Shakespeare's sonnets' relationship with his dark lady: 'my five wits nor my five senses can | Dissuade one foolish heart from loving thee,' says Shakespeare the sonneteer; 'I must from this enchanting queen break off,' says Antony; 'Ten thousand harms more than the ills I know | My idleness doth hatch' (1.2.121–3).

Cleopatra may not be married now, but her long amatory experience is emphasized by repeated references to former lovers. Compared to her passion for Antony what she felt for Julius Caesar, who fathered children on her—'he ploughed and she cropped'—showed her to be 'green in judgement, cold in blood'. Antony repeatedly calls her a whore, and, for all his infatuation, admits 'She is cunning past men's thought.' She is one that 'trade[s] in love' (2.5.2). Experience has steeped her in the tricks of the courtesan's trade, like those in the brothels described by Thomas Nashe (p. 29). She puts her manipulative techniques into practice as she waits to hear what news Antony has had from Rome. Her mimic eloquence in describing how he spoke of love is no less than his—

> When you sued staying,
> Then was the time for words; no going then.
> Eternity was in our lips and eyes,
> Bliss in our brow's bent; none our parts so poor
> But was a race of heaven.   (1.3.33–7)

And when she hears news of Fulvia's death, though she may be momentarily disconcerted—'Though age from folly could not give me freedom, | It does from childishness. Can Fulvia die?'—she is quick to turn the situation to her own advantage as she rebukes Antony for showing so little grief: 'Now I see, I see, | In Fulvia's death how mine received shall be.' Fulvia's death does not relieve Antony of the guilt of adultery; before long he marries Octavia, giving Cleopatra still further opportunities for jealous tantrums.

The observer within the play is Enobarbus, who brings to his view of Cleopatra a sceptical perspective combined with a full if detached awareness of the power of her sexuality. As a technique for gaining attention she can, he says, feign death at a moment's notice, and he elaborates this with the sexually charged 'I do think there is mettle [sexual vigour, semen] in death, which commits some loving act upon her, she has such a celerity in dying'—a speedy readiness to swoon—and we remember the 'little death' that is sexual orgasm. For all this, even Enobarbus acknowledges the reality of her attractions: 'Age cannot wither her, | Nor custom stale her infinite variety'—perhaps a delicate way of suggesting virtuosity in sexual techniques.

Though Cleopatra is calculating and unscrupulous in her dealings with Antony, her manipulative mastery of the techniques of love, far exceeding that displayed by Cressida, is shown to be compatible with an obsessive intensity of desire for him. Fooling around with the eunuch Mardian—she takes no pleasure in 'aught an eunuch has'—and her attendant women, she imagines Antony in terms of the world conqueror that he once was, 'the demi-Atlas of this earth, the arm | And burgonet of men', and expresses envy of the very horse that bears his weight—as she has borne it. And she longingly recollects the language of their love-making in which he would call her his 'serpent of old Nile' (1.5.19–33).

Shakespeare shows us an Antony who is torn apart between the demands of his past as the great warrior of Rome, whom he still aspires to be, and his present as the besotted lover of an Egyptian siren whom even in his infatuation he can say that he 'found…as a morsel cold upon | Dead Caesar's trencher'. That which remains in him of his past self acknowledges and deplores his folly even as his present self indulges it. After Cleopatra has betrayed him at the battle of Actium his disillusionment and fury find bitter expression. She is a 'foul Egyptian', a 'Triple-turned whore', 'this false soul of Egypt'. And, he threatens,

> The witch shall die.
> To the young Roman boy she hath sold me, and I fall
> Under this plot. She dies for't.

But she tricks him out of his revenge with that skill in feigning death that Enobarbus had praised in her. The false news of her death softens Antony's wrath and causes him to call on Eros to fulfil his promise to help him to die. When Eros turns the sword upon himself, Antony takes his servant's death, and what he believes to be Cleopatra's, as examples for his own, which he sees as a sexual consummation:

> I will be
> A bridegroom in my death, and run into't
> As to a lover's bed.   (4.15.99–101)

But bungling his intended death blow, he has to be carried to Cleopatra in her monument where he hopes to delay death for long enough to be able to give her the 'poor last' of 'many thousand kisses'. In his dying moments he begs her to temporize with Caesar, but she promises that 'My resolution and my hands I'll trust, | None about Caesar.' She mourns Antony's dissolution as a melting of 'the crown o'th'earth', and though the notion of detumescence underlies her words 'The soldier's pole is fall'n' any hint of bawdy fades in the poetry of the image.

Remarkably, the generally impassive Caesar hears news of Antony's death with an emotional tribute to him as he had been in his greatest days:

> The breaking of so great a thing should make
> A greater crack. The rivèd world

214

> Should have shook lions into civil streets,
> And citizens to their dens. The death of Antony
> Is not a single doom; in that name lay
> A moiety of the world.   (5.1.14–19)

And he weeps.[6]

The final stretch of the play centres on the shifting relationship between Octavius and Cleopatra. Though Octavius is an austere figure, his love for his sister is apparent; indeed it has occasionally been interpreted as bordering on the incestuous, as in the fine interpretation of the role by John Hopkins in Gregory Doran's Stratford production of 2006. Octavius wants to take Cleopatra captive to Rome and show her led in triumph before the people. But she has promised Antony that she will kill herself rather than submit to such degradation, and repeats her determination to die an Egyptian death when Caesar's ambassador Proculeius, whom Antony has told her to trust, captures her:

> Rather a ditch in Egypt
> Be gentle grave unto me; rather on Nilus' mud
> Lay me stark naked, and let the waterflies
> Blow me into abhorring; rather make
> My country's high pyramides my gibbet,
> And hang me up in chains.   (5.2.56–61)

To Dolabella she presents a glorious vision of Antony as the greatest of men, a vision which enhances our view of her as well as of him, but Shakespeare continues to present her in multiple perspectives. Though she kneels in apparent subservience to Caesar when he enters, it is soon revealed that she is up to her old tricks still, attempting to cheat him by retaining for herself treasure which she pretends to have given up to her conqueror, and berating the hapless Seleucus, who has revealed her deceit, with all her old vigour: 'Slave, soulless villain, dog! | O rarely base!' To omit this episode, as directors sometimes do, is to sentimentalize: she remains to the end the manipulative, cunning woman we have seen earlier.

The information from Dolabella that Caesar plans to send her and her children to Rome ahead of him, and there to display them to public ignominy, provokes from her an outraged vision of a pageant in which 'some squeaking Cleopatra' will 'boy my greatness | I'th'posture of a whore.' The ironies would have been multiple as the boy actor spoke these lines. She prepares for her suicide as if for a combined wedding and coronation, and again there is comic deflation in the episode in which the Clown brings her the asps, instruments of her death (5.2.237–74). It is a worm, a 'pretty worm', that will dispatch her, and there is a hint of phallicism in the worm 'that kills and pains not'. The days of revelry are over: 'Now no more | The juice of Egypt's grape shall moist this lip.' Imagining Antony waiting for her where, as he had said, 'souls do couch on flowers'—picturing heaven as a place rather like the barge in which he had first seen her—she addresses him for the first time as husband: 'Husband, I come.' She sees death as the ultimate consummation of her relationship with Antony, and there may be a hint of the orgasmic in 'come'. Certainly death is identified with love-making: 'The stroke of death is as a lover's pinch, | Which hurts and is desired.' She is still capable of jealousy, fearing that if Charmian dies first Antony will 'make demand of her'. And she dies with the name of Antony on her lips. Caesar himself acknowledges her seductiveness even in death: 'she looks like sleep, | As she would catch another Antony | In her strong toil of grace.' This tragedy ends, like a romantic comedy, with the expectation of marriage. A play that ultimately defies generic classification, it is Shakespeare's most complex exploration of the intricate entanglements of lust and love.

9

⤛∽⤜

Whores and Saints

'The middle of humanity thou never knewest, but the extremity of both ends,' says Apemantus of Timon in *Timon of Athens* (4.3.302–3). In this chapter we will look at Shakespeare's depictions of female sexuality encompassing the extremes of whore to (almost) saint, which appear almost entirely in plays written during the second part of his career. (A possible exception is the Courtesan in *The Comedy of Errors*, but her status, like that of Bianca in *Othello* (see p. 182), is uncertain, and she owes less to Shakespeare's imagination than to the conventions of Plautine comedy.) Shakespeare's earliest portrayals of prostitutes are in the Henry IV plays, of around 1597 to 1598, and his most idealized patterns of female virtue appear in his final plays, from 1607 onwards. This is perhaps an indication of the increasing stylization of his dramatic technique, akin to the symbolic characterization of the wicked Queen in *Cymbeline*, the artificiality of the conclusion of *The Winter's Tale*, and the contrasts between Caliban and Ferdinand, and Ariel and Prospero, in *The Tempest*.

Both *Henry IV Part One* and *Part Two* include scenes set in a tavern which clearly, like the establishments with which George Wilkins (p. 29) was associated, doubled as a brothel, at least to the extent of offering its clients the services of a resident whore. Complaining that he has had his pocket picked, Falstaff says, 'This house is turned bawdy-house' (Part One 3.3.98–9). Prince Harry's first speech addressed to Falstaff accuses him of taking an interest in 'the time of the day' only if 'hours were cups of sack, and minutes capons, and clocks the tongues of bawds, and dials the signs of leaping-houses [brothels], and the blessed sun himself a fair hot wench in flame-coloured taffeta' (1.2.6–10). And Falstaff retaliates by asking the Prince, 'Is not my Hostess of the tavern a most sweet wench?' The Prince's response associates the Hostess with venereal disease: 'Why, what a pox have I to do with my Hostess of the tavern?' and Falstaff's reply, 'Why, thou hast called her to a reckoning many a time and oft', puns on 'call to a reckoning' in the sense of 'asked her for your tavern bill' and 'arranged a rendezvous with her' or 'called her to [sexual] account'. The Prince appears to acknowledge the truth of Falstaff's accusations in his solil-oquy 'I know you all', at the end of the scene, in which he declares his determination ultimately to 'throw off' his 'loose behaviour'. The King too, in the interviews in which he rebukes Harry for his unprincely behaviour, speaks of his 'inordinate and low desires', of the 'barren pleasures', 'rude society', and 'vulgar company' to which his son is addicted (3.2.12–14, 41).[1]

Shakespeare takes the opportunity offered him for comedy of sexual wordplay in the teasing of the Hostess by the Prince and Falstaff. She is, says Falstaff, 'an otter' because 'She's neither fish nor flesh; a man knows not where to have her.' The innocent sense of his words is 'how to understand her', and, as David Bevington writes in his Oxford edition, she 'seemingly remains unaware of the sexual implications' of what he says in replying 'Thou or any man knows where to have me, thou knave, thou', but when the Prince purports to come to her aid by agreeing with her—'Thou sayst true, Hostess, and he slanders thee most grossly'—he 'hints that she is to be commended for her sexual availability.'[2] Falstaff's words could also be taken to imply 'to have her vaginally or anally'.[3]

The sexual resonances of *Henry IV Part Two* are both more numerous and far darker than those of *Part One*. Whereas Mistress Quickly's prime function is that of hostess—tavern-keeper—here she employs a resident prostitute, the significantly named Doll Tearsheet. (Doll was a common name for a prostitute, as in Ben Jonson's Doll Common in *The Alchemist*; 'Tearsheet' carries connotations of sexual fun and games amounting to violence.) Falstaff speaks of getting 'a wife in the stews' (1.2.52), and seems to allude to syphilis in calling for 'A pox of this gout, or a gout of this pox!—for the one or the other plays the rogue with my great toe.' Mistress Quickly says of Falstaff that he has 'stabbed me in mine own house, most beastly, in good faith. A cares not what mischief he does; if his weapon be out, he will foin like any devil, he will spare neither man, woman, nor child' (2.1.15–18).

On the surface this is innocent enough—'he has stabbed me cruelly in my own house; when his sword is drawn he will thrust with it.' But unconscious bawdy wordplay is as inescapable here as in some of the Nurse's speeches in *Romeo and Juliet*: 'house' could mean 'brothel' or even 'vagina'; 'beastly' could imply 'unnaturally'; 'weapon' commonly has the innuendo of 'penis' and 'foin' of 'copulate', as a little later when Doll asks Falstaff when he will 'leave fighting o'days, and foining o'nights' (2.4.233–4); and in this context the idea of sparing 'neither man, woman, nor child' could imply both sodomy and pederasty. Whether the Hostess should be taken to be seriously accusing Falstaff of these irregularities, or whether Shakespeare is merely allowing his audience the pleasure of seeing unintended bawdy significance in what she says, is, however, a matter of interpretation. If she really means what she seems to be saying it casts a dark light on Falstaff. Similarly it is uncertain whether we should take seriously the Prince's statement that Doll is 'such kin' to Falstaff 'as the parish heifers are to the town bull', which would imply that she is his daughter, and thus that his association with her is incestuous. But there can be no doubt that she is a whore, 'as common as the way between St Albans and London', as Poins says (2.2.159–60).

Doll is seriously—and comically—drunk when she totters on to entertain Falstaff, and allusions to, and fear of, syphilis abound in his talk with her. It is not unreasonable to see the sexual allusiveness of this play as a response to the growing anxiety about syphilis in Shakespeare's own time. Doll curses Falstaff with 'A pox damn you'; his interpretation of her phrase 'our chains and our jewels' as 'brooches, pearls, and ouches [carbuncles, sores on the skin]', alludes to the 'outward manifestations on the skin...of venereal infection',[4] and speaking of diseases he says 'We catch of you, Doll, we catch of you'; his language is riddled with innuendo related to infection with syphilis, and to treatment of it—'to serve bravely [succeed sexually] is to come halting [damaged] off, you know; to come off the breach [vagina] with his pike [penis] bent bravely, and to surgery [treatment for disease] bravely; to venture upon the charged chambers ['that part of a gun's bore in which the charge is placed—but charged here with pox, not powder'] bravely' (2.4.46–51).[5]

Falstaff jests bawdily about the Hostess with Pistol: 'Do you discharge upon mine hostess'—'I will discharge upon her'—ejaculate over her—'Sir John, with two bullets [balls]', and Doll becomes vicious in response to his threat to 'charge' her. 'By this wine, I'll thrust my knife in your mouldy chaps an you play the saucy cuttle [slang for a knife used by cutpurses] with me!' A brawl seems inevitable as he draws his sword on her, threatening to tear her ruff—a word which, according to Gordon Williams, 'serves as vaginal metaphor', which would give a violent edge to the image. She abuses Pistol harshly—'You a captain? You slave! For what? For tearing a poor whore's ruff in a bawdy-house!'—and serious violence is averted only when Bardolph tries, with difficulty, to calm the infuriated Pistol, with Mistress Quickly in characteristic dogberryisms beseeching the man she calls 'Master Pizzle' (bull's penis, her pronunciation of Pistol) to 'aggravate your choler', and Falstaff drawing Doll aside, placating her with whatever business the actor and director between them care to devise.

After at last the blustering, drunken Pistol has been ejected—or discharged—wounded in the shoulder by Falstaff and pursued by Bardolph, we see a gentler side to Doll as she comforts and flatters the old man, sitting on his knee as they hear the music provided by 'Sneak's noise'—the name of the group they have summoned. The mood becomes elegiac as, calling him her 'whoreson little tidy Bartholomew boar-pig',[6] she bids him 'leave fighting o'days, and foining [copulating] o'nights, and begin to patch up thine old body for heaven.' A chill falls momentarily on the scene as he begs 'do not speak like a death's-head, do not bid me remember mine end', but the mood is broken by the entry of the Prince and Poins prepared to play their practical joke on the old man.

The chiaroscuro of the scene flickers rapidly between sentiment and sarcasm. The young men bring a new perspective to bear as Harry comments satirically on 'the withered elder', and Poins marvels that 'desire should so many years outlive performance'. But Shakespeare switches momentarily back to a more affective mode as, in response to Falstaff's 'I am old, I am old', Doll declares that she loves him 'better than I love e'er a scurvy young boy of them all.' And soon Falstaff is demanding 'a merry song' and more sack, and the Prince mockingly calls Doll an 'honest, virtuous, civil gentlewoman', asking 'Is she of the wicked? Is thine hostess here of the wicked?' Falstaff's answer is sombre: 'one of the women'—Doll—'is in hell already, and burns poor souls'—that is, infects men with syphilis—'For the other'—Mistress Quickly—'I owe her money, and whether she be damned for that I know not.'

At the end of the scene Shakespeare tugs at the audience's heart-strings again, inviting them to allow human feeling to supplant moral judgement as Falstaff is called to the wars and the women, also abandoning their critical faculties, bid him a tearful farewell. But sentiment is abjured when, just before the Prince's coronation, we see them haled off to prison (5.4). The jesting is over. 'There hath been a man or two killed about' Doll. In the hope of evading the gallows she claims to be pregnant, but the Beadle reveals that she has stuffed herself with a cushion, and both women abuse their captors in fishwife-like terms as they are hauled off to what Pistol calls 'base durance and contagious prison'.

Shakespeare counterpoints Falstaff's sexual present with nostalgic reflections of his and some of his contemporaries' sexual past. The tavern scenes have established an elegiac mode through the aged but still sexually active—or at least sexually desirous—Falstaff's consciousness of failing powers and of the approach of death. In the first orchard scene (3.2) this mode is still further enhanced by his coevals' reminiscences of sexual exploits long since past and by Falstaff's comments on them. Justice Shallow boasts of what he did as a young man in the Inns of Court: 'we knew where the bona-robas [high-class prostitutes] were, and had the best of them all at commandment.' Rather as Falstaff had said, 'I am old, I am old', so Shallow knows that 'all shall die'. But in the meantime he is enough in touch with the present to take an interest in the current price of bullocks at Stamford fair (3.2.37). He recalls one of the bona-robas, Jane Nightwork, still living but, says Falstaff 'Old, old, Master Shallow.' And his co-justice Silence chips in with 'That's fifty-five year ago' (3.2.207). But left alone Falstaff casts doubt on the truth of the old man's reminiscences of 'the wildness of his youth and the feats he hath done about Turnbull Street'—the original name of Turnmill Street, which was the most notorious location of brothels in Shakespeare's as in Henry IV's London (see p. 74). 'Lord, Lord, how subject we old men are to this vice of lying!' Shallow had been skinny 'like a man made after supper of a cheese paring', though 'lecherous as a monkey, and the whores called him "mandrake"—a plant whose forked root was said to be like the figure of a naked man. He 'came ever in the rearward of the fashion'—possibly, as Partridge hinted, an accusation of buggery—and frequented 'overscutched'—worn-out—'hussies', not 'the classy "bona-roba" girls he brags about'.[7]

*

As we have seen, prostitution and brothels feature in *Measure for Measure*, written some five or six years after *Henry IV Part Two*, but the most extensive depictions of brothel life in Shakespeare's plays come in *Pericles* in which he collaborated with the real-life brothel-keeper and part-time writer George Wilkins. Regrettably the play survives only in a badly damaged text, with odd disjunctions of plot and incon-sistencies of characterization which may be the result of this. How much, if any, of it derives directly from Wilkins's personal and profes-sional experience we cannot say; much of its raw material in fact, including some details of the brothel scenes, is fairly closely based on two main sources. One is the story of Apollonius of Tyre as told by the poet John Gower, who narrates the play, in his *Confessio Amantis*, which Shakespeare had already drawn on for the framing story of Egeon in *The Comedy of Errors*, the other, a short novel called *The Pattern of Painful Adventures* by Laurence Twine, published about 1594. The story of the play's survival is further complicated by the existence of another novel, *The Painful Adventures of Pericles, Prince of Tyre*, published in 1608, shortly after the play had first been performed, written by Wilkins himself in which he exploited its theatrical success, and appears to have incorpo-rated and paraphrased parts of its dialogue.

Pericles, a play of extremes, features incest and prostitution as well as a heroine of saintly purity. Incest was regarded with abhorrence, and Shakespeare rarely portrays, or even mentions, it. As we have seen, Hamlet deplores Claudius's union with his dead brother's widow, Gertrude, as incestuous, and indeed Queen Elizabeth's father, King Henry VIII, had divorced Catherine of Aragon so that he could marry Anne Boleyn, on the specious grounds that his marriage had been incestuous as Catherine had previously been married to his brother. Shakespeare's only other direct references to the crime both portray it as an extreme of sin. In *Measure for Measure*, Isabella asks her brother Claudio 'Is't not a kind of incest to take life | From thine own sister's shame?' (3.1.140–1), and in *King Lear*, Lear speaks of 'Thou perjured and thou simular of virtue | That art incestuous' (3.2.54–5). In *The Winter's Tale* Shakespeare actually removes almost all hint of the incestuous desire that the character who corresponds to Leontes feels for his daughter in the source story, Robert Greene's *Pandosto*.[8]

Pericles ranges in its human characters from an incestuous father and daughter to a chaste young woman of saintly virtue, and even brings on stage in a vision the goddess of chastity herself. Incest figures in the opening scene of the first act, which is generally thought to have been written mainly by Wilkins, though Shakespeare is the only author to be named on the title page of the first edition, of 1609. The episode is closely indebted both to Gower and to Twine, who narrate it at some length. In the play it functions mainly as a plot device to set the action in motion. The protagonists, the Syrian king Antiochus and his beautiful daughter (she is not given a personal name), with whom he has a long-standing incestuous union, are cardboard figures, lacking any depth of characterization. The riddle that Antiochus has devised in order to keep his daughter unmarried and which her suitors must either solve or die in the attempt—as many, the 'grim looks' of whose severed heads are on display, have found to their cost—does not prove intellectually taxing to Pericles:

> I am no viper, yet I feed
> On mother's flesh which did me breed.
> I sought a husband, in which labour
> I found that kindness in a father.
> He's father, son, and husband mild;
> I mother, wife, and yet his child.[9]

He speaks eloquently of the daughter's beauty:

> You're a fair viol, and your sense the strings
> Who, fingered to make man his lawful music,
> Would draw heav'n down and all the gods to hearken.
>
> (Sc. 1.107–12, 124–6)

(The last line resembles Biron's 'And when love speaks, the voice of all the gods | Make heaven drowsy with the harmony.' See p. 102.) But his awareness of her sin immediately puts him off the idea of marrying her.

In the later scenes of the play, for which probably Shakespeare was principally responsible—though dramatic collaboration may be pervasive rather than unitary—the ugliness of incest of the opening episode is set off by the virginal purity of Pericles's daughter, Marina. It is significant that his wife's first words after being cast coffined on the waters, shipwrecked, and then restored to life, are 'O dear Diana' (Sc. 12.102). Diana, the Greek goddess of chastity, is to be this play's tutelary goddess. When Pericles leaves his infant daughter in the care of the apparently virtuous but actually wicked Dionyza, he swears 'By bright Diana' that his hair will remain 'unscissored' until she is married (Sc. 13.27–30). It is in Diana's temple at Ephesus that Thaisa becomes a handmaid soon after she is rescued, and in the concluding episodes Diana appears to Pericles and to us in a vision that guides him to reunion with Thaisa. Marina's call on Diana to help her to preserve her chastity after she has grown to maturity and the pirates have sold her into a brothel thus becomes more than a mere passing allusion. It links her with the mother she does not know and with the supernatural forces which she hopes will guard her. But the brothel-keeper turns her prayer into a ribald jest—'What have we to do with Diana?'

Despite the extremes of virtue and vice portrayed in the brothel scenes, they have far more psychological verisimilitude and theatrical vitality than the opening episodes of incest. Admittedly the figure of the Governor of Mytilene, Lysimachus, who comes to the brothel to 'do the deed of darkness' but leaves ashamed of his 'corrupted mind', rewarding Marina with gold not for sexual services but for her virtue, and cursing the proprietors of the brothel, is inconsistent, possibly because of deficiencies in the text as it has come down to us. There is comedy in the descriptions of the lustful reactions of those in the marketplace who hear Marina's attractions advertised, and in the reaction of the Gentleman who, finding 'divinity preached' in the whorehouse, departs declaring, 'I am for no more bawdy houses. Shall's go hear the vestals'—Diana's virginal attendant priestesses—'sing?' (Sc. 19.4–7). And the Pander and Bawd, who run the establishment, are colourful characters in whom villainy lightly worn achieves a degree of moral complexity. Their realistic, earthy attitude to sex, their total failure to comprehend Marina's scruples, their horror that 'she has here spoken holy words to the Lord Lysimachus', have comic reality. There is brilliant black comedy in these scenes, but they, even more than the Eastcheap scenes of *Henry IV Part Two*, leave us in no doubt that trading in the flesh, with the diseases and deaths consequent upon it, is a sordid calling:

> BAWD   The stuff we have, a strong wind will blow it to pieces,
> they are so pitifully sodden.
> PANDER   Thou sayst true. They're too unwholesome, o' conscience.
> The poor Transylvanian is dead that lay with the little
> baggage.
> BAWD   Ay, she quickly pooped him, she made him roast meat for
> worms.   (Sc. 16.17–23)

On stage even more than in print Marina is a desperately touching figure as she stands listening to their materialistic assessment of the commercial value of her body, and the instruction to Boult to 'Crack the ice of her virginity' is horrifying. But Boult, like other Shakespearian rogues and villains before and after him, such as Paroles in *All's Well That Ends Well*, has his moment of self-defence as he responds to Marina's protests.

What would you have me do? Go to the wars, would you, where a man may serve seven years for the loss of a leg, and have not money enough in the end to buy him a wooden one?   (Sc. 19.195–8)

Gower describes Marina's virtues after she has escaped from the brothel to be a teacher in 'an honest house' in semi-divine terms—'She sings like one immortal, and she dances | As goddess-like to her admirèd lays.' And when, by one of those chances common in romance literature, Pericles, who 'hath not spoken | To anyone, nor taken sustenance | But to prorogue his grief' for three months, arrives on his barge in Mytilene (Sc. 21), Lysimachus commends Marina as one who, 'with her sweet harmony | And other choice attractions, would alarum | And make a batt'ry through his deafened ports' with her *sacred* physic'. Her healing powers are 'sacred', as if of a saint.

The profoundly moving and deeply protracted scene in which she attempts to drag from the depths of despair that is close to death the ageing, unkempt old man who is a stranger to her has antecedents in many of Shakespeare's earlier plays, including the reunion of twin brother and sister in *Twelfth Night* and that of another father and daughter in *King Lear*. Like Lear, Pericles is a reluctant Lazarus, initially resisting attempts to bring him back to life. But Marina is a miracle worker, a chaste repository of secrets like the Diana of *All's Well That Ends Well*. In what she has said she has been 'godlike perfect', and the reunion of father and daughter is hailed by the sound of music of the spheres which induces a vision of the goddess Diana herself, directing them to her temple at Ephesus. There Pericles is reunited with his wife Thaisa, who is also Marina's mother, and the virginal Marina, her mission done, can be betrothed to Lysimachus.

For almost the entire action of the play Marina has been depicted as innately virtuous, chaste by nature. There is no suggestion that she is ever even tempted to be otherwise. Lysimachus's initially lustful desire for her is quenched by her eloquent appeal to his better nature

(Sc. 19.98–142), and when she enters to attempt her father's cure, the governor rather snobbishly says that she would suit him as a bride if only she were of better family:

> She's such a one that, were I well assured
> Came of gentle kind or noble stock, I'd wish
> No better choice to think me rarely wed.   (Sc. 21.57–9)

When it is revealed that she is a princess Pericles tells Lysimachus he could marry her if he wanted to do so, and the next we hear of the affair is when Pericles tells Thaisa that Lysimachus is 'the fair betrothèd of your daughter'. There is no hint that she desires a husband, or that her wishes have been consulted, or even that anyone thinks they should have been. In this she comes closer to the Isabella of *Measure for Measure* than to the Helen of *All's Well That Ends Well*.

*

The plays discussed so far in this chapter, along with *Measure for Measure* (see pp. 122–34), which feature inns doubling as brothels or brothels themselves, are the most likely to include references to venereal diseases, which occur notably also in *Troilus and Cressida* (p. 192), *King Lear* (p. 210), and *Timon of Athens*, a play of even more pronounced extremes than *Pericles*. No other play in the canon is more schematic in structure, almost certainly because, written in collaboration with Thomas Middleton, it was never put into final form. It has been called 'the still-born twin of *Lear*',[10] and Timon is like Lear in that the shock of disillusionment after being betrayed by those they have trusted brings both men to a rejection of the society in which they have lived and to a series of bitter reflections on mankind, and especially on human sexuality. Timon, all philanthropy in the earlier part of the play, undergoes such an extreme reversal of character in the second part that he can say 'I am Misanthropos, and hate mankind' (4.3.53). Exiling himself from Athens he indulges in a generalized diatribe against humanity which indiscriminately attributes all kinds of sin, sexual and otherwise, to men, women, and children alike:

> Maid, to thy master's bed!
> Thy mistress is o'th' brothel. Son of sixteen,
> Pluck the lined crutch from thy old limping sire;
> With it beat out his brains! (4.1.12–15)

And he invokes upon them the punishment of sexually transmitted diseases:

> Plagues incident to men,
> Your potent and infectious fevers heap
> On Athens, ripe for stroke! Thou cold sciatica [i.e. syphilis],
> Cripple our senators, that their limbs may halt
> As lamely as their manners! Lust and liberty,
> Creep in the minds and marrows of our youth,
> That 'gainst the stream of virtue they may strive
> And drown themselves in riot! Itches, blains [venereal symptoms],
> Sow all th'Athenian bosoms, and their crop
> Be general leprosy [also used of syphilis] ! (4.1.21–30)

Sexual satire becomes more specific on the entrance of the Athenian captain Alcibiades with his army and their camp followers, the whores Phrynia and Timandra. Timon calls the gold that he finds in the woods 'Thou common whore of mankind', and contrasts Phrynia's outward glamour with her inward corruption:

> This fell whore of thine
> Hath in her more destruction than thy sword,
> For all her cherubin look. (4.3.61–3)

And Shakespeare refers specifically to the methods used in his own time for the treatment of syphilis as Timon tells Timandra

> Make use of thy salt hours: season the slaves
> For tubs and baths, bring down rose-cheeked youth
> To the tub-fast and the diet. (4.3.86–8)

He inveighs bitterly against 'the counterfeit matron': 'It is her habit only that is honest, | Herself's a bawd.' And the whores' demands for more and more gold which he pours into their outstretched aprons provoke him to increasingly strident invective, referring specifically to symptoms of syphilis including rotting of the bones and loss of hair:

> Down with the nose,
> Down with it flat; take the bridge quite away
> Of him that his particular to foresee
> Smells from the general weal. Make curled-pate ruffians bald,[11]
> And let the unscarred braggarts of the war
> Derive some pain from you. Plague all,
> That your activity may defeat and quell
> The source of all erection.   (4.3.157–64)

Their clients will be rendered impotent by disease.

Timon's emotion is, as T. S. Eliot said of Hamlet's, 'in excess of the facts as they appear',[12] which perhaps is why his obsession with the symptoms and cure of venereal diseases has been taken to reflect a similar preoccupation within Shakespeare himself, as well as why Alcibiades thinks Timon is mad: 'Pardon him, sweet Timandra, for his wits | Are drowned and lost in his calamities'   (4.3.89–90).

*

There are no virtuous women in *Timon of Athens*, if we except the 'masque of Ladies as Amazons' who dance almost wordlessly in Act 1, Scene 2—and even their virtue is called into question by the cynic Apemantus. By contrast each of the last four plays that bring Shakespeare's solo playwriting career to an end—the tragicomedies, or romances—features a heroine of exceptional virtue. Innogen, in *Cymbeline*, stands out from the others in that she is already married at the start of the action, though recently and secretly. There is no doubting the intensity of her love for Posthumus, but—interestingly in the light of the purity of the heroines of the other three plays—it appears to be presented as a kind of married chastity like that of 'The

Phoenix and Turtle' (pp. 80–1). Posthumus, under the mistaken belief that she has been unfaithful to him, says that 'Me of my lawful pleasure she restrained, | And prayed me oft forbearance; did it with | A pudency so rosy the sweet view on't | Might well have warmed old Saturn.' He goes on to say that Giacomo, in trying to seduce her,

> found no opposition
> But what he looked for should oppose and she
> Should from encounter guard.   (2.5.9–12, 17–19)

The exact meaning of all this is disputed. Innogen's restraint of her husband has usually been taken to imply simply that she limited his sexual access to her within bounds of moderation; but Anne Barton has argued that it means that, though married, she was still a virgin, on the grounds that '"opposition" here "does not seem to be an abstraction—his wife's honour, for instance—nor a vague allusion to the vagina" but "is a specific reference to the hymen."'[13] No final answer is possible, but Posthumus does say that she 'prayed me oft'—not 'always'—'forbearance', and it is certain both that Innogen is married and that she regards herself as Posthumus's wife and sexual partner.

By contrast, two other heroines of late plays by Shakespeare are presented as chaste but—unlike Marina—sexually desirous. Both *The Winter's Tale* and *The Tempest* lay great significance on the importance of premarital chastity, and suggest that it is not easily preserved. In Act 4, Scene 4 of *The Winter's Tale* the opening dialogue between Florizel and Perdita makes clear that they are passionately in love and have sworn to marry. Shakespeare gives them some of the richest and most sensuous love poetry that he ever wrote, but is at pains to emphasize the purity of their desires. Perdita's royal status is as yet unknown, and the young Prince, responding to her fears lest his father should see them together, assures her that even gods such as Jupiter, Neptune, and Apollo, who transformed themselves into human shape to woo mortal women, never did so

> for a piece of beauty rarer,
> Nor in a way so chaste, since my desires
> Run not before mine honour, nor my lusts
> Burn hotter than my faith.

Perdita, too, has 'desires', even 'lusts', and is no less physical in her desires than Florizel; she would strew her lover with flowers

> like a bank, for love to lie and play on,
> Not like a corpse—or if, not to be buried,
> But quick and in mine arms.   (4.4.32–5, 130–2)

And we have external witnesses to their love: the Old Shepherd, who has brought Perdita up, thinks 'there is not half a kiss to choose | Who loves another best.' But she acquiesces in Florizel's resolution to remain chaste till marriage.

Rather as, in *Love's Labour's Lost* and *As You Like It*, Shakespeare sets off the more idealized, courtly lovers with characters of rustic earthiness, so in *The Winter's Tale* he juxtaposes the romantic love of Florizel and Perdita with Autolycus's sexual astringencies. The Servant speaks naively of the pedlar's 'love songs for maids, so without bawdry, which is strange, with such delicate burdens of dildos and fadings, "Jump her, and thump her"' (4.4.194–6). In fact of course these 'burdens' are laden with sexual innuendo: 'Jump and Thump are coital terms, and probably "fading" too'.[14] And Autolycus sings of 'summer songs for me and my aunts [used for 'prostitutes'] | While we lie tumbling in the hay' (4.3.11–12). He has a ballad of a woman who was 'turned into a cold fish for she would not exchange flesh [have sex] with one that loved her' (4.4.276–7). The country lasses Mopsa and Dorcas squabble over the Clown's favours, and Dorcas hints jealously that he 'hath promised', even paid, Mopsa more than gloves; to which Mopsa retaliates with 'He hath paid you all he promised you. Maybe he has paid you more, which will shame you to give him again' (4.4.238–40).

But when the Prince's father, Polixenes, and Camillo come disguised before them, Shakespeare again gives the lovers eloquent expressions of both the intensity and the purity of their passion: 'By th' pattern of mine own thoughts', says Perdita, 'I cut out | The purity of his.' They remain steadfast in their faith even when Polixenes reveals his identity as Florizel's father, forbids their union, and threatens to disinherit his son as he has not been consulted and to devise a cruel death for Perdita if ever she 'hoop his body more with [her] embraces'.

Shakespeare glosses lightly over the fact that Florizel lies when he refers to Perdita as his wife on their arrival at her father's court (5.1.166); later the young man is forced to admit that they are not married, but in the play's final speech Leontes tells Polixenes that Florizel 'is troth-plight to your daughter'. The self-restraint of the young lovers in *The Winter's Tale* relates to Leontes's sixteen-year period of sexual continence after Hermione has apparently died. Each of them succeeds in exercising the art that subdues nature, and all receive their reward, Leontes in finding that art becomes nature.

*

In *The Tempest* emphasis on premarital chastity forms part of the larger pattern of a play that is exceptionally concerned with the presentation of moral absolutes and that offers perhaps Shakespeare's most thoughtful and extended consideration of the relationship between love and lust, chastity and virtuous desire. This play, too, works within a dialectic of extremes. In the King's party, the cynical Antonio and Sebastian—harsh, insolent, and uncharitable—are contrasted with the idealistic Gonzalo, good-humoured, tolerant, and urbane. In the remainder of the play these contrasts are mirrored most strongly in the relationship between Ferdinand, the King's son, and Caliban. In them Shakespeare employs a symbolical mode of characterization which helps both to distinguish between the two characters and to point to similarities between them. Before we see Caliban, Prospero tells his daughter, Miranda

> He does make our fire,
> Fetch in our wood, and serves in offices
> That profit us. (1.2.313–15)

And Caliban's first words, spoken '*within*'—that is, behind the tiring-house wall of the Jacobean theatre—are 'There's wood enough within.' The carrying of wood is a symbolical burden, in Caliban's case a punishment imposed upon him for the crime of attempting to rape Miranda who declares that her 'modesty' (chastity) is 'the jewel in [her] dower'. The uncontrolled sexual urge is seen as part of the destructive disorder of which thunder and lightning, with which the play opens, had been the initial symbols. It can be emphasized in production: when Peter Hall directed the play at the National Theatre in 1988 his Caliban was padlocked over his genitals. (See Plate 13)

It is a clear aspect of the play's design that Shakespeare immediately follows the exit of the lustful and rebellious figure of Caliban with the entrance of the play's romantic lover, Ferdinand. Where Caliban resists control, Ferdinand, who enters under the magic control of Ariel (and thus of Prospero, since Ariel is his agent), willingly accepts it as a means of proving his love for Miranda. His love is a power, a bondage, but one that illustrates the Christian paradox that in some kinds of service lies perfect freedom:

> My spirits, as in a dream, are all bound up.
> My father's loss, the weakness which I feel,
> The wreck of all my friends, nor this man's threats
> To whom I am subdued, are but light to me,
> Might I but through my prison once a day
> Behold this maid. All corners else o'th'earth
> Let liberty make use of; space enough
> Have I in such a prison. (1.2.489–96)

And Prospero imposes on him a love test such as those to which the heroes of chivalric romance were customarily subjected, and which

Benedick parodies in *Much Ado About Nothing* when he says to Don Pedro:

> Will your grace command me any service to the world's end? I will go on the slightest errand now to the Antipodes that you can devise to send me on. I will fetch you a tooth-picker now from the furthest inch of Asia, bring you the length of Prester John's foot, fetch you a hair off the great Cham's beard, do you any embassage to the pigmies, rather than hold three words' conference with this harpy. (2.1.246–53)

The test imposed on Ferdinand is less arduous than any of these. All he has to do is, like Caliban, to fetch and chop Prospero's firewood. The opening stage direction of Act 3 reads: '*Enter Ferdinand, bearing a log.*' His subsequent soliloquy, followed by the dialogue between him and Miranda, bases itself on his attitude to his task, along with Miranda's concern that he 'Work not so hard'. Whereas the first words we have heard Caliban speak are a complaint against his task—'There's wood enough within'—Ferdinand accepts his 'mean task' gladly because 'The mistress which I serve quickens what's dead, | And makes my labours pleasures.'

One of the minor problems in staging the play is to determine the nature and quantity of the wood to be shifted. If the logs are too heavy, Miranda's offer to relieve him of the task will seem absurd and Prospero will appear to be punishing rather than testing him. If they are too light, the scene will be trivialized. The significance of the symbolism is brought home at the end of the scene when Ferdinand, betrothing himself to Miranda, declares himself her husband 'with a heart as willing | As bondage e'er of freedom.' Nicholas Hytner found a solution to the problem in a Stratford production of 1988 when he had the log-bearing Ferdinand enter more than once as the lights were going down after the interval, channelling off the audience's laughter before the action proper resumed.

Prospero has been an unseen witness of the conversation between the lovers, and at the end of the scene declares his satisfaction at their betrothal. But he is constantly concerned to sustain the distinction between lust and love as symbolized in Caliban's uncontrolled desire and Ferdinand's acceptance of the need for self-restraint. Giving his daughter to Ferdinand he says:

> All thy vexations
> Were but my trials of thy love, and thou
> Hast strangely stood the test. Here, afore heaven,
> I ratify this my rich gift.   (4.1.5–8)

Still he insists on the importance of self-control:

> If thou dost break her virgin-knot before
> All sanctimonious ceremonies may
> With full and holy rite be ministered,
> No sweet aspersion shall the heavens let fall
> To make this contract grow,

And again,

> Look thou be true. Do not give dalliance
> Too much the rein. The strongest oaths are straw
> To th'fire i'the'blood.   (4.1.15–19, 51–3)

The explicit moralizing here is unusual for Shakespeare, though it has its parallels in other late plays. It may be seen as an aspect, perhaps even an unpleasant one, of the characterization of Prospero. Psychoanalytical critics have suggested that it reflects incestuous desire on his part for his daughter.[15] But it clearly relates to the play's over-riding concern, adumbrated in its opening scene, with mankind's attempts to control and tame the potentially anarchic forces of nature both within and outside himself, and both the importance of sexual self-control and the rewards that it may reap will be the theme of the masque that Prospero conjures up for the lovers' entertainment and instruction.

This masque is designed to reinforce the injunctions to premarital chastity that precede it. Iris alludes explicitly to the temptations with which Venus and Cupid have beset the lovers, and praises the strength of will—the self-control—with which these temptations have been resisted:

> Here thought they to have done
> Some wanton charm upon this man and maid,
> Whose vows are that no bed-right shall be paid
> Till Hymen's torch be lighted—but in vain.
> Mars's hot minion is returned again.
> Her waspish-headed son has broke his arrows,
> Swears he will shoot no more, but play with sparrows,
> And be a boy right out.   (4.1.94–101)

The next time that we see the lovers after the masque, they are playing chess,[16] a game that requires serious exercise of the brain. This play is full of symbols: I see this as an emblem of the need for intellectual control, a game in which the partners are equal though in a state of constant readjustment, as in a well-balanced partnership. Sexual desire is but one element in the truly loving and virtuous relationship.

10

Just Good Friends?

I n writing about Shakespeare's Sonnets I discussed how he writes about deeply loving relationships between two males in a way that does not necessarily imply a sexual component while leaving open the possibility that one exists. The same is true of relationships between pairs of both male and female friends in some of his plays. I have referred in passing to gay interpretations of, particularly, Slender in *The Merry Wives of Windsor*, Don John in *Much Ado about Nothing*, Mercutio in *Romeo and Juliet*, and Iago in *Othello*. Richard II has often been thought of and portrayed as homosexual; Shakespeare shows him as being influenced by 'Caterpillars of the commonwealth' (*Richard II*, 2.3.16) who are said to have 'Made a divorce betwixt his queen and him, | Broke the possession of a royal bed' (3.1.12–13), and this interpretation has frequently been carried through into performance.[1] And the relationship between Falstaff and the Prince in the Henry IV plays has been similarly interpreted, notably (if enigmatically) in Gus van Sant's 1991 film *My Private Idaho*.

There are other friendships, and at least one love/hate relationship, in which both critics and actors have discerned a sexual component. Its identification depends on a number of factors including intimacies of expression, forms of address, and descriptions of behaviour. Moreover the topic needs to be considered in the context of the extensive Renaissance debate about the relative merits of friendship and of love, especially married love, a debate which often privileged male friendship over the demands of heterosexuality. It underlies many of Shakespeare's plays, from *The Two Gentlemen of Verona* to *The Two Noble Kinsmen*.

The interpretation of intimacy of language is indissolubly linked with social and linguistic conventions. Are there, for instance, differences between the way two same-sex friends address or speak of one another that might enable us to tell whether they are just good friends, or that they love each other non-sexually, or that one of them feels unreciprocated desire for the other, or that the two are lovers in the fullest sense of the word? In some of the Sonnets, including some of those in which it is clear that a male is addressing another male, we have seen an intensity of feeling that seems entirely compatible with the deepest and most physically fulfilled kind of love relationship, even though such an interpretation must depend on subjective reaction. And in many of the plays men and women address persons of the same sex with expressions of affection such as might imply to a modern reader or theatregoer that their relationship was of extraordinary intimacy.

But is there a danger of judging too much by the conventions of our own time? In English and American society of the present day heterosexual females, especially younger ones, are allowed, or allow themselves, considerable intimacy of expression both in language and in physical contact with no imputation of sexuality. Among heterosexual men, however, relatively laconic modes of address prevail. For one man to use terms of endearment, such as 'sweetheart', 'love', 'darling', or 'beloved' to another, and to embrace warmly or to kiss, would render them liable to be supposed to be in a sexual relationship.

In the past it would seem that greater freedoms prevailed. In Shakespeare's time, it has been said, 'the proper signs of friendship could be the same as those of same-gender passion.'[2] Take for example the opening dialogue of *The Two Gentlemen of Verona*, a play discussed earlier in Chapter 5 in the context of sexual desire and courtship between men and women. In the first line, Valentine addresses his friend as 'my loving Proteus', and Proteus replies with 'Sweet Valentine'; in the ensuing conversation—about love of women, which Valentine decries as a state 'where scorn is bought with groans'—they use the familiar second person singular 'thy', and on departing Valentine says 'Sweet Proteus'. This is mild enough, and can easily be taken as no more than adolescent expressions of affection; but the relationship between the young men has also been interpreted as indicative of an emotional bond that includes sexuality while being also a natural step on a journey towards heterosexuality—'only a phase', as the saying goes. In an extended discussion of the play within this context, it has been asserted that the opening lines 'insert the play into a discourse of homoerotic male friendship from its first conversation,'[3] and the play's Arden editor, William Carroll, notes that in production Proteus has been depicted as 'a confused young man sexually attracted to Valentine as well as Julia and then Silvia'.[4] This is an interpretation that the text allows even if it does not positively endorse it. But undoubtedly the play ends in heterosexual unions for both men.

Far stronger is the relationship in *The Merchant of Venice* between Antonio and Bassanio. Like Romeo, Bassanio is the wooer of a woman from the opening of the action, and is clearly young, whereas Antonio—like Mercutio (see p. 157)—is unattached, and will remain so throughout the play. There is no indication of his age. He expresses unexplained melancholy in the play's opening words—'In sooth, I know not why I am so sad.' When Solanio says he must be in love, Antonio replies enigmatically with 'Fie, fie.' There is nothing to suggest that he is interested in women. Bassanio speaks of Antonio's 'love' for him (at e.g. 1.1.131–2), as does Antonio of Bassanio (e.g. 1.1.154), but in the context of a promise to raise as much money as he can to assist Bassanio in his wooing of Portia. During the course of the action Antonio behaves with extraordinary, self-sacrificing generosity in assisting his friend to woo his bride, even putting his life at risk in Bassanio's service by wagering a pound of his own flesh on his friend's behalf. When news arrives that Antonio is in serious danger of having to pay the forfeit, an onlooker, Salerio, speaks with admiration and wonder of Antonio's kindness—'A kinder gentleman never trod the earth'—and of the depths of Antonio's love for his friend. Describing how the two parted, he reports, in a curiously precise visualization of bodily action, that

> his eye being big with tears,
> Turning his face, he put his hand behind him
> And, with affection wondrous sensible,
> He wrung Bassanio's hand; and so they parted.   (2.8.46–9)

To which Solanio responds with 'I think he only loves the world for him.' A strong testimonial to their love.

After Bassanio has successfully wooed Portia, and when he learns that Antonio's fortunes have all been lost, Bassanio speaks nobly of him as

> The dearest friend to me, the kindest man,
> The best-conditioned and unwearied spirit
> In doing courtesies, and one in whom
> The ancient Roman honour more appears
> Than any that draws breath in Italy.   (3.2.290–4)

All Antonio wants is that Bassanio should 'come | To see me pay his debt, and then I care not.' And when he believes himself about to die at Shylock's hands, he again speaks lovingly to and of Bassanio:

> Say how I loved you. Speak me fair in death,
> And when the tale is told, bid her [Portia] be judge
> Whether Bassanio had not once a love.

Bassanio responds in kind:

> Antonio, I am married to a wife
> Which is as dear to me as life itself,
> But life itself, my wife, and all the world
> Are not with me esteemed above thy life.
> I would lose all, ay, sacrifice them all
> Here to this devil, to deliver you.   (4.1.279–84)

Even allowing for the fact that the extremity of the situation might encourage hyperbole, this is a passionate avowal. There is no doubt that Bassanio's feelings for Portia are heterosexual. But that is not incompatible with the possibility that, as directors and actors have often suggested with fond looks, embraces, and kisses, Antonio loves Bassanio sexually, that Bassanio is emerging from a sexual relationship with Antonio, and even that Bassanio sustains bisexual affections with his friend to the end of the play. We cannot say that Shakespeare explicitly portrays a sexual relationship, but equally— as with the Sonnets—we cannot deny that the text permits such a subtextual reading. As Alan Sinfield remarks, Shakespeare's 'plays are pervaded by erotic interactions that strike chords for lesbians and gay men today'.[5]

Perhaps even stronger is the bond between another Antonio, the sea-captain in *Twelfth Night*, and Sebastian, whom he has rescued from shipwreck. Here there is a clear age difference. Antonio is an experienced seaman, Sebastian young enough to be the twin of a young woman, Viola, who in her disguise is several times addressed as 'boy' and who would have been played by a boy actor—as Sebastian too very likely was: the play has only three women characters, and the company for which the play was written probably numbered at least four boys among its numbers. This brings their relationship within the parameters of the sexual friendship between an adult male and an adolescent youth familiar to readers of Shakespeare's time from Greek and Roman literature which influenced, among others, Marlowe and

Barnfield. We have seen too that such sexual relationships existed between, for instance, the Earl of Oxford and young men in his household, though it is not easy to tell to what extent, if any, these were consensual. In two of Shakespeare's sonnets the poet addresses a 'boy'—'sweet boy' in Number 108, and 'my lovely boy' in 126. The transitoriness of a boy's love was proverbial—in *King Lear*, the Fool advises his master 'He's mad that trusts in the tameness of a wolf, a horse's health, a boy's love, or a whore's oath' (Sc. 13.14–15, Quarto only).

When we first see Antonio in *Twelfth Night* he is pressing his help upon Sebastian, who speaks explicitly of Antonio's love for him, as Antonio himself does: 'If you will not murder me for my love, let me be your servant' (2.1.31–2). And after the boy has left, rejecting Antonio's help, the older man declares

> I do adore thee so
> That danger shall seem sport, and I will go.

His statement bears a curious resemblance to the couplet of Sonnet 36 (which is repeated in Sonnet 96):

> But do not so; I love thee in such sort
> As thou being mine, mine is thy good report.

Go he does, despite danger, and when we next see them he says

> I could not stay behind you. My desire,
> More sharp than filèd steel, did spur me forth... (3.3.4–5)

Sebastian graciously accepts his assistance.

It is not surprising in view of Antonio's expression of intense 'desire'—the sexual connotations of the word cannot be avoided, especially in conjunction with the phallic image of the filed—sharpened— steel blade, that his feelings for Sebastian have been interpreted as homoerotic. During the course of the action Sebastian cheerfully accepts Olivia's sexual advances, but Antonio's resentment when, as he mistakenly believes, his 'god' rejects his plea for help (3.4.333) is bitter. He had 'snatched' him 'out of the jaws of death, | Relieved him with such sanctity of love, | And to his image' had done 'devotion'. Defending himself before Orsino in the final scene he repeats the claim that he had redeemed Sebastian 'From the rude sea's enraged and foamy mouth' and that, like that other Antonio in *The Merchant of Venice*, he had risked his life for the young man's sake, speaking of the 'witchcraft' that the 'most ingrateful boy' exercised, and of his 'love without retention or restraint'.

Olivia, understandably bewildered on hearing the person she believes to be her husband swearing that 'he' loves Orsino 'More by all mores than e'er I shall love wife', exclaims 'Ay me detested, how am I beguiled'—which is tantamount to saying that she thinks Sebastian must be gay.[6] And Orsino's torments over Cesario/Viola, as he declares that he will 'Kill what I love' and 'sacrifice the lamb that I do love' (5.1.117, 128) might imply the same about him. Olivia soon learns otherwise, but Sebastian continues to express affection for Antonio, addressing him, after the complications of the action have been sorted out, as 'my dear Antonio', and exclaiming 'How have the hours racked and tortured me | Since I have lost thee!' This is almost the last we hear of Antonio, though he is given no clear exit from the scene. Like his namesake in *The Merchant of Venice*, he is not included in the play's happy ending—unless, that is, the director decides otherwise.

Stephen Orgel has described Antonio and Sebastian as being 'the only overtly homosexual couple in Shakespeare except for Achilles and Patroclus'.[7] They have been portrayed so in performance, notably in Lindsay Posner's Stratford *Twelfth Night* of 2001 in which we first saw Antonio embracing a youthful Sebastian on a bed; the warmth of Antonio's embraces of the boy made it clear that they had just slept together. (See Plate 14) But while I agree with Orgel that the text portrays sexual desire for Sebastian on Antonio's behalf, and that Sebastian has loving feelings for the older man, I am less certain that Shakespeare intended to portray a fully realized sexual union. The play is full of the yearning of unreciprocated love, portrayed both comically and seriously; this may well be one of the instances of it.

The case is different with Achilles and Patroclus in *Troilus and Cressida*. Their relationship was well known from Greek legend:

> The conquering Hercules for Hylas wept;
> And for Patroclus stern Achilles drooped,

wrote Marlowe in *Edward II*.[8] The exact nature of the relationship was much discussed. Within the play itself the scurrilous Thersites expresses a characteristically reductive view. 'Thou art thought to be Achilles' male varlet', 'his masculine whore', he says to Patroclus, who does not deign to reply. This is the only derogatory remark in the whole of Shakespeare to what may be regarded as homoerotic behaviour. Shakespeare, unlike many of his contemporaries, never uses potentially scornful words such as 'ingle' and 'ganymede' to refer to boys who love men ('cat', as an abbreviation of catamite, is a possible exception: *All's Well That Ends Well*, 4.3.242–3, 267, 277.)

Many critics have aligned themselves with Thersites, often in homophobic terms. A. P. Rossiter, in 1961, described Patroclus as Achilles's 'catamite',[9] and Jan Kott was even more scornful than Thersites, writing that 'The great Achilles, the heroic Achilles, the legendary Achilles wallows in his bed with his male tart—Patroclus. He is a homosexual, he is boastful, stupid and quarrelsome like an old hag.'[10] There is no bed in the play's stage directions—this, like much of what Kott wrote, is a fantasy taking off from the text, not a valid reading of it.

Shakespeare, however, places a far more romantic view of the relationship in the mouth of Patroclus himself. After Ulysses has accused him of cowardice, Patroclus says:

> To this effect, Achilles, have I moved you.
> A woman impudent and mannish grown

Is not more loathed than an effeminate man
In time of action. I stand condemned for this.
They think my little stomach to the war
And your great love to me restrains you thus.
Sweet, rouse yourself, and the weak wanton Cupid
Shall from your neck unloose his amorous fold
And like a dew-drop from the lion's mane
Be shook to air.   (3.3.209–18)

There is ambiguity here. The word 'effeminate' could mean over-influenced by women. Achilles is married, to Polyxena—though we never see her—and the phrase 'the weak wanton Cupid' could refer to his love for her, not to Patroclus. But 'your great love to me' is strong and unambiguous; I see no reason to doubt that Shakespeare was imagining a fully realized sexual relationship between the two men. This is certainly how it is usually portrayed in production. But, as Sinfield notes, Patroclus, like Achilles, 'is also interested in women; he kisses Cressida enthusiastically, and Thersites says he is eager to hear of promising whores'.[11]

Achilles and Patroclus are warriors. So are Coriolanus and Aufidius. Indeed for much of *Coriolanus* they are deadly enemies. Nevertheless after Coriolanus has defected to the enemy camp, Shakespeare causes Aufidius to clasp his former adversary in a warm embrace and to address him in terms loaded with homoerotic implications:

Here I clip
The anvil of my sword, and do contest
As hotly and as nobly with thy love
As ever in ambitious strength I did
Contend against thy valour. Know thou first,
I loved the maid I married; never man
Sighed truer breath. But that I see thee here,
Thou noble thing, more dances my rapt heart
Than when I first my wedded mistress saw
Bestride my threshold.   (4.5.110–19)

Though the lines include an assertion of heterosexuality in their reference to Coriolanus's wife, Virgilia, it is impossible not to take them as an expression of a passionately homoerotic attraction at least on the part of Coriolanus to Aufidius. It would be easy to interpret Coriolanus in Freudian terms as an emotionally immature, over-mothered warrior. Roger Warren's description of the encounter in Elijah Moshinsky's television production shows how this subtext can be brought to the surface:

> Coriolanus and Aufidius fought the duel virtually naked. After they had beaten the weapons out of each other's hands, they continued to grapple, their hands around one another's throats—but the stranglehold became almost an embrace: as they stared infatuated into each other's eyes, there was a cross-cut back to Rome. The effect was repeated when Coriolanus went to Antium. Aufidius took Coriolanus by the throat before embracing him and massaging his chest slowly and intently as he said that to see Coriolanus there 'more dances my rapt heart | Than when I first my wedded mistress saw | Bestride my threshold'.[12] (See Plate 12)

*

Just as King James addressed Buckingham as his 'wife' (pp. 37–8), so, in the last play in which Shakespeare had a hand, *The Two Noble Kinsmen*, the imprisoned Arcite says to his cousin Palamon 'We are one another's wife, ever begetting | New births of love' (2.2.80–1). Like *The Two Gentlemen of Verona*, this play, written jointly by Shakespeare and John Fletcher, draws on the common Renaissance debate between the claims of friendship and of heterosexual love. Arcite's declaration comes during a long conversation in which, though he has bemoaned the likelihood that they will never know 'The sweet embraces of a loving wife | Loaden with kisses', they have consoled themselves with the thought of their love for one another, and in which Palamon has asked 'Is there record of any two that loved | Better than we do, Arcite?' They sustain an antiphon of mutual admiration and of expressions of eternal love which with calculated, and typically Fletcherian, irony reaches its climax—'after death our spirits shall be led | To those that love eternally'—at the very moment that the woman with whom they are both destined simultaneously and instantly to fall in love comes within their view. Palamon is the first to see her—later, rather childishly, he lays claim to her on this account—'I saw her first'—and within seconds they are quarrelling over her affections. Their rivalry for her love forms the backbone of the play, leading to theatrically effective if psychologically implausible episodes which exploit the tension between their mutual affection and their rivalry for the hand of Emilia.

There seems little doubt that the dramatists—the scene is generally attributed to Fletcher, but both authors must be held responsible for it—have calculated the scene to titillate by raising homoerotic expectations while later denying their implications. This impression is strengthened by the fact that the play includes from Emilia what is probably the strongest expression of love of one female for another in the canon, which asserts that such love may be valued above that between man and woman, and which uses physically erotic imagery to do so. Recalling her childhood love for Flavina, who died when they were both aged eleven, Emilia says

> The flower that I would pluck
> And put between my breasts—O then but beginning
> To swell about the blossom—she would long
> Till she had such another, and commit it
> To the like innocent cradle, where, phoenix-like,
> They died in perfume. On my head no toy
> But was her pattern. Her affections—pretty,
> Though happily her careless wear—I followed
> For my most serious decking. Had mine ear
> Stol'n some new air, or at adventure hummed one,
> From musical coinage, why, it was a note
> Whereon her spirits would sojourn—rather dwell on—
> And sing it in her slumbers. This rehearsal—
> Which, seely innocence wots well, comes in

Like old emportment's bastard—has this end:
That the true love 'tween maid and maid may be
More than in sex dividual.[13]   (1.3.66–82)

And she declares that she will never love a man. In the end, however, despite her devotion to 'chaste Diana', Emilia accepts Palamon as a gift from the dying Arcite.

The intricate style of her speech about Flavina, typical of late Shakespeare, proclaims him as its chief, if not only, author. Shakespeare portrays other intense female friendships, between for instance Hermia and Helena in *A Midsummer Night's Dream* and Rosalind and Celia in *As You Like It*. These too have been interpreted homoerotically: Valerie Traub writes, for example, that 'Cheek by Jowl's 1991 *As You Like It* portrayed Celia in love with Rosalind, but did so through the mediation of an all-male cast.'[14] And for her *A Midsummer Night's Dream* is 'suffused' with 'homoerotics'.[15]

It is inescapable that both readers and performers react to the characters in a play as if they were real people. In doing so they respond to what lies underneath the surface of the text—its 'subtext'—as well as to the words themselves. In this they may be influenced, as we have seen that Laurence Olivier was in his portrayal of Iago, by the findings of psychoanalysis. If they find homosexuality it seems right that they should project it to their readers and their audiences. This does not necessarily mean that they will be expressing Shakespeare's implicit meanings. Dramatic texts take on lives of their own in relation to the society in which they are performed and to the personalities of those who experience them. The plays read us, just as we read them.

CONCLUSION

Throughout his career Shakespeare was interested, both as a writer and no doubt as a man, in human sexuality. When I began to write this book I called it *Shakespeare and Sex*. Shakespeare found in sex an inexhaustible topic for poetry and for drama of all kinds, both comic and tragic, and one that grew in him as he developed in experience of life and of art. As I went on, and especially as I wrote about Shakespeare's own work, I came to feel that he continually saw sex as an instrument of relationships between people, and one that cannot—or should not—be divorced from love. I came to feel that I knew him a little better as I traced his involvement with the topic, not entirely in chronological order of the composition of his work but with some sense of development and change. He knew of the dangers of mistaking animal desire for a higher passion, that the sexual instinct is one that may be misused, that it can lead to rape and murder, to a prostitution of all that is best in man. But he knew too that sex is an essential component of even the highest forms of human love, that it can lead to a sublime realization of the self in a near-mystical union of personalities such as he figures forth in his poem 'The Phoenix and Turtle'.

Understanding of Shakespeare's attitudes to sex has grown along with studies of language and of sexuality. We know more than our ancestors did about the complexities of our inner selves. Scholars of human psychology and physiology as well as of literature and drama, critics, directors, and actors have deepened our understanding of what he wrote in itself and of the ways that it can be reinterpreted, even adapted, to figure forth the emotional complexities of successive generations. Shakespeare gives us no easy answers, but he goes on helping us, if not to understand, at least to explore ourselves through his depiction of an amazing range of human sexual experience.

NOTES

Introduction

1 See e.g. Marvin Rosenberg, *The Masks of Othello* (Berkeley/Los Angeles: University of California Press, 1961), 56–60.

2 Robert Bridges, *Collected Essays Papers* etc., 30 parts (Oxford: Oxford University Press, 1927–36), i.28.

3 Jonathan Bate and Russell Jackson (eds), *Shakespeare: An Illustrated Stage History* (Oxford: Oxford University Press, 1996), 204–5.

4 I write about this in my *Looking for Sex in Shakespeare* (Cambridge: Cambridge University Press, 2004), 73–5.

5 Gordon Williams, *A Dictionary of Sexual Language and Imagery in Shakespearean and Stuart Literature*, 3 vols (London: Athlone Press, 1994), under 'soul'.

6 Christopher Marlowe, *Complete Plays*, ed. M. T. Burnett (London: J. M. Dent, Everyman, 1999), 4.1.92.

7 Pauline Kiernan, *Filthy Shakespeare* (London: Quercus, 2006).

Chapter 1: Sexuality in Shakespeare's Time

1 A. L. Rowse, *Simon Forman: Sex and Society in Shakespeare's Age* (London: Weidenfeld and Nicolson, 1974).

2 Jeanne Jones, *Family Life in Shakespeare's England: Stratford-upon-Avon 1570–1630* (Stroud: Shakespeare Birthplace Trust, 1996), 90.

3 Ibid.

4 Ibid. 86.

5 E. R. C. Brinkworth, *Shakespeare and the Bawdy Court of Stratford* (London/Chichester: Phillimore, 1972), 75–6.

6 Jones, *Family Life*, 86.

7 Brinkworth, *Bawdy Court*, 86–7.

8 David Cressy, 'Espousals, Betrothals, and Contracts', in *Birth, Marriage and Death: Ritual, Religion and the Life-Cycle in Tudor and Stuart England* (Oxford: Oxford University Press, 1997).

9 Ibid. 277.

10 Brinkworth, *Bawdy Court*, 70–1.
11 Bruce R. Smith, *Homosexual Desire in Shakespeare's England: A Cultural Poetics* (Chicago: Chicago University Press, 1991, rpt 1994), 87.
12 Germaine Greer, *Shakespeare's Wife* (London: Bloomsbury, 2007), 96.
13 Lena Cowen Orlin, *Locating Privacy in Tudor London* (Oxford: Oxford University Press, 2008), 141.
14 Duncan Salkeld, 'The Case of Elizabeth Evans', *Notes and Queries* 50:1 (2003), 60–1. I am grateful to Dr Salkeld for allowing me to see and use his complete transcripts of the case. Salkeld's article corrects the references in Park Honan, *Shakespeare: A Life* (Oxford, Oxford University Press, 1998), 310–11.
15 The case is recorded in C. J. Sisson's *Lost Plays of Shakespeare's Age* (Cambridge: Cambridge University Press, 1936), to which my account, adapted from my book *Shakespeare & Co* (London: Allen Lane Press, 2007), is deeply indebted.
16 B. T. Boehrer, 'Bestial Buggery in *A Midsummer Night's Dream*', in D. L. Miller et al. (eds), *The Production of English Renaissance Culture* (Ithaca/London: Cornell University Press, 1994), 123–50; quoted from 149.
17 Peter Laslett, *The World We Have Lost Further Explored*, 3rd edn (London: Methuen, 2000), 156–7.
18 Orlin, *Locating Privacy*, 218–19.
19 An earlier playhouse, the Red Lion, of 1567, lasted for only a few months.
20 This is, incidentally, a piece of evidence to be held against the Chorus in *Romeo and Juliet*'s reference to the 'two-hours' traffic of our stage'.
21 E. K. Chambers, *The Elizabethan Stage*, 4 vols (Oxford: Clarendon Press, 1932), iv.195.
22 Ibid. iv.197.
23 Ibid. iv.223–4.
24 Clare Williams (trans. and ed.), *Thomas Platter's Travels in England 1599* (London: Jonathan Cape, 1937), 175.
25 In Thomas Middleton, *Complete Works*, gen. ed. Gary Taylor and John Lavagnino (Oxford: Oxford University Press, 2007), 5.2.33–40.
26 Quoted in Glynne Wickham et al. (eds), *English Professional Theatre, 1530–1660* (Cambridge: Cambridge University Press, 2000), 173.
27 The ballad is reprinted in my *Shakespeare & Co.*, 242–3.
28 Wickham, *English Professional Theatre*, 17.
29 Duncan Salkeld, 'Literary Traces in Bridewell and Bethlem, 1602–24', *RES* NS 56:225 (2005), 379–85, quotation from 382.

30 An interesting account of him is given by Roger Prior, 'The Life of George Wilkins', *Shakespeare Survey* 25 (1972), 137–52.

31 *The Works of Thomas Nashe*, ed. R. B. McKerrow (Oxford: Basil Blackwell, rpt 1958), ii.152–3.

32 Rowse, *Simon Forman*, 288.

33 Smith, *Homosexual Desire*, 8.

34 Rowse, *Simon Forman*, 99.

35 Michael Wood, *In Search of Shakespeare* (London: BBC, 2003), 200–3. René Weis, *Shakespeare Revealed: A Biography* (London, John Murray, 2007), 148.

36 William Googe, *Of Domestical Duties* (London, 1622), 500. I owe this reference to Dr Jane Kingsley-Smith.

37 Smith, *Homosexual Desire*, 48–51.

38 Ibid. 53.

39 Alan Sinfield, *Shakespeare, Authority, Sexuality* (London: Routledge, 2006), 59–60; also 77, where 'people' becomes 'gay and bisexual people'.

40 Ibid. 60.

41 Smith, *Homosexual Desire*, 84.

42 Cited by Russ McDonald, *The Bedford Companion to Shakespeare* (Boston: Bedford Books, 1996), 291.

43 Mary Bly, *Queer Virgins and Virgin Queans on the Early Modern Stage* (Oxford: Oxford University Press, 2000), 6.

44 A. L. Rowse, *Shakespeare's Southampton: Patron of Virginia* (London: Macmillan, 1965), 162.

45 Alan Nelson, *Monstrous Adversary: The Life of Edward de Vere, 17th Earl of Oxford* (Liverpool: Liverpool University Press), 213–17.

46 Quoted in Alan Stewart, *The Cradle King: A Life of James VI and I* (London: Chatto and Windus, 2003), 341.

47 Kyd's note is reprinted in Park Honan, *Christopher Marlowe, Poet and Spy* (Oxford: Oxford University Press, 2005), 381.

48 Ibid. 374.

49 Quoted in Lisa Jardine and Alan Stewart, *Hostage to Fortune: The Troubled Life of Francis Bacon 1561–1626* (London: Victor Gollancz, 1998), 465.

50 Daphne du Maurier, *Golden Lads: A Study of Anthony Bacon, Francis and their Friends* (London: Victor Gollancz, 1975; rpt. Virago Press, 2007), 227–8. See also Jardine and Stewart, *Hostage to Fortune*, 107–9.

51 But see Valerie Traub, *The Renaissance of Lesbianism in Early Modern England* (Cambridge: Cambridge University Press, 2002).

52 Quoted in Louis Crompton, *Homosexuality and Civilization* (Cambridge, MA: Harvard University Press, 2006), 398.
53 Thomas Middleton, *The Roaring Girl*, ed. P. Mulholland (Manchester: Manchester University Press, 1997), appendix E, p. 262.
54 Middleton, *Complete Works*, 721.

Chapter 2: Sex and Poetry in Shakespeare's Time

1 See Gary Taylor, 'Shakespeare and Others: The Authorship of *Henry the Sixth, Part One*', *Medieval and Renaissance Drama in English* 7 (1995), 145–205.
2 Thomas Nashe, *Selected Writings*, ed. S. Wells (London: Edward Arnold, 1964), 231.
3 Lawrence Stone mistakenly writes that 'Native English pornography as a literary genre seems to have had its tentative beginnings in the scurrilous and mildly obscene poems about sexual life at the court in the 1620s, which circulated widely in manuscript' (*The Family, Sex and Marriage in England 1500–1800* (New York: Harper and Row, 1977), 335). Valerie Traub (*The Renaissance of Lesbianism in Early Modern England* (Cambridge: Cambridge University Press, 2002), 104) writes, 'It is a peculiarity of the history of English censorship' that the poem 'was not burned among other obscene, scurrilous, and satiric texts in London during the Bishop's Ban of 1599— perhaps because it had not yet come to the attention of the authorities.' But surely it is because it had not been printed.
4 *The Works of Thomas Nashe*, ed. R. B. McKerrow (Oxford: Basil Blackwell, rpt 1958), v.141.
5 The *OED* explains this phrase as 'comports oneself vaingloriously'.
6 Gordon Williams, *Glossary of Shakespeare's Sexual Language* (London: Athlone Press, 1997), under 'conscience'.
7 Louis Crompton, *Homosexuality and Civilization* (Cambridge, MA: Harvard University Press, 2006), 398.
8 This stanza, remarks Alan Sinfield, 'surely promises fellatio followed by sodomy' (*Shakespeare, Authority, Sexuality* (London: Routledge, 2006), 146).
9 Could Shakespeare have remembered Barnfield's lines in writing his play?
10 Richard Barnfield, *The Complete Poems*, ed. George Klawitter (Selinsgrove: Susquehanna University Press, 1990), 126.
11 Ibid. 127.

12 Paul Hammond, *Figuring Sex between Men from Shakespeare to Rochester* (Oxford: Oxford University Press, 2002), 72–84.

13 Andrew Worrall, 'Richard Barnfield: A New Biography', *Notes and Queries* (Sept. 1992), 170–1, corrects Klawitter on Barnfield's biography, showing that he died in 1620, not 1627, and that there is no evidence that he married and had a son as was previously believed, but that he had been disinherited in favour of his younger brother.

14 Anne Lake Prescott, 'Drayton, Michael (1563–1631)', in *Oxford Dictionary of National Biography* (Oxford: Oxford University Press, 2004).

15 Lemuel Whitaker, 'The Sonnets of Michael Drayton', *Modern Philology* 1:4 (April 1904), 563–7.

16 Prescott, 'Drayton'.

17 That is, the light sock worn by comic actors in Greek and Roman comedy.

18 Mary Bly, *Queer Virgins and Virgin Queans on the Early Modern Stage* (Oxford: Oxford University Press, 2000), 98, citing Alan Stewart, *Close Readers: Humanism and Sodomy in Early Modern England* (Princeton: Princeton University Press, 1997), 152–3. Stewart's pp. 148–60 are devoted to a study of 'Friendly Reading Together: Or, Studying for Action?: Another "Profe" of Amicitia'.

19 Barnfield, *Complete Poems*, 82 (emphasis mine).

20 Bruce Smith remarks that Barnfield's epistle 'To the courteous gentlemen readers' in *The Affectionate Shepherd* 'is addressed to one group of gentlemen in particular, the gentlemen of the Inns of court' (*Homosexual Desire in Shakespeare's England: A Cultural Poetics* (Chicago: Chicago University Press, 1991, rpt 1994), 102).

21 Bly, *Queer Virgins*, 103.

22 Quoted in e.g. E. K. Chambers, *William Shakespeare: A Study of Facts and Problems*, 2 vols (Oxford: Clarendon Press, 1930), ii.194.

23 In Thomas Middleton, *Complete Works*, gen. ed. Gary Taylor and John Lavagnino (Oxford: Oxford University Press, 2007), 1.2.46–9.

24 Cited by Lawrence Danson, *Wilde's Intentions* (Oxford: Oxford University Press, 1997), 120–1.

25 Katherine Duncan-Jones, *Ungentle Shakespeare* (London: Thomson Learning, 2001), 73.

26 Paul Edmondson, 'The narrative poetry of Marlowe and Shakespeare', in *The Cambridge History of English Poetry*, ed. Michael O'Neill (Cambridge: Cambridge University Press, 2010), 188–9.

27 Quoted in Chambers, *William Shakespeare*, ii.218.

28 Paul Edmondson and Stanley Wells, *Shakespeare's Sonnets* (Oxford: Oxford University Press, 2004), 30–1. They are reprinted, along with the narrative poems, in Stanley Wells (ed.), *Shakespeare Found!* (Stratford-upon-Avon: Cobbe Foundation and The Shakespeare Birthplace Trust, 2009).

29 See e.g. Germaine Greer, *Shakespeare's Wife* (London: Bloomsbury, 2007), 260–1.

30 Edmondson and Wells, *Shakespeare's Sonnets*, 30.

31 Andrew Gurr, 'Shakespeare's First Poem', *Essays in Criticism* 21:3 (July, 1971), 221–6.

32 See Chapter 10, 'The Critical Reputation of the Sonnets', in Edmondson and Wells, *Shakespeare's Sonnets*, 131–44.

33 Ibid.

34 Joseph Pequigney, *Such Is My Love: A Study of Shakespeare's Sonnets* (Chicago: University of Chicago Press, 1985), 155–88.

Chapter 3: Shakespeare and Sex

1 Louis Crompton, *Homosexuality and Civilization* (Cambridge, MA: Harvard University Press, 2006), 367.

2 Cited in S. Schoenbaum, *Shakespeare's Lives* (Oxford: Oxford University Press, 1991), 239.

3 Quoted in Lawrence Stone, *The Family, Sex and Marriage in England 1500–1800* (New York: Harper and Row, 1977), 497.

4 Modernized from the citation by Bruce R. Smith, *Homosexual Desire in Shakespeare's England: A Cultural Poetics* (Chicago: Chicago University Press, 1991, rpt 1994), 147.

5 Mary Edmond, *Rare Sir William Davenant* (Manchester: Manchester University Press, 1987), 14.

6 Smith, *Homosexual Desire*, 229. Presumably he refers only to the poems concerning a woman.

7 William Shakespeare, *Complete Sonnets and Poems*, ed. Colin Burrow, Oxford Shakespeare (Oxford: Oxford University Press, 2002), note to Sonnet 153, l.

8 Katherine Duncan-Jones, *Ungentle Shakespeare* (London: Thomson Learning, 2001), 224.

9 Michael R. G. Spiller, *The Development of the Sonnet* (London: Routledge, 1992), 156.

10 Germaine Greer, *Shakespeare's Wife* (London: Bloomsbury, 2007), Chap. 7.

11 Paul Edmondson and Stanley Wells, *Shakespeare's Sonnets* (Oxford: Oxford University Press, 2004), 4–5.

12 E. K. Chambers, *William Shakespeare: A Study of Facts and Problems*, 2 vols (Oxford: Oxford University Press, 1930), ii.12–13.

13 E. R. C. Brinkworth, *Shakespeare and the Bawdy Court of Stratford* (London/ Chichester: Phillimore, 1972), 143.

Chapter 4: The Fun of Sex

1 The same pun occurs in *The Taming of the Shrew*, Induction 2.122, where Sly says, 'Ay, it stands so that I may hardly tarry so long.' Perhaps most memorably, it underlies the Porter's remarks in *Macbeth* that drink 'provokes the desire but it takes away the performance'; it makes a man 'stand to and not stand to' (2.3.28–33).

2 Gordon Williams, *A Dictionary of Sexual Language and Imagery in Shakespearean and Stuart Literature*, 3 vols (London: Athlone Press, 1994).

3 *Much Ado About Nothing*, ed. Claire McEachern, Arden Shakespeare (London: Thomson Learning, 2006), note to 5.2.16–17.

4 Ibid. note to 5.2.21.

5 Gordon Williams, *Glossary of Shakespeare's Sexual Language* (London: Athlone Press, 1997), 75.

6 This situation is turned on its head in Fletcher's sequel, *The Tamer Tamed*: see my *Shakespeare & Co.* (London: Allen Lane Press, 2007), 20–5.

7 Printed as an Additional Passage in the Oxford *Complete Works*.

8 Paul Edmondson, 'Liking It', in Irina S. Prikhod'ko (ed.), *Rubrica's Shakespeare Studies* (Moscow: Polygraph-Inform, 2006), 112–22, quotation from 117.

9 Pete Kirwan, '*The Merry Wives of Windsor* @ Shakespeare's Globe', *The Bardathon* (published online August 26, 2008) <http://blogs.warwick.ac.uk/ pkirwan> accessed 22 February 2009. The production was directed by Christopher Luscombe, who had offered a similar interpretation when he played the role at Stratford in 1996.

Chapter 5: Sexual Desire

1 In performance this can be used to indicate that he is experiencing an erection.

2 The notion of wooing 'like a soldier' recalls Theseus's paradoxical claim to Hippolyta: 'I wooed thee with my sword, | And won thy love doing thee injuries' (*A Midsummer Night's Dream*, 1.1.16–17), but Theseus might mean

that Hippolyta came to love him out of admiration for his military prowess, even though it was directed against her.

3 See e.g. Brian Vickers, *Shakespeare: Co-Author* (Oxford: Oxford University Press, 2002), Chap. 3.

4 Barbara Everett has written that 'Shakespeare "knew", in some sense, all the rules of his art, and then some. He probably knew from the beginning what he wanted to do, and he spent the whole of his career learning how to do it' ('Making and Breaking in Shakespeare's Romances', *London Review of Books* (22 March 2007), 19).

5 It has always seemed odd that characters in a play set in Vienna should have Italian names; the theory that the play was originally set in Italy, possible Ferrara, is strongly propounded by John Jowett, 'The Audacity of *Measure for Measure* in 1621', *Ben Jonson Journal* 8 (2001), 229–48.

6 *Measure for Measure*, ed. N. W. Bawcutt, Oxford Shakespeare (Oxford: Oxford University Press, 1991), note to 2.4.102–3.

7 Brian Gibbons (ed.), *Measure for Measure*, New Cambridge Shakespeare (Cambridge: Cambridge University Press, 1991), notes to 2.4.101 and 103.

8 Frank Kermode, who regards the second half of the play as 'a muddle', says that 'as a tragicomedy it fails because the contrivances of the poet too much resemble those of the Duke' (*Shakespeare's Language* (London: Allen Lane Press, 2000), 164).

9 There is a parallel in *King Lear* when Edgar says, 'Why I do trifle thus with his despair | Is done to cure it' (4.5.33–4). In both plays this can be seen as Shakespeare offering his audience an excuse for morally dubious behaviour on the part of his characters.

10 Matthew 7:1–2, Geneva Bible.

11 Matthew 5:38.

12 *Measure for Measure*, ed. Bawcutt, 40.

13 *All's Well That Ends Well*, ed. Susan Snyder, Oxford Shakespeare (Oxford: Oxford University Press, 1993), note to 1.1.34.

14 Gordon Williams, *Glossary of Shakespeare's Sexual Language* (London: Athlone Press, 1997), 'blow up'.

15 Susan Willis, *The BBC Shakespeare Plays: Making the Televised Canon* (Chapel Hill: University of North Carolina Press, 1991), 149.

16 It is not clear whether Bertram is one of these lords, or whether he stands aside with Lafeu and Paroles. See *All's Well That Ends Well*, ed. Snyder, n. to 2.3.52.1.

Chapter 6: Sex and Love in *Romeo and Juliet*

1 Roger Allam, 'Mercutio in *Romeo and Juliet*', in Russell Jackson and Robert Smallwood (eds), *Players of Shakespeare* 2 (Cambridge: Cambridge University Press, 1988), 114.

2 *Romeo and Juliet*, ed. James N. Loehlin, Shakespeare in Production series (Cambridge: Cambridge University Press, 2002), 80.

3 John Downes, *Roscius Anglicanus*, cited ibid. 7.

4 I modernize Brooke from the reprint in Geoffrey Bullough, *Narrative and Dramatic Sources of Shakespeare*, 7 vols (London: Routledge and Kegan Paul, 1957–75), i.284–363.

5 Ibid. 284.

6 Ibid. 285.

7 Gordon Williams, *A Dictionary of Sexual Language and Imagery in Shakespearean and Stuart Literature*, 3 vols (London: Athlone Press, 1994).

8 So also Dogberry, in *Much Ado About Nothing*: 'and which is more, as pretty a piece of flesh as any is in Messina' (4.2.79–80).

9 Punning on the sense of carrying a child.

10 Dover Wilson/G. I. Duthie's New Cambridge edition of 1955 read 'open ars and'.

11 Allam, 'Mercutio in *Romeo and Juliet*', 112.

12 Quoted by Peter Holding, *Romeo and Juliet*, Text and Performance series (Basingstoke: Macmillan, 1992), 55.

13 Allam, 'Mercutio in *Romeo and Juliet*', 115.

14 It could also mean 'semen', a sense that is relevant here.

15 'I will bite thee by the ear for that jest' (2.3.72).

16 Paul Hammond, *Love between Men in English Literature* (New York: St Martin's Press, 1996), 59.

17 Russell Jackson (ed.), *Romeo and Juliet*, Shakespeare at Stratford series (London: Arden Shakespeare, 2003), 99.

18 According to Loehlin (ed.), *Romeo and Juliet*, 123, this originated with Zeffirelli's film.

19 Niamh Cusack, 'Juliet in *Romeo and Juliet*', in Jackson and Smallwood (eds), *Players of Shakespeare* 2, 125.

20 Peter Holland, *English Shakespeares* (Cambridge: Cambridge University Press, 1997), 269.

21 Loehlin (ed.), *Romeo and Juliet*, 106.

22 4.3.12–13, 4.4.31–3.

23 See T. J. B. Spencer, 'English (English, Scots, Anglo-Irish and American)', in A. T. Hatto (ed.), *Eos: An Enquiry into the Theme of Lovers' Meetings and Partings at Dawn* (Mouton: The Hague, 1965), 505–53.

24 Loehlin (ed.), *Romeo and Juliet*, 193.

25 Ibid. 194.

26 Jackson (ed.), *Romeo and Juliet*, 165.

27 In Baz Luhrmann's film, the Liebestod from Wagner's *Tristan und Isolde* sounded at this point. In a hangover from David Garrick's adaptation, Juliet showed signs of life to the viewer—though not to Romeo—before he died.

28 Romeo's mother is not there, having suddenly died, I suspect from grief because Shakespeare knew that the boy who had taken her role was needed for another part.

Chapter 7: Sexual Jealousy

1 Song of Solomon 8.6, Geneva Bible.

2 *Much Ado About Nothing*, ed. Claire McEachern, Arden Shakespeare (London: Thomson Learning, 2006), 18.

3 See e.g. Penny Gay, *As She Likes It* (London: Routledge, 1994), 161, and McEachern (ed.), Arden Shakespeare edn, 18.

4 McEachern (ed.), Arden Shakespeare edn, 260.

5 S. T. Coleridge, *Coleridge's Shakespeare Criticism*, ed. T. M. Raysor, 2 vols (London: Dent, 1960), i.49.

6 Bruce Smith, *Homosexual Desire in Shakespeare's England: A Cultural Poetics* (Chicago: Chicago University Press, 1991, rpt 1994), 61.

7 Lois Potter, *Othello*, Shakespeare in Performance series (Manchester: Manchester University Press, 2002), 92.

8 Cited in my *Looking for Sex in Shakespeare* (Cambridge: Cambridge University Press, 2004), 86.

9 Potter, *Othello*, 174.

10 Ibid. 195, referring to Oliver Parker's film (1994).

11 'Peevish' seems to have had a stronger sense than now; Michael Neill, in his edition in the Oxford Shakespeare series (2006), glosses it as 'foolish, mad; malignant; headstrong'.

12 A. C. Bradley, *Shakespearean Tragedy* (London: Macmillan, 1904; rpt 1957), 161.

13 T. S. Eliot, 'Shakespeare and the Stoicism of Seneca', in *Selected Essays* (London: Faber and Faber, 1951), 130–1.

14 Gordon Williams, A *Glossary of Shakespeare's Sexual Language* (London: Athlone Press, 1997), 'nectar'.

15 Claire M. Tyler, 'The Text of Cressida and Every Ticklish Reader: *Troilus and Cressida*, the Greek Camp Scene', *Shakespeare Survey* 41 (1990), 63–76.

16 The Bishop of Winchester had jurisdiction over the South Bank.

17 Antony Sher, 'How I Got into the Mad Bard's Head', *The Guardian*, 2 January 1999.

18 Stephen Orgel, 'The Poetics of Incomprehensibility', *Shakespeare Quarterly* 42 (1991), 431–7.

Chapter 8: Sex and Experience

1 E. A. M. Colman, *The Dramatic Use of Bawdy in Shakespeare* (London: Longman, 1974), 115.

2 Gordon Williams, A *Glossary of Shakespeare's Sexual Language* (London: Athlone Press, 1997).

3 Heeds not his own advice.

4 Gordon Williams, A *Dictionary of Sexual Language and Imagery in Shakespearean and Stuart Literature*, 3 vols (London: Athlone Press, 1994).

5 *King Lear*, ed. Kenneth Muir, Arden Shakespeare (London, 1972), note to 5.3.238.

6 Paul Edmondson points to an interesting parallel between the last sentence and John Donne's 'Meditation XVII': 'No man is an island, entire of itself; every man is a piece of the continent, a part of the main. If a clod be washed away by the sea, Europe is the less, as well as if a promontory were, as well as if a manor of thy friend's or of thine own were: any man's death diminishes me, because I am involved in mankind.'

Chapter 9: Whores and Saints

1 E. A. M. Colman, however, says that the Prince 'does not include women in his much-discussed "loose behaviour"' (*The Dramatic Use of Bawdy in Shakespeare* (London: Longman, 1974), 99).

2 *Henry IV, Part One*, ed. David Bevington, Oxford Shakespeare (Oxford: Oxford University Press, 1998), note to 3.3.125.

3 Another possible reference is Abraham Slender's reaction to his discovery that he has taken a boy for a girl: 'If I had been married to him, for all he was in woman's apparel, I would not have had him' (*The Merry Wives of Windsor*, 5.5.188–90).

4 *Henry IV, Part Two*, ed. René Weis, Oxford Shakespeare (Oxford: Oxford University Press, 1997), note to 2.4.48.

5 Gordon Williams, *A Glossary of Shakespeare's Sexual Language* (London: Athlone Press, 1997).

6 A Bartholomew pig was a pig traditionally roasted at the Bartholomew Fair.

7 *Henry IV, Part Two*, ed. Weis, note to 3.2.302. Parts of this speech are found only in the Quarto text, and therefore are printed among Additional Passages in the Oxford Complete Works edition.

8 *The Winter's Tale*, ed. Stephen Orgel, Oxford Shakespeare (Oxford: Oxford University Press, 1996), 58.

9 This is rather easier to solve than the riddle posed in Gower:

> With felony I am upbore,
> I eat, and have it [yet?] not forlore
> My mother's flesh, whose husband
> My father for to seek I found,
> Which is the son eke of my wife.

Twine offers a variant on this, also rather more cryptic than that in the play:

I am carried with mischief, I eat my mother's flesh; I seek my brother my mother's husband, and I cannot find him.

Between them, Shakespeare and Wilkins have made it easier for Pericles, perhaps out of theatrical necessity.

10 John Dover Wilson, *The Essential Shakespeare* (Cambridge, Cambridge University Press, 1932), 131.

11 Both destruction of the nose and baldness are symptoms of syphilis.

12 T. S. Eliot, 'Hamlet and his Problems', in *The Sacred Wood* (London: Methuen, 1920), 101.

13 *Cymbeline*, ed. Roger Warren, Oxford Shakespeare (Oxford: Oxford University Press, 1998), 32, citing Anne Barton, 'Wrying But a Little', in her *Essays, Mainly Shakespearean* (Cambridge: Cambridge University Press, 1994), 3–30; quotation from 24.

14 Williams, *Glossary*, under 'dildo'.
15 e.g. A. D. Nuttall, *The Stoic in Love* (London: Rowman and Littlefield, 1989), 11: 'There is of course no mention of possible incest between Prospero and Miranda, but the thought may be there.'
16 The word occurs nowhere in the dialogue of Shakespeare's plays, only in this stage direction.

Chapter 10: Just Good Friends?

1 See e.g. my *Looking for Sex in Shakespeare* (Cambridge: Cambridge University Press, 2004), 73–6.
2 Alan Sinfield, *Shakespeare, Authority, Sexuality* (London: Routledge, 2006), 63.
3 Jeffrey Masten, *Textual Intercourse* (Cambridge: Cambridge University Press, 1997), 39.
4 *The Two Gentlemen of Verona*, ed. William C. Carroll, Arden Shakespeare (London: Thomson Learning, 2004), 88.
5 Sinfield, *Shakespeare, Authority, Sexuality*, 180.
6 I owe this point to Dr Paul Edmondson.
7 Stephen Orgel, *Impersonations: The Performance of Gender in Shakespeare's England* (Cambridge: Cambridge University Press, 1996), 51.
8 1.4.392–3.
9 A. P. Rossiter, *Angel with Horns* (London: Longmans, Green, 1949), 137.
10 Jan Kott, *Shakespeare Our Contemporary* (London: Methuen, 1964), 62.
11 Sinfield, *Shakespeare, Authority, Sexuality*, 90.
12 Roger Warren, 'Shakespeare in England', *Shakespeare Quarterly* 35 (Autumn 1984), 334–40; quoted from 336.
13 'Dividual' is an emendation of 'individuall'; but Masten retains the original reading on the grounds that '*individual* once signified the opposite of its modern meaning; so Emilia may be concluding that the love between the two maids is *more* than the love between the individual ("indivisible") sexes', or that 'the speech may conclude that the true love between two maids is indivisible *in more than simply sex*' (*Textual Intercourse*, 51–2).
14 Valerie Traub, *The Renaissance of Lesbianism in Early Modern England* (Cambridge: Cambridge University Press, 2002), 39.
15 Ibid. 152.

FURTHER READING

Bergeron, David M., *Royal Family, Royal Lovers: King James of England and Scotland* (Columbia: University of Missouri Press, 1991)

Bray, Alan, *Homosexuality in Renaissance England* (London: Gay Men's Press, 1992)

Brinkworth, E. R. C., *Shakespeare and the Bawdy Court of Stratford* (London/Chichester: Phillimore, 1972)

Colman, E. A. M., *The Dramatic Use of Bawdy in Shakespeare* (London: Longman, 1974)

Crompton, Louis, *Homosexuality and Civilization* (Cambridge, MA: Harvard Univeristy Press, 2003)

DiGangi, Mario, *The Homoerotics of Early Modern Drama* (Cambridge: Cambridge University Press, 1997)

Edmondson, Paul and Stanley Wells, *Shakespeare's Sonnets* (Oxford: Oxford University Press, 2004)

Fabricius, Johannes, *Syphilis in Shakespeare's England* (London: Jessica Kingsley, 1994)

Goldberg, Jonathan, *Sodometries: Renaissance Texts, Modern Sexualities* (Stanford: Stanford University Press, 1992)

Hammond, Paul, *Figuring Sex between Men from Shakespeare to Rochester* (Oxford: Clarendon Press, 2002)

Haynes, Alan, *Sex in Elizabethan England* (Stroud: Sutton, 1997)

Hulme, Hilda, *Explorations in Shakespeare's Language* (Aberdeen: Aberdeen University Press, 1962)

Jones, Jeanne, *Family Life in Shakespeare's England: Stratford-upon-Avon 1570–1630* (Stroud: Shakespeare Birthplace Trust in association with Sutton Publishing, 1996)

MacFaul, Tom, *Male Friendship in Shakespeare and his Contemporaries* (Cambridge: Cambridge University Press, 2007)

Masten, Jeffrey, *Textual Intercourse* (Cambridge: Cambridge University Press, 1997)

Nordlund, Marcus, *Shakespeare and the Nature of Love* (Evanston, IL: North-western University Press, 2007)

Orgel, Stephen, *Impersonations: The Performance of Gender in Shakespeare's England* (Cambridge: Cambridge University Press, 1996)

Partridge, Eric, *Shakespeare's Bawdy* (London: Routledge and Kegan Paul, 1947)

Pequigney, Joseph, *Such Is My Love: A Study of Shakespeare's Sonnets* (Chicago: University of Chicago Press, 1985)

Rowse, A. L., *Simon Forman: Sex and Society in Shakespeare's Age* (London: Weidenfeld and Nicolson, 1974)

Rubinstein, Frankie, *A Dictionary of Shakespeare's Sexual Puns and Their Significance*, 2nd edn (London: Macmillan, 1989)

Sinfield, Alan, *Shakespeare, Authority, Sexuality* (London: Routledge, 2006)

Smith, Bruce R., *Homosexual Desire in Shakespeare's England: A Cultural Poetics* (Chicago, University of Chicago Press, 1991, rpt with a new Preface, 1994)

Stewart, J. I. M., *Character and Motive in Shakespeare* (London: Longmans, 1949)

Stone, Lawrence, *The Family, Sex and Marriage in England 1500–1800* (New York: Harper and Row, 1977)

Traub, Valerie, *The Renaissance of Lesbianism in Early Modern England* (Cambridge: Cambridge University Press, 2002)

Wells, Stanley, *Looking for Sex in Shakespeare* (Cambridge: Cambridge University Press, 2004)

——*Shakespeare & Co* (London: Allen Lane Press, 2007)

Williams, Gordon, *A Dictionary of Sexual Language and Imagery in Shakespearean and Stuart Literature*, 3 vols (London: Athlone Press, 1994)

——*Shakespeare, Sex and the Print Revolution* (London: Athlone Press, 1996)

——*A Glossary of Shakespeare's Sexual Language* (London: Athlone Press, 1997)

INDEX